Relinquished

Relinquished

The Politics of Adoption
and the Privilege
of American Motherhood

Gretchen Sisson

ST. MARTIN'S PRESS
NEW YORK

First published in the United States by St. Martin's Press, an imprint of St. Martin's Publishing Group

RELINQUISHED. Copyright © 2024 by Gretchen Sisson. All rights reserved. Printed in the United States of America. For information, address St. Martin's Publishing Group, 120 Broadway, New York, NY 10271.

www.stmartins.com

Designed by Meryl Sussman Levavi

The Library of Congress Cataloging-in-Publication Data is available upon request.

ISBN 978-1-250-28677-2 (hardcover)
ISBN 978-1-250-28678-9 (ebook)

Our books may be purchased in bulk for promotional, educational, or business use. Please contact your local bookseller or the Macmillan Corporate and Premium Sales Department at 1-800-221-7945, extension 5442, or by email at MacmillanSpecialMarkets@macmillan.com.

First Edition: 2024

10   9   8   7   6   5   4   3   2   1

To all the mothers who shared their stories with me,
and their children

Contents

Author's Note

With the exception of one participant (who chose to be named), all names and identifying information throughout the book have been changed. Participant narratives have been edited for continuity, length, and to protect the privacy of individuals who were interviewed, but they otherwise reflect the stories of participants as they were told to me. Additional information on the research methodology is available in Appendix A.

Relinquished

Introduction

In the winter of early 2009, nineteen-year-old Haley was adrift. Her parents had kicked her out of their house, and her four-year-old son, Jacob, was temporarily staying with her sister. Haley was moving from couch to couch, staying with an aunt, some friends, or her boyfriend (whom her parents hated). Haley had been adopted as a baby but was in contact with her biological family; it was while she was staying with her birth mother* that she began to suspect she might be pregnant again. She was correct. "I was in the doctor's office, right after they told me I was pregnant," Haley told me in 2010. "I just wanted to get out of it, but I knew I couldn't handle an abortion. I thought adoption would fix everything."

This first thought of adoption was fleeting. A few weeks later, Haley—still rootless, still single-parenting Jacob, still deeply uncomfortable with abortion—was determined to figure out how to raise her second child. "I was going to keep him. I just knew I was going to keep him. That's how it was going to be. I was going to get a job, and I started going to school because I wasn't getting any jobs because I wasn't qualified for anything. I didn't need

---

* Please see Appendix B, "A Note on Adoption Language," for a discussion of the diction in use throughout this book, particularly with regard to the use of "birth mother."

my parents, and I didn't need anyone else. Me and Jacob and the baby were going to make it."

Haley was already familiar with this hustle. When she became pregnant with Jacob at fifteen, she was a below-average student, uninvested in her schoolwork. But she was deeply motivated by becoming a mother to finish high school and provide a good example for her child. She "immediately knuckled down" and eventually graduated from high school with a 4.0 grade point average. Haley was proud of herself. She'd gotten herself together to parent Jacob. She could do it again for this baby.

But a month later, Haley's determination was hitting a wall. It was now spring, and while the snow in the nearby Rocky Mountains remained deep, her suburban hometown was starting to thaw. She felt that the baby's father would be a danger to her and their child if she told him about the pregnancy, so she simply had not. Her parents—who had been so supportive after Jacob was born—told her that they didn't want to have anything to do with this baby. They said it was because the baby's father was dangerous (which Haley agreed he was; he had a history of being physically rough with her), but Haley thought it might also have been because the baby's father was Black. Whatever their reasons for refusing to help, the result was the same: Haley's support network was thin, her bank account was empty, and her housing prospects were few.

One night Haley was parked outside a Safeway, making use of the store's free Wi-Fi to do her homework while Jacob slept in the back seat. "I just suddenly burst into tears," she remembered. "I just realized I couldn't take him. I couldn't take care of him. I think that's when I really knew adoption was right for Elijah, and not just my way of getting out of trouble."

When Haley relinquished her son Elijah for infant adoption, she joined a cohort of American women that is remarkably small. In recent years, only about 19,000 women have relinquished newborns annually, out of approximately 4 million births and in contrast to just under 1 million abortions. These rates mean that while over the course of their reproductive lives nearly 86 percent of American women will give birth and 25 percent will have an abortion, less than 1 percent will relinquish an infant for private adoption. Yet the discourse around adoption—in our politics, in our popular culture, in how we think about family building broadly—gives the decisions of these comparably few women an outsized role in American ideas about pregnancy, reproductive choice, and motherhood. However, these cultural narratives are centered on a politicized ideal of what mother-hood and family ought to look like; they are almost never rooted in the lived experiences of people like Haley, a single teen mom who desperately wanted to find a way to parent and just couldn't make it work.

* * *

In 2009, while Haley was grappling with what to do about her pregnancy, I was on the other side of the country working my way through graduate school. I was writing my master's thesis on infertility treatments, driving my Zipcar through Boston sub-urbs to speak with couples about their struggles to conceive and build their hoped-for families. In between schoolwork, I spent my days interning at the Massachusetts Alliance on Teen Preg-nancy, considering the rights and well-being of young mothers and their children across the commonwealth. I spent my eve-nings volunteering with the Eastern Massachusetts Abortion Fund, taking calls from countless people who wanted an abor-tion but needed help affording one. I saw all these types of work as parallel, critical efforts to understand and support people in having the families they wanted, on their own terms.

Just a few years earlier, in 2006, Ann Fessler's *The Girls Who Went Away: The Hidden History of Women Who Surrendered Children for Adoption in the Decades Before* Roe v. Wade had been published, opening the eyes of many in my academic and advocacy circles to the grim realities of adoption in decades past.

In her book, Fessler probes the stories of women who not only lacked access to abortion but also lacked sex education or knowledge about their own bodies and the means to make choices for themselves and their children. For these women, adoption was often coercive, always secretive, and unambiguously traumatizing.

But in 2009, these haunting stories of pre-*Roe* adoptions seemed light-years away as soon as you turned on the television. This was the same year that *16 and Pregnant* began chronicling the lives of young mothers on MTV. The show's reality TV lens was—by the intention of the content creators—designed to present the lives of these young women as so disrupted and unappealing that other young people would go to any length to avoid early parenthood. The one exception to this dismal portrayal in that first season was the story of Catelynn and Tyler, a teen couple who relinquished their daughter Carly for adoption. During the season finale, Catelynn and Tyler sat beside Dr. Drew Pinsky, who lauded them as "courageous," "strong," and "extraordinary." "I feel so passionately that you need to be honored," he gushed.

And of course, this cultural narrative praising adoption wasn't just on MTV. The film *Juno*, portraying a spunky, sarcastic teen mother happily biking away after relinquishing her baby, was still fresh in moviegoers' memories. In contrast to a string of series finales punctuated by adoptions on *Sex and the City* and *Friends*, where viewers had been rooting for the adoptive parents all along, *Juno* felt novel for depicting a birth parent with any nuance at all. This was also the year that Sandra Bullock won an Academy Award for her role as a "white savior" adoptive mother in *The Blind Side*, a film in which the Black birth mother is continuously villainized for not having the wisdom to give up her child.

It was this cultural zeitgeist of adoption promotion that helped me understand connections between my own work and the social conditions underlying infant relinquishment. The couples experiencing infertility, the marginalized young mothers, the hotline callers in need of money for their abortions: I saw them all as moving on parallel paths in creating the families that they wanted at that time in their lives. These paths were not mutually exclusive over the course of a lifetime, of course—many women who become mothers have had previous abortions, and most people seeking abortions are already parenting children. But adoption puts these individual paths into intersection, with the premise that the path of this young mother or that woman struggling to afford an abortion should be part of the story of the couple trying to conceive. By transferring infants from poor, young, underprepared, or unsupported women to mostly married, often heterosexual, typically white families of financial means, private adoption is believed to avert the need for abortion, nullify the purported adverse outcomes of teen parenting, alleviate the social burden of caring for under-resourced families, appease the pain of infertility, and uphold the value of the two-parent heteronormative family structure or accommodate nontraditional families. In this common vision, adoption is a conservative panacea; it represents a particular, effective, *private* solution to myriad *social* problems.

This context does not mean that adoption is embraced solely by the political right. In the decade since I began this project, American politics have changed dramatically—yet adoption remains one of the few bipartisan areas of political agreement. On an anniversary of *Roe v. Wade,* President Barack Obama framed adoption as mutually agreeable "common ground" in the abortion debate; a decade later President Donald Trump would showcase a redemptive story about a nameless drug-addicted birth mother and the heroic police officer adoptive father in his State of the Union address. The March for Life's 2014 theme of "Thank you, birthmom!" reflects the long-term investment of the anti-abortion movement in adoption promotion, while the inclusion of the rights of adoptive parents in *Obergefell v. Hodges,* the Supreme Court case allowing gay marriage, reflects the ways many gay, lesbian, transgender, and queer people use adoption as a means of family building. The Congressional Coalition on Adoption is the largest bipartisan bicameral caucus in the federal government. To the extent that adoption has been understood as a feminist issue, it has broadly been with the aim of upholding the practice of adoption and making it more widely accessible. Adoption makes possible the maintenance of both the heteronormative family ideal beloved by the right and the nontraditional, chosen family ideals embraced by the left. But all these ideals prioritize the families that are being created with little reliance on—or accountability for—the families that are separated.

*   *   *

On June 24, 2022, the Supreme Court of the United States ruled in *Dobbs v. Jackson Women's Health Organization* to overturn *Roe v. Wade,* the 1973 case that had established a legal right to abortion across the country. The *Dobbs* decision thus allows the states to regulate and limit abortion provision (assuming the absence of federal law that protects abortion access). During the oral arguments for *Dobbs* in December 2021, the questions the Supreme Court justices asked did little to probe what the burden would be for American women who were denied abortion access: what it would mean for their physical and mental health, their families, their futures, their communities. Instead, given the opportunity to reverse fifty years of constitutionally protected access to abortion, many questions centered on adoption. Justice Amy Coney Barrett asked if all those potential burdens could be averted if more women terminated their parental rights after giving birth. Essentially: Isn't adoption the solution?

History has already answered this question, and told us definitively that no, it is not. But the traumatized voices of pre-*Roe* birth mothers seem distant. Fessler's "girls who went away" are now a generation or more removed. The practices of adoption today seem different enough that it is plausible to convince ourselves that we are not doomed to repeat those traumas. But even if the stories of birth mothers today do not precisely repeat the history of their pre-*Roe* counterparts, they still echo the stories of earlier generations.

The reversal of *Roe v. Wade* will deny some Americans access to abortions that they would otherwise choose to have, potentially dramatically increasing the number of domestic adoptions. This increase will not be because women frequently decide between abortion and adoption—as this book will explore, they do not—but because as people's options are constrained, as abortion is unavailable and parenting is untenable, adoption becomes the only path forward. If we wish to understand what adoption means today, we must listen to relinquishing mothers now. *Relinquished* provides a comprehensive account of their stories: what their life was like during their pregnancies, how they came to decide on adoption, and what consequences the adoption has had for their lives and their children.

*   *   *

The stories that I have collected over the last decade illuminate what types of motherhood, which children, and whose families are most valued by our society, and how individual life trajectories are shaped when the looming forces of abortion politics, religion, conservative family values, and nontraditional family building intersect to create narratives about adoption that are not rooted in the experiences of those who live it. This book seeks to correct this error by recentering the experiences of Haley and of so many women like her. The failure to listen to their stories means continuing to misunderstand the complexity of modern adoption and to misalign our public policy with the needs of those most impacted. Most important, neglecting the stories of women who relinquish infants will mean we fail to understand what happens when women are not in control of their own reproductive lives and futures, and when families are not supported at a very basic level—it will mean carrying the injustices and traumas forward for a new post-*Roe* generation, and beyond.

This book is the result of over a hundred interviews with women who have relinquished infants for domestic adoption. In 2010, I met with women across the country, from a living room with panoramic windows overlooking the Atlantic Ocean, to the conference room of a law firm, the lobby of a quiet Quaker meetinghouse, a bench outside a sandwich shop that had no empty tables, a pizza parlor in Massachusetts, and a Starbucks in Texas (which required my transcriptionist to strain to hear the conversation over the sound of the coffee grinder). In 2020, I met with women over Zoom, as we all socially distanced inside our homes during the COVID-19 pandemic.

While I interviewed mothers who relinquished as early as 1962, this book focuses on women whose adoptions took place between 2000 and 2020. They live in every region of the United States. At the time of our interviews, these women were lawyers, stay-at-home mothers, college students, psychologists, teachers, an acupuncturist, a sex worker, a professor, a hairstylist, a grocery store cashier, and a photographer. Several were unemployed, a few were formerly incarcerated, some were formerly homeless, and a few others had histories of addiction. Many were religious, some used to be but weren't anymore, and a few had never been. Many were married (or remarried, newly divorced, or avowedly single); one had just broken up with her boyfriend and was hoping it would "stick." Several of them were adopted themselves, which impacted how they understood their pregnancies and relinquishments. Most of them were raising children. In short, they represented the full range of American life—their paths had all led them to adoption at one point, one way or another, but they were often on different trajectories. They had a tremendous range of experiences and feelings around their relinquishments.

In the context of the sweeping history of family separation and adoption in the United States, this book offers a close examination of just one twenty-year period from the perspective of mothers who relinquished infants for private domestic adoption. My participants terminated their parental rights by signing adoption papers, and their children were adopted privately through adoption agencies and independent attorneys; their rights were not terminated by the state, and their children, for the most part, were not placed in foster care.* Accordingly, I do not speak to the experiences of families targeted by the family regulation system (e.g., foster care) unless they also engaged with private adoption. However, as we will see, the presence of such threatening systems does shape the experiences of many mothers, particularly women of color. This book focuses solely on domestic adoption and the experiences of American mothers; I do not examine the way international relinquishment is structured within the political systems of other countries. Nor does my sample include relinquishing fathers—while I interviewed a few fathers, I ultimately did not include them in this analysis; birth fathers remain under-considered in the ways adoption is practiced and understood. Finally, and most critically, I do not study the experiences of adopted people, though I do consider other research that has examined the impact of adoption on their lives and work to incorporate their voices wherever possible. Ultimately, my research provides one meaningful piece in the large and complex puzzle that is American adoption.

The stories shared in this book are not about faraway people. While the families formed by adoption are often visible to us, the families separated by adoption are often unseen. As I interviewed these mothers, I found that their lives—and the lives of many other women like them—intersected with my own. Two participants took classes at the same small college I attended, with the same professors. Several women worked with adoption

---

* Some infants relinquished for private adoption spend brief periods in foster care or crisis care. Increasingly, however, infants in private adoptions are released directly to their adoptive families (even before the adoptions are legally finalized).

agency professionals that I had met at conferences for work. One had—years ago, at the time of her adoption—lived just down the street from the house where I was then working, interviewing her over the phone. Another participant, Natalie, lived several states away. However, her daughter had been adopted by a couple who lived in San Francisco (where I lived with my children, including my son who was about the same age as her relinquished daughter). The adoptive parents had given their daughter a distinctive name. One sunny Saturday while attending my son's soccer game, I heard that name called out on an adjacent playing field, and I knew from the details Natalie had shared with me that I was watching her daughter dribble the ball toward the goal, surrounded by her classmates. The fact that Natalie had not seen her child in years while I now sat yards away from her made Natalie's separation feel all the sharper. The cultural erasure of families separated by adoption often makes these stories invisible. But they are often right in front of us.

My analysis and curation of these stories is rooted in my perspective as a feminist scholar who values autonomy and care in the pursuit of reproductive justice. In this effort, I am indebted to the women of color theorists who have articulated reproductive justice as a critical feminist theory, the women of color activists who have built the reproductive justice movement, and the impacted people—not just my participants but the myriad scholars, writers, and advocates, particularly transracially and transnationally adopted people—who have shaped the connections between adoption and reproductive justice in their work (many of whom are cited throughout this book). This book represents my effort to preserve the accounts of my participants and contribute to this collective production of knowledge. While I did not set out to write a polemic, my commitment to listening to the voices of relinquishing mothers and adopted people and my belief in reproductive justice as the best way forward in our post-*Dobbs* world have both led me to understand the current practices of domestic infant adoption in the United States as anathema to that pursuit of justice.

*   *   *

When I first spoke with Haley, it was just over a year since her second son, Elijah, was born. She had initially wanted a semi-open adoption—which, for her, meant exchanging pictures and updates, and having occasional visits. But the agency she worked with gave her a profile for prospective adoptive parents Rachel and Mark, and Haley was immediately drawn to them. Rachel and Mark wanted a fully open adoption, having learned that research supported the idea that openness was better for the adopted child. Haley agreed.

"I couldn't handle not ever hearing from Rachel and Mark again. It wasn't just because of Elijah, it was because of them. I just really love them. I couldn't really imagine not having them be part of my life. Rachel is practically a sister to me now . . . I definitely consider them part of my family. I think they consider me part of theirs? I talk to Rachel pretty much every day. And it's not always about Elijah. I think she cares about me, too."

Haley seemed satisfied with where she was in life. She felt that the adoption helped her gain the respect of her parents, which she "never really had." When we spoke, she'd just become a certified nursing assistant and was about to begin a new job that paid eleven dollars an hour—more money than she'd ever made. She couldn't yet hold Elijah without crying, but she loved that Rachel never put him down. "I couldn't do that, if I'd kept him," she said. "I'd have to be working, and most likely it would have to be two jobs, and I wouldn't have time to not put him down." Haley was excited that Rachel, Mark, and Elijah had moved much closer to where she lived—just an hour away!—and was hopeful that she'd see them often.

In many ways, this was a successful adoption narrative, and Haley's story seemed to confirm our best ideas about what adoption today could be. Rachel and Mark cared about Haley, and they were so committed to open adoption that they pushed for it when Haley was initially reluctant. Haley, the young woman who was so alone during her pregnancy, felt the support and friendship of her son's adoptive mother. Elijah was loved and healthy, in a stable family. Haley felt respected by her parents, had achieved an educational goal, and was eagerly on a path toward financial self-sufficiency. If Haley's feelings about her own adoption were unexplored, if it seemed that Haley needed Rachel's friendship in an asymmetrical way, if that Haley's inability to hold Elijah without crying was mentioned just passingly, and if there was an implied question mark lingering in Haley's voice when she talked about being part of Rachel and Mark's family, surely the foundation was strong enough to weather all that for a lifetime.

It would take ten years, and hundreds of interviews with women like Haley, for me to understand why it wasn't.

1

The Domestic Suppliers of Infants

In the United States, the nationwide legal right to abortion started with an adoption.

In 1969, twenty-one-year-old Norma McCorvey was pregnant for the third time. Her life had not been easy; she was not parenting either of her two children. She had lost custody of her first daughter to her own mother, Mary, one night when Mary manipulated a drunk Norma into terminating her parental rights. She never laid eyes on her second child, who she relinquished for adoption at birth. Now pregnant again, Norma wanted an abortion. Her doctor refused to perform one and referred her to an adoption attorney who, seeing how much Norma wanted an abortion, referred her to two young lawyers. That was how Norma ended up at Columbo's Pizza in Dallas, Texas, meeting with Linda Coffee and Sarah Weddington, signing the affidavit that would turn her into Jane Roe of *Roe v. Wade*.

Of course, the Supreme Court's decision in *Roe v. Wade* would not come until 1973, years after Norma had given birth to her third child. She was furious when she realized the *Roe* case would not help her get the abortion she wanted and felt like she was "nothing more than just a name on a piece of paper" to Linda and Sarah. Without access to abortion, she felt "hopeless," "worthless," and utterly unable to parent. Norma was left with only one constrained choice: adoption.

After a grueling labor, Norma gave birth to a baby girl. She didn't expect to be allowed to see the baby, but a nurse made a mistake and brought the baby in to breastfeed:

> Then she handed me the baby. . . . Was this my baby? Why were they giving it to me? Should I look at it? Or not look at it? I was too full of pain to say anything. . . . The nurse must have seen the expression on my face, because she quickly realized that she'd done something awful. . . . She pulled the baby out of my arms and handed it to an orderly, who left. Then the baby was gone forever. . . . I turned my face to the wall and wept.

Later in her life, Norma disclosed that the sense of loss lingered: "I spent years searching the faces of children I passed on the streets and in supermarkets. *Is that her?* I'd ask myself. *Could that be my child?*" She described her later conversion—to both fundamentalist Christianity and to the anti-abortion movement—through her relationship with Emily, the daughter of an Operation Rescue volunteer who did "clinic rescue" at the abortion clinic where Norma worked: "My heart melted when I saw Emily sitting quietly on the couch. . . . A maternal side of me that had long laid dormant was being resurrected. You see, though I had been pregnant three times, I was never allowed to be much of a mom." While Norma would go on to give us plenty of reasons to doubt her motivations for involvement in the anti-abortion movement, her love for Emily is clear throughout her story. The idea that she could be maternal and love a child seems to have been a source of joy for her.

Norma had a great deal of trauma in her life: a brutal childhood in poverty, an absent father, a violent mother, repeated sexual assault, ongoing domestic abuse, alcoholism and drug use, and later, a conservative church that required her to renounce her longtime same-sex romantic partner. Yet her most enduring sorrow seems to be the adoption relinquishments:

I am a rough woman, born into pain and anger and raised mostly by myself. I went to reform school, not high school or college. I have had many jobs, but no professions. I have abused drugs and alcohol. I was married to a man who beat me when I was pregnant. I have sought out and pulled close bad people, and I have lashed out and pushed away the people who love me. I have a bad temper, and oftentimes, at the worst times, I lose it. I am my own worst enemy. I have had three children—but two of them, for better or worse, are unknown to me. Of my many sorrows, this is without a doubt the worst.

Over the course of her life, Norma McCorvey would prove to be an unreliable narrator of her own story.* She wrote two very different memoirs and participated in a documentary film about her life; together, these tell about her role as a Supreme Court plaintiff, her time working at an abortion clinic, her alienation from the abortion rights movement, her conversion to Christianity, her deep involvement in the "pro-life" movement, and her late-in-life confession that her anti-abortion work was entirely financially motivated. Given all this, her accounting at different moments should be considered with a critical eye. But her position as a birth mother seems to have been little understood, even though the constraints that led her to adoption were at the root of the case that bears her pseudonym.

If Norma's story marks one point in the history of adoption and abortion politics in this country, then the end of *Roe,* the legal precedent bearing Norma's pseudonym, marks another. In its

---

* Norma McCorvey wrote *I Am Roe* (1994) as a testament to the necessity of legal abortion and a proud documentation of her own role in the Supreme Court case. Just three years later, she published *Won by Love* (1997), the story of her conversion to Christianity, her embrace of the anti-abortion movement, and her guilt over the case bearing her pseudonym. Toward the end of her life, Norma participated in the documentary *AKA Jane Roe* (2020) as her "deathbed confession," stating that her anti-abortion activism was financially motivated and that "if a young woman wants to have an abortion, that's no skin off my ass. That's why they call it choice."

June 2022 ruling in *Dobbs v. Jackson Women's Health Organization*, the Supreme Court overturned *Roe* and asserted there was no constitutional right to privacy that protected abortion access nationwide. During the *Dobbs* oral arguments, Justice Amy Coney Barrett postulated that requiring women to continue pregnancies was a negligible burden: "In all fifty states, you can terminate parental rights by relinquishing a child. . . . It seems to me that the choice more focused would be between, say, the ability to get an abortion at twenty-three weeks or the state requiring the woman to go fifteen, sixteen weeks more and then terminate parental rights at the conclusion." Relinquishment, Justice Coney Barrett argued, would allow women to continue pregnancies while still avoiding the "consequences of parenting and the obligations of motherhood that flow from pregnancy." In other words: Who needs access to abortion if adoption exists?

In the majority opinion for *Dobbs,* Justice Samuel Alito went one step further, offering the thin reassurance to those denied access to abortion under the new court ruling that "a woman who puts her newborn up for adoption today has little reason to fear that the baby will not find a suitable home." In a footnote citing a Centers for Disease Control and Prevention (CDC) report, he implied that an increased availability of infants would in fact serve a broader social good: "the domestic supply of infants relinquished at birth or within the first month of life and available to be adopted has become virtually nonexistent." In a way, Alito is right: estimates provided in the same CDC report would suggest that there are at least forty-five prospective families waiting to adopt for every infant relinquished for domestic adoption. But the justices' arguments that adoption is a meaningful alternative to abortion, that the availability of suitable homes is of consoling relevance to those denied abortion, or that the state has a vested interest in ensuring the availability of children for adoption all ignore not just how pregnancy decisions are made, but how a long trajectory of oppressive and traumatic American history has shaped the practice of adoption today.

* * *

To understand contemporary adoption, it is essential to understand the long and far-reaching tradition of family separation throughout American history. These historical traumas shape how adoption is practiced, which infants and children are valued for what purposes, which communities engage with systems of adoption, and whom adoption aims to serve. It requires visiting the darkest moments in our country's past.

Many of America's earliest relinquishing mothers were enslaved Black women whose children were often sold away from them. Of all the core violations of American slavery, including the systemic rape and forced childbearing, these separations were among the harshest losses. The narratives of enslaved people are rife with mothers begging to be bought along with their children or to not have their children sold away. "Still holding me in her arms . . . [she] honestly and imploringly besought my master to buy her and the rest of the children," wrote Charles Ball, remembering his own separation from his mother. But the selling away of children from their parents, or vice versa, was systematic—an estimated half of all slave trades separated nuclear families—and intentional, as the ongoing threat of separation was used to induce terror and extract obedience from enslaved parents. In *Incidents in the Life of a Slave Girl,* Harriet Jacobs spoke of this threat: "When my master found that I still refused to accept what he called his kind offers, he would threaten to sell my child. 'Perhaps that will humble you,' said he." The practice of separation incentivized a callous indifference to the family relationships of enslaved people, and it continued after the end of the Civil War, when former slave owners argued that liberated Black people could not care for their own families and took their children into forced indentured servitude.

In this same tradition were the Native American mothers who fled to the hills every day with their children and grandchildren to try to hide from government officials who rounded up the children and sent them to military-run boarding schools. They could rarely hide well enough and long enough. At the schools, the children faced abuse and coercive assimilation into white American culture: their belongings were burned; they were beaten for speaking their own languages; they were physically and sexually abused, involuntarily sterilized, and starved. In an infamous 1892 speech, Colonel Richard Henry Pratt—dubbed the "father of the movement in getting Indians out from their old life into citizenship"—argued that these schools allowed the government to "kill the Indian in him, and save the man."

Also in the nineteenth century, poor white mothers in eastern cities, many of them immigrants, struggled to care for their children due to poverty, widowhood, illness, or simply having more children than they had the capacity to parent. They surrendered them to foundling homes or institutions that labeled the children "orphans" despite the fact they had living parents. Many of these children became Orphan Train riders, sent west for rehoming. One such child was Hazelle, who fondly recalled trips to the Bronx Zoo and the Metropolitan Museum of Art with her widowed mother from her early childhood. However, when her mother was hospitalized, Hazelle was sent to Texas. She protested, saying, "I can't go. I'm not an orphan. My mother's still living. She's in a hospital right here in New York," but the social worker ignored her objections. The Orphan Trains were framed as a benevolent way to move children toward safe Christian homes.* As Charles Loring Brace, founder of the New York Children's Aid Society, put it: "The best of all asylums for the outcast child is the farmer's home." Yet many of these homes were often

---

* Many of these organizations were run by abolitionists who decried the selling of enslaved children from their mothers but saw no conflict in their own work separating children from their families via Orphan Trains.

more interested in fostering laborers than in expanding their families. Accordingly, the Children's Aid Society often marketed the children as a source of helpful and low-cost labor: "Boys . . . handy and active . . . could be employed on farms, in trades, in manufacturing. . . . Girls could be used for the common kinds of housework."

These examples were usually focused on older children; they were rarely about infants.* It wasn't until the twentieth century that a social demand for babies came into existence. As sociologist Viviana Zelizer states, the early 1900s saw a cultural shift: "While in the nineteenth century a child's capacity for labor had determined its exchange value, the market price of a twentieth-century baby was set by smiles, dimples, and curls." As children came to be understood as an inherent source of fulfillment and joy for parents, the demand for them soared. This shift does not mean that parents of previous centuries loved their children less; it does mean that the economic incentives around having children—and the motivations for adoption—had changed. Adoption had previously included temporary fostering or kinship arrangements, but now increasingly involved the full and permanent legal transfer of parental rights. Prospective adoptive parents were eager to participate. "The woods are full of people eager to adopt," a Boston probate court judge remarked in 1919. The supply and demand dynamics of adoption had inverted. By 1927, The New York Times reported that a new challenge was "one of finding enough children for childless homes rather than that of finding enough homes for homeless children." These early

---

* Indeed, when abolitionists made family separation a focus of their antislavery message, it was an easy concession for some southern states to outlaw the selling of infants away from their enslaved mothers beginning in the 1850s. (This policy cost them almost nothing, as there was no real market for small children, but—they hoped—would make the institution of slavery appear more humane and thus more resistant to the attacks of abolitionists, as gender studies scholar Laura Briggs describes in Taking Children.) And while some babies rode the Orphan Trains (especially toward the later years of the Orphan Train period, into the twentieth century), most riders were older children.

laments about the limited supply of adoptable babies would continue throughout the century and beyond. As gender studies and adoption scholar Laura Briggs describes, "Every generation in the twentieth century faced a 'baby famine.'"

Into this opportunity for profit stepped Georgia Tann, who served as director of the Tennessee Children's Home Society beginning in 1924, but who impacted the practice of adoption far beyond her tenure. As chronicled by reporter Barbara Bisantz Raymond in her book *The Baby Thief*, thousands of women had their children stolen by Tann. There was Irene Green, who after groggily waking from anesthesia was told by a labor and delivery nurse that she'd delivered a stillborn baby. When Green protested that she'd heard the baby cry, the nurse told her she was wrong. When she asked to see her newborn's body, she was told they had already disposed of it. In fact, Tann had taken the baby. There was Grace Gribble, a poor widow who signed papers at the behest of a social worker employed by Tann, believing they would help her children get health insurance, only to realize they were adoption relinquishments. Her children were sold for adoption in three different states; by the time she found a lawyer to take her case, the judge ruled: "This is one of the sad tragedies of life that even a mother must endure for the best interests of her children." There was Mary Owens, who wrote to one of Tann's agents: "Please help me git my baby back. I am so heartbroken about the way it has bin taken from me. . . . I would gladly lay down my life just to see her one time." Tann would take sick children from doctors' offices and tell their parents they had died; she would remove children from nursery schools while their parents were at work. Over the course of her career, she would facilitate over 1,000 adoptions and earn over $1 million. To protect herself, Tann facilitated adoptions for prominent celebrities, authors, and politicians, including actress Joan Crawford, writer Pearl S. Buck, and New York governor Herbert H. Lehman. These connections made those at the highest levels of society complicit in the secrecy of her work. Tann lobbied for sealed birth certificates, meaning that adopted people would never have access to their original parents, and this secrecy was legally issued in nearly every state—including New York, where Governor Lehman closed access himself. Adopted people had only one legal identity, and it was as the children of their adoptive parents.

After World War II, the United States embraced a Cold War conformity that centered value around the traditional white heteronormative nuclear family. In that society, parenthood was a path toward the constructed ideal of middle-class stability, and thus adoptable infants continued to increase in market value. In contrast to baby farmers of the 1870s, who were *paid* by desperate families to assume custody of their babies, by the 1950s, a healthy baby would *cost* adoptive parents up to $10,000. Given the social value of parenthood and the sentimental value of children, what price could be too high? However, the same cultural forces that made parenting so desirable for white married couples also worked to categorically exclude and stigmatize variations of parenthood that did not conform to this ideal. Thus began the "baby scoop" era, a time of extractive, coercive, and secretive adoptions that lasted until 1973.

During this time—from the end of World War II to the legalization of abortion—about 4 million American infants were relinquished for adoption, including 1.5 million to unrelated adoptive parents; there were between 33,000 and 89,000 adoptions to unrelated petitioners per year. These dramatically high adoption numbers were the result of a collision of social factors: an increase in nonmarital sexual relationships, the inaccessibility of contraception for unmarried couples, and the illegality of abortion. These social forces intersected with strictly enforced cultural ideas about appropriate femininity, sexuality, and motherhood. Unmarried pregnancy was viewed as deeply shameful, not just for the pregnant woman, but for any child born, who would be branded with the stain of illegitimacy and the label "bastard." Many women were desperate to avoid this outcome, and as we'll examine in more detail in the next chapter, most of them did. However, for many young women and their parents, immediate marriage, unmarried parenthood, and abortion were all unthinkable. These expectant mothers were sent to maternity homes, where they were given no choice but to relinquish their infants. Sue, one of the many mothers included in Ann Fessler's *The Girls Who Went Away,* shared:

> One of the questions that come up when you go to court and relinquish is they ask you if you have been coerced in any way, and I thought it was the height of hypocrisy. Of course, you're coerced. You're coerced by your parents, who said, "Don't come home again if you plan to keep that child. We're not going to help you." You're coerced by everyone around you because of the shame and the lack of acceptance by society and your community. You're not acknowledged as a fit mother because you had sex before marriage. The judge congratulated me on how courageous I was. I was furious that he would tell me it was about courage. It was about defeat. It was about total shame and defeat.

These adoptions were closed—mothers had no say in where their children would go, and they were told never to search for them. But they were framed as a path toward redemption for white women, who, it was argued, would be able to move past the shame of the pregnancy, maintain a guise of virginity, and resume their intended journey toward marriage and more appropriate motherhood.

The vast majority of relinquishing mothers during the baby scoop era were white: while nearly 9 percent of all infants born to unmarried mothers were relinquished during that period, that included nearly 20 percent of infants born to white unmarried mothers and only 1.5 percent of infants born to Black unmarried mothers. This disparity is often attributed to traditions of single motherhood and extended kinship care in Black communities, and the fact that Black single mothers faced less stigma and shame from their immediate families and communities. This explanation is likely true—but there was also less of a market for Black babies, and most maternity homes would not accept Black women. (Most white prospective parents would refuse to consider adopting a Black child, even if that meant forgoing parenthood.) During the 1940s, not a single Black child was placed for agency adoption in Florida and Louisiana. Efforts to promote adopting to families of color were often fruitless, as Black parents were alienated from the process by income requirements, proof of infertility, and predominantly white agency staffs. But Black families were not protected from family separation. Those separations were more rooted in punishment, rather than in facilitating adoptions. For example, in 1960 Louisiana governor Jimmie Davis responded to school desegregation by cutting thousands of Black children off from public assistance programs. When the federal government intervened and said that states could not deny aid to families living in suitable homes, Louisiana responded by deeming the homes of Black families "unsuitable" and removing their children. Faced with the possibility of losing their children, Black mothers were effectively deterred from seeking the benefits that would have allowed them to better support their families.

The 1950s and '60s also saw the systematic removal of Native children reemerge as the Indian Adoption Project (IAP). Whereas Black children were deemed "unadoptable" because of the exclusion of prospective Black adoptive families and a lack of interest in transracial adoption, Native infants and children were specifically targeted for adoption by white families who believed the children could more easily pass as white. This transfer would continue the destructive assimilative work of the Indian boarding schools. Anthropologist Susan Devan Harness, herself an IAP adoptee from the Confederated Salish and Kootenai

Tribes, describes how she and her fellow adopted people "became lightning rods for beliefs and attitudes rooted deep in a history of extermination." In her memoir, Devan Harness writes about reuniting with her birth family and trying to understand her mother's inability to parent her: "I am now in my homeland, where it all began. I could make a lot of people uncomfortable with my experiences laid out, boned and fileted for all to see. *This is what happens,* the wind whispers, as if agreeing with me, *when you let your children go.*"

The dislocations and fractures of these decades shifted by the 1970s and through the 1980s, as the legality of abortion lowered unintended birth rates—and, consequently, adoption rates. By this time, transracial adoption was becoming not just more acceptable to white families, but even aspirational, in vogue. Adoption historian Ellen Herman chronicles how the "love makes a family" ideology was prolific, and transracial adoption was a "longed-for symbol of national progress" and "a triumphal narrative in which bright lines separate the eras of Jim Crow and old-fashioned empire from our own age of multiculturalism and postcolonialism." However, the earlier rarity of transracial adoption broadly (specifically the adoption of Black children) was rooted not *just* in white racism and a deep desire to credibly pass adopted children as biological offspring (though those factors played a role), but also in communities' desire to defend their rights to raise their own children. In 1972, the National Association of Black Social Workers issued a statement that read in part: "We affirm the inviolable position of Black children in Black families where they belong." A few years later, the Indian Child Welfare Act (ICWA) was enacted to require Native children to be kept within their tribal communities; advocates argued: "We know that our children are our greatest resource, and without them we have no future . . . we have been here many times before with the same message: 'we know what is best for our children.'"

By the 1990s, the domestic adoption rates were at an all-time low: relinquishment rates for private adoption were only 1.7 percent among white women, and virtually zero among Black and Latina women. But demand for adoption remained high, and if American mothers were relinquishing at far lower rates than in previous generations, there were still means by which their children could be made available for adoption. The increased acceptability of transracial adoption meant that these children could come via the foster care system (which disproportionately impacts families of color) and international adoption.

Black mothers were increasingly targeted to have their children removed, not because of abuse or real risk, but for parenting within the constraints of poverty. These efforts were reinforced federally: in 1996, Congress passed the Personal Responsibility and Work Opportunity Reconciliation Act (known as "welfare reform"), which replaced categorial aid to families with temporary aid tied to work requirements; in effect, the law pushed more families into economic vulnerability. Soon after, Congress passed the Adoption and Safe Families Act of 1997 (ASFA), which fast-tracked the termination of parental rights for families with children in foster care. While this policy was intended to move children to permanency more quickly, it also framed adoption as preferable to reunification with their families; its aim was to double the number of foster care children available for adoption. It worked. The position the National Association of Black Social Workers had advanced in 1972 was rendered moot in these acts. Legal scholar Dorothy Roberts tells the story of Valerie, a Black mother trying to parent her young children in a cold, roach-infested apartment in 1998—just a year after ASFA was passed. Her children were sick, her housing was unstable, her utilities were cut off, and her mental health was wavering. She turned to the Department of Children and Family Services (DCFS) for help, hoping to place the children in foster care temporarily while she worked to build a safer and more stable life.

But even after successfully completing parenting classes, Valerie was not reunited with her children. After more and more delays and escalating mental distress, DCFS changed the goal from reunification to termination of parental rights and adoption. The child welfare system (or family regulation system, as it is often referred to by critics) had always been used to police Black families with the threat of child removal, but this now involved children being made available for adoption.

At the same time, international adoption into the United States doubled during the 1990s. Most of these adopted people came from countries with political instability, very high rates of poverty, or their own coercive reproductive policies, and most of them were children of color being adopted by white families. International adoption reached its peak in 2004 with nearly 23,000 adoptions. That number soon plummeted rapidly, as countries limited the exporting of their children for a variety of reasons: increasing economic stability (South Korea), the ending of the one-child policy (China), political retaliation against the United States (Russia), high-profile cases of coerced or exploitative adoptions (Ethiopia, Guatemala, Haiti), and well-publicized cases of abuse and "rehoming" of internationally adopted people (Russia, again). The culture around international adoption also shifted, with increased awareness of coercion, abuse, and child-trafficking. Much of this decrease was in line with the recommendations of the United Nations Convention on the Rights of the Child, which asserted that children should "not be adopted internationally when there is suitable care for them available within their own country." In 2020, there were only 1,622 children brought into the United States for adoption.

Throughout this history, the people forcing or facilitating family separations always argued that what they were doing was in the best interest of the children and their birth parents. Before the Civil War, slavery apologists argued that "negroes are themselves both perverse and comparatively indifferent about this matter. Sometimes it happens that a negro prefers to give up his family rather than separate from his master." Even the Freedmen's Bureau, established to help formerly enslaved people, sometimes facilitated the forced indenture of Black children, on the premise that those families could not support their own children. Family separations nearly always took place within the context of charitable or child welfare organizations. Proponents of Indian boarding schools framed their work as saving Native children from their savage ways and assimilating them into American culture. The Orphan Trains were run by many of the country's most prominent and well-funded Christian missionary and child welfare organizations—including the New York Children's Aid Society, the New York Foundling Hospital, and similar charities in Boston and Philadelphia—with the stated purpose "to raise the fallen and to save the lost." (In fact, their work was considered progressive at the time, because they viewed poverty not as a moral failing, but as a social crisis.) The Indian Adoption Project was run by the Child Welfare League of America, who believed Native children would be better cared for within white families. The baby scoop era maternity homes were often run by Catholic Charities, the Florence Crittenton Mission, and the Salvation Army, and were designed to redeem unmarried mothers and their children. One social worker described the religious calling she felt to do this work: "There entered a God-given purpose in my heart, which had never left me from that day to this, that [the unmarried mother] should have a chance." This ongoing language of charity, welfare, and salvation elides the harm done by family separation, and frames the practice of adoption solely as a social good. Whether those practicing the work—in any decade through today—believe the honorable motives they purport to serve remains an open question.

Those people today who remain devoted to adoption's promotion often claim that it is quite different than it used to be. Mostly these differences are best attributed to cultural and legal shifts, rather than to changes in the practice of adoption. The diminishing taboos around nonmarital pregnancy and single motherhood and the availability of abortion in many states mean that the social context of adoption is very different and will ensure that our post-*Roe* era is not a full return to the deeply constrained choices and coercive practices that relinquishing mothers faced before 1973. The most meaningful shift in adoption practice in recent decades is that most adoptions are, to some degree, open. "Open adoption" is not clearly or singularly defined, nor is it legally enforceable. Instead, openness broadly encompasses any number of arrangements: relinquishing parents selecting their child's adoptive family, receiving pictures or letters in the mail for a few years, visiting with their child once a year, or in some instances, becoming an integrated part of the extended kinship circle around their child. Yet as we will see, there are many things about adoption that preserve the conservative values and inequities on which adoption is premised, and that ultimately do not serve those most impacted by adoption.

The history of adoption is essential to understand because it has never gone away. Instead, the social forces that have always shaped family separation and the market forces that have incentivized adoption have become increasingly intertwined. Family regulation systems—under the guise of child welfare—both punish and oppress poor families and families of color and *also* make children available for adoption; private adoption systems are motivated to increase the supply of adoptable infants, *and* they do so by marginalizing vulnerable families and allowing relinquishment to be the only path forward. The memory of family separation during American enslavement haunts a family regulation system that polices and threatens Black communities today. The echoes of Native boarding schools and the Indian Adoption Project reverberate not just through ongoing judicial challenges to the Indian Child Welfare Act, but also through the removal of refugee and immigrant children on the southern U.S. border to "special schools" run by private adoption agencies. (Indeed, the Trump administration used the legal precedents in Indian policy to justify family separation at the border.) And while international adoption into the United States remains extremely low, at times of crises it reemerges: when there's a tsunami in the Indian Ocean in 2005, an earthquake in Haiti in 2010, or a war in Ukraine in 2022, American missionaries and nonprofit organizations routinely work to remove children, not just from danger, but from their families.

Even the definition of "orphan" endures: the U.S. Citizenship and Immigration Services still defines an "orphan" as a child who may have a living parent. The practices established in the early 1900s by Georgia Tann and others—sealed birth certificates, lack of openness, high payments, prioritized secrecy—still shape the experience of adopted people who do not have access to their original birth certificates or who have minimal access to their full identities due to closed adoptions or limited contact. Critical adoption scholar Kimberly McKee describes these as "adoption's residues," which are "both visible and invisible, their legibility dependent on whether we want to recognize how the systems governing adoption are inextricably tied to other systems used to control, discipline, and surveil." But this is not just a consideration of how historical injustices are relevant to today's adoptions. The mothers who lost children during the baby scoop era and through the Indian Adoption Project are still here; their stories are still ongoing, and their children's are, too. They are still part of our present. And while—as the following discussion details—these mothers of previous generations may seem different from mothers who relinquish today, their experiences are all too similar.

*   *   *

Understanding even the basic contours of adoption today is more challenging than might be expected. As a researcher, I have found it continually frustrating that the U.S. government does not track private domestic adoptions. The U.S. State Department tracks international adoptions because they involve bringing noncitizen children into the country, and there is some accounting of children in foster care and public adoptions nationwide. The National Council for Adoption (NCFA), an organization that advocates for adoption agencies and adoption-promotive policies, does compile reports tabulating state-level data to come up with national numbers. But even the NCFA numbers are vague, because it's exceedingly difficult to appropriately count adoptions that may be identical legally, but quite different for the people living them—or, conversely, rooted in similar circumstances, but with very different legal understandings. For example, the most frequent private adoptions are stepparent adoptions, where a parent's new spouse gains parental rights to their children. Because these adoptions are usually of older children and because they preserve a legal relationship to at least one biological parent, they are quite different than a pregnant woman choosing an unrelated family to raise her child from birth—even if they are legally the same. On the other hand, the state's intervening and terminating a mother's parental rights to her infant soon after birth, or a parent's leaving their newborn at a safe haven site, would possibly both involve public adoptions but might feel more similar to a new mother who terminates her own parental rights to her child in a private adoption.* Because of the lack of integrated and systematic tracking, even seemingly simple questions about adoption are difficult to answer.†

---

* The lines between public and private adoptions are often blurred because—even in voluntary, private adoptions—only the state (via a family court judge) can terminate parental rights. Even in adoptions where a newborn is discharged from a hospital into the immediate physical custody of their adoptive parents, legal custody will often be held by the state or an adoption agency working in partnership with the state until the adoption is finalized. Several states have laws that allow for the custody of infants who are abandoned at safe haven sites to be given over to private agencies.

† I am not the only researcher with this frustration. Most NCFA reports tabulating state-level data make note of the lack of federal data, with the specific recommendation that this be corrected. In 2005, adoption researchers Victor Flango and Mary Caskey remarked in

Looking at the overall birth rates in the United States and the best available accounting for private adoptions, I found that adoptions represented approximately 0.5 percent of all births from 1982 through 2014. This estimate translates to 18,300 to 20,000 private infant adoptions every year for the last decade. This number is out of 3.8 to 4 million births per year, and in contrast to 850,000 to 1 million abortions per year (with the numbers of both births and abortions currently declining every year—though this may change with the shifting legal context of abortion). Compared to birth and abortion rates, the adoption rate is merely a blip. Yet, compared to other developed countries, particularly those that invest highly in their children and families, the U.S. rate is extremely high—between three and thirty-five times higher than the domestic adoption rates in such countries.*

For most of the 1990s, researchers found that demographic profiles of relinquishing mothers still reflected those of the baby scoop era: middle-class teenage girls, who had a reasonable expectation of a college education and middle-class stability—who perceived (and whose parents perceived) the opportunity cost of parenting at a young age to be high. Compared to young mothers who chose to parent their children, relinquishing mothers in the 1980s and 1990s were more likely to be white, to be enrolled in school and earning good grades, and to have better-educated

---

their report *Adoptions, 2000–2001*: "Most private adoption agencies neither compile data on the number of children adopted through their agencies, nor on the characteristics of the children, their adoptive parents and their birth parents. They assume these data are captured by public agencies, which in turn are often under the impression that private agencies keep comprehensive information on their own adoptions. Most do not, and so it is not possible to compile totals from private adoption agencies."

* For example, Iceland—which ranks at the top of the OECD (Organisation for Economic Co-operation and Development) measures for supporting families—had just *nine* non-stepparent domestic infant adoptions in 2019. This number is actually a marked increase over 2018, when the number was just one. Even controlled for differences in population, the U.S. rates are two to twenty times higher. Similar patterns hold true for Denmark (about thirty domestic infant relinquishments annually in recent years), New Zealand (about twenty), and Norway (about eight).

parents; they were less likely to have been raised by a single parent or have received public benefits. Importantly, though, women who had worked at a paid job for at least six months were *less* likely to relinquish. When they made their own money, rather than being dependent on their parents' support, adoption was far less likely.

However, these profiles were already outdated when I began my research, and little new data was being collected on relinquishing mothers today. Only one source had in-depth data on these mothers: the adoption agencies.* So I asked them. Six agencies sent me demographic information on the relinquishing mothers with whom they worked, including information on 8,658 infant adoptions that took place between 2011 and 2020.

That profile of young middle-class white women does not seem to reflect relinquishing mothers today.

While the majority of mothers in my sample were white, that majority was only 55 percent—a meaningful reduction from the over 90 percent just twenty years ago. In contrast to studies from the 1990s, in which relinquishment was found to be nearly nonexistent among Black and Latina women, at least 17 percent of my sample were Black women and over 7 percent Latina, with an additional 7 percent identifying as multiracial. Numbers of Asian American women were low (around 2 percent), and the reported number of Native American women was very low (less than 1 percent, most likely because the Indian Child Welfare Act

---

* This is not entirely true—California's Department of Social Services (DSS) has these data available for all private adoptions that happen in California. However, the DSS does not aggregate these data and make them available. When I requested access, they told me to ask the agencies. They also told me I could speak with relinquishing mothers only if I asked permission of their adoption service providers first—but as there was no reason rooted in research ethics to do so, I did not, and my institutional review board did not require me to. However, this interaction illustrates both how dependent the state is on private agencies to collect these data, and how willing they are to allow private agencies to be gatekeepers to accessing information about how adoption is practiced in this country.

ensures that tribal adoptions are often managed separately from the private adoption system—and as Chapter 6 discusses, this regulation likely impacts how tribal membership is recorded in private adoptions). In comparison to the overall American population, this means that while most relinquishing mothers are white, women of color (and particularly Black women) are currently overrepresented among birth mothers relinquishing infants.

Only 14 percent of the women in my sample were teenagers; about 56 percent were in their twenties. Compared to data for all American births, this does skew younger—but the idea that most relinquishing mothers are teens is no longer true. Importantly, adoption no longer represents a way of deferring motherhood: a majority of relinquishing mothers had other children at the time of the adoption.

Why, then, are they relinquishing their babies? The answer is clear when we look at the variables that speak to their financial resources: most of them are unemployed; 64 percent reported less than $5,000 in personal annual income. If we look at their health insurance, 88 percent of relinquishing mothers had coverage from Medicaid—this proportion is over twice the rate of Medicaid coverage for all women who give birth in the United States. The data provided by one larger agency showed that 28 percent of their birth mothers lived in chronic poverty, and 20 percent were homeless at the time of relinquishment.

None of these findings suggest that all relinquishing mothers are living in abject poverty, though it is clear that some of them are. As you'll see in the stories to come, some of them might have low personal income because they are still teenagers or students relying on their family's financial support. Some of them might be unemployed at the time of the adoption because they had to quit their jobs due to the pregnancy. What these numbers do show, however, is that—at the time of the adoption—many of these mothers have few financial resources within their own control, and the support of others or the ability to resume paid employment might be contingent on the decision they make about who will parent their child.

These data also suggest that the racial demographics of relinquishing mothers are changing rapidly, as transracial adoption has become more common, as the private adoption systems are increasingly entwined with family regulation systems that target Black families and women of color, and as poverty (which, given the racial capitalism of our country, disproportionately shapes the lives of people of color) becomes the most common reason for relinquishment. Because my interview sample includes women who relinquished from 2000 (when private domestic adoption was still overwhelming white) to 2020 (as it was becoming more racially diverse), my sample is disproportionately white when compared to relinquishing mothers today. The shifting demographics and increasing participation of women of color in private adoption suggests their stories should carry particular weight as we consider the future of adoption in the United States.

Most important, though, the attempt to profile birth mothers is descriptive only of those who have already relinquished, and not at all predictive of who will relinquish in the future. Women of every race, ethnicity, age, and income are far, far more likely to choose either abortion *or* parenting rather than adoption. But this pattern suggests that for those who do relinquish infants, their lack of economic power is relevant to why they do. In her work looking at the experiences of mothers in the baby scoop era, historian Rickie Solinger writes: "Almost everybody believes that on some level, birthmothers *make a choice to give their babies away. . . .* I argue that adoption is rarely about mothers' choices; it is, instead, about the abject choicelessness of some resourceless women." For the women that Solinger was considering, "choicelessness" was rooted in class-based ideas about sexuality, gender, motherhood, and legitimacy. For women today, it is increasingly about access to money and the stability it provides.

* * *

Ultimately, knowing who relinquishing mothers are is only part of understanding contemporary adoption, because so many ideas of adoption are not rooted in the experiences of those who live it but instead in the political, religious, and cultural narratives that we have about building families, caring for children, finding common ground in the abortion debate, and fulfilling a religious calling.

Most adoption facilitators in the United States (and around the world) are closely affiliated with conservative churches and thus, either by proxy or directly, with the anti-abortion movement. In a 2014 report, the Heritage Foundation identified the largest adoption agencies in the country: Bethany Christian Services, Catholic Charities, and LDS Family Services. Due to legal requirements that they serve same-sex couples, along with a diminishing number of mothers interested in relinquishment, several of those agencies have reduced or eliminated their child-placing services in the years since. However, most of the largest agencies remain church-affiliated, and most of those that no longer directly facilitate adoptions still provide counseling and services to pregnant women in the hope of encouraging adoption.

In her 2013 book *The Child Catchers,* Kathryn Joyce describes "the new gospel of adoption":

Across the United States a much wider spectrum of evangelical churches . . . had begun to view adoption as a perfect storm of a cause: a way for conservative churches to get involved in poverty and social justice issues that they had ceded years before to liberal denominations, an extension of pro-life politics and a decisive rebuttal to the taunt that Christians should adopt all those extra children they want women to have, and, more quietly, as a window for evangelizing, as Christians get to "bring the mission field home" and pass on the gospel to a new population of children, effectively saving them twice.

However, the "quiet part"—that adoption is a way of evangelizing, and thus a core part of being a Christian—is increasingly less quiet. Adoption theologians, most prominently Russell Moore, have argued that Christians are "adopted" by God, and that that is the source of their salvation. An adoptive father, Moore argues that adoption is a way of living the gospel, a mission, an inheritance from God. Even prior to the fall of *Roe,* conservative Christians were already ready and eager to adopt.

This eagerness allows them to look past a persistent truth: that the children these prospective adoptive parents are intent on "saving" are often not babies and are rarely orphans. In fact, they often have living parents, or at least extended kinship networks within their own communities, that would *like* to care for them; they are also often older children.*

These narratives of child-saving reach beyond the church and infuse popular news media. Looking specifically at the crisis in Haiti after the 2010 earthquake that destroyed the developing country's infrastructure, Joyce told the story of agency after agency that removed Haitian children from the country, often illegally. Yet this grim reality was misunderstood in popular coverage. CNN's Soledad O'Brien made a TV documentary on an evangelical orphanage in Haiti entitled *Rescued; The Times* of London reported, "The paperwork can wait . . . everyone wins with adoption." While UNICEF worked in line with the Hague Adoption Convention guidelines limiting international adoptions to children for whom reunion with their birth families or in-country adoption was impossible, this work was dismissed as against "the good of the children" and "nation-pandering" by evangelical leaders looking to broker adoptions, one saying

---

* Evangelicals are not alone in their embrace of the "orphan crisis." In 2005, Angelina Jolie appeared on the cover of *People* magazine under the headline "Angelina adopts a baby girl: The star welcomes little Zahara, an African orphan." Except Zahara was not an AIDS orphan, as *People* said—her mother was alive and had wanted to raise her child, but poverty made it impossible for her to keep the baby properly nourished, so she relinquished her to an agency. Jolie's story is just one high-profile case.

Haitian children were being "held hostage by UNICEF's agenda." Then senator Mary Landrieu said: "Either UNICEF is going to change or have a very difficult time getting support from the U.S. Congress. Americans take this call very seriously." She was joined by fellow Democratic senator Amy Klobuchar, who boasted of the thirty-nine children brought from Haiti to her state of Minnesota and expressed pride in encouraging Haitian president René Préval to remove barriers to international adoption.

Klobuchar and Landrieu are both Democrats, and Landrieu is an adoptive mother who made adoption her signature issue during her time in office. As their advocacy demonstrates, conservative Republicans do not have a political monopoly on adoption. After all, the Adoption and Safe Families Act of 1997, which facilitated the faster termination of parental rights for those in foster care, was championed by then first lady Hillary Clinton, passed under President Bill Clinton, and was invoked by Secretary of State Clinton during her own presidential campaigns. (The left-leaning think tank Center for American Progress cited ASFA as one of Secretary Clinton's "great accomplishments" in 2015.) In 2021, President Joe Biden noted the beginning of National Adoption Month to "celebrate all of the children and families nurtured, enriched, and made whole by adoption"—but he was also the first president to acknowledge the history of harms against Black and Native families by the family regulation systems and articulate that "we must improve our efforts to keep families together, prevent the trauma of unnecessary child removal." When Russia invaded Ukraine in early 2022, the first response of many U.S. elected officials was not so different from the reaction to the Haitian crisis twelve years earlier: seventy-three members of the House and Senate (of both parties) signed a letter to Secretary of State Antony Blinken requesting that this not delay international adoptions from Ukraine.

Yet beyond these political statements and legislation by Democratic leaders, many on the political left support progressive ideas of family building that rely on the concept of chosen family, of allowing kinship bonds to be forged regardless of biological relationships—ideas that segue quite readily to an embrace of adoption, particularly for queer couples who cannot conceive biological children without the use of assisted reproductive technologies. In his work on creative family building through adoption, surrogacy, and gamete donation for gay and lesbian couples and single mothers by choice, sociologist Joshua Gamson acknowledges the progressive tension of the dual narratives of "rough, rewarding individual parenthood quests and of the troubling structural inequalities that shape family making." Critical perspectives on these underlying inequalities, Gamson suggests, "might be a buzz kill [when] placed against the happy endings" of the families that are *formed* by nontraditional family building, "but they are also not wrong."

As I wrote with fellow sociologist Jessica Harrison,

> All these things can be true: that parental love is full and valid without a biological relationship; that children do not need a "traditional" family to thrive; that children adapt to a range of normalcies and benefit from having many adults who care about them. And all of these things can also be true: that the families made whole by adoption are more visible to us than the families separated by adoption, and adopted people are always part of both; that adoption is almost universally the transfer of infants from families with fewer resources and less power to families with more resources and more power; that the idyllic appeal of adoption is such that it has moved those otherwise very deeply immersed in the work of creating a more just world to overlook the systemic issues of privilege upon which adoption functions, and without which adoption would be inconceivable.

Americans of all religions and political parties believe adoption to be a fundamentally necessary and social good; they see adoption as a way of ensuring better lives for children who might otherwise not have homes or parents at all. These beliefs are rarely rooted in reality.

We have collective cultural ideas about what good parents can offer and what incapable parents look like: most often, those incapable parents are young, poor, and unmarried, possibly unemployed or without stable housing, occasionally with histories of addiction or incarceration, or more rarely with demonstrated patterns of neglect or abusiveness. But many of our ideas about what constitutes a "better life" are rooted in politicized social mythologies. The trajectory of completing college, then securing a job, housing, and marital stability, and *then* having children within the context of a two-parent household is a distinctly middle-class life course. Deviations from this path—a teen pregnancy or single motherhood, for example—might really derail that aspirational life course, and birth mothers often cite their own youth or lack of a stable relationship as reasons for considering adoption, with the belief that a family that conforms to their middle-class ideals is better able to provide their child with this "better life." There are truisms in our society that women who delay parenthood past adolescence have better outcomes for themselves and their children, and that children raised in two-parent families accrue advantages throughout their lives. But *compared to whom*?

When we look at teen mothers, for example, we attribute any number of adverse outcomes in their own and their children's lives to their early childbearing. But it remains a demographical fact that adolescent motherhood is almost exclusively the domain of girls and families who were *already poor* before becoming pregnant. What do these young women have to lose by having their children earlier in life? Because of their circumstances, they are not often college-bound, and they have few expectations of upward social mobility. And it's not clear that the decision is costly to them or their children. Social science research has found that when this cohort is compared to appropriate groups (such as their sisters who delayed childbearing, or women in their community who had miscarriages as teenagers), there are almost no adverse outcomes best attributed to maternal youth. One longitudinal analysis found that the teen mothers worked more hours, earned more money, received more support from spouses, and were not more likely to be reliant on long-term public assistance. In poor communities, the children of teen mothers score as well, if not better, on measures of cognitive development from preschool through early adolescence. After studying adolescent childbearing for over forty years, sociologist Frank Furstenberg wrote: "Many of the apprehensions about the powerful and lasting consequences of early parenthood . . . have not been substantiated by social science research. But many policymakers and most Americans continue to believe that eliminating early childbearing would produce great dividends for young people, their families, and society at large." He goes on to argue: "rather than being the primary source of social disadvantage, early childbearing is better understood as a product of disadvantage." Essentially: they have children earlier because they are poor; they are not poor because they have children earlier—and it is the poverty that shapes their lives, trajectories, and outcomes.

Additionally, while many unpartnered birth mothers relinquish because they want their child to have two parents, this ideal also lacks realistic nuance. Unsurprisingly, children raised by parents in high-conflict marriages are no better off than peers in single-parent households. For Black children, researchers have found that living in a one-parent household does not have the same cost as it has for their white peers, nor does living in a two-parent family carry a comparable benefit. Examining thirty years of longitudinal data, sociologist Christina Cross found that for Black teens, family structure had a far weaker relationship to their educational success than it did for their white classmates. Cross demonstrated that it was the difference in access to resources—money, housing, good jobs—that accounted for this different relationship between success and family structure. Another study found that the particularly ungenerous social supports available to single American mothers (compared to single mothers in other rich democratic countries) puts them—and their children—at greater likelihood of poverty. Such stringent ideas about who deserves to parent almost always come back to money, support, and the lack thereof.

True, children are expensive, and it's easy to say that financial stability is needed to raise children—but we must then acknowledge the vast number of people that parent without such stability. Over 37 million Americans live in poverty, including 11.6 million children; estimates suggest that nearly one in six American children live in poverty, and almost 71 percent of children living in poverty are children of color. Over 6.4 million children live in households with food insecurity, and on any given night, 175,000 children experience homelessness. For many families, these are not the challenges of a moment, but struggles for a lifetime. Such inequities are damning for our country and its future. American poverty is not an indication of personal failing but instead a vast and systemic social problem to which infant adoption cannot possibly offer a solution. While it might be understandable that some individual mothers view relinquishment as a path out of poverty for their child—or out of their own stigmatized position as someone who might need public support—framing it as a solution to poverty that offers a "path to a better life" fails to recognize that we are offering a small, private response to a problem that requires massive public engagement. Adoption is not, broadly, a solution to the precarious conditions under which millions of Americans consider and seek parenthood, for whom dreams of financial stability are illusory or unattainable.

* * *

In April 2020, I was invited to attend a meeting hosted by the U.S. Department of Health and Human Services. This convening of adoption researchers, advocates, and lobbyists was intended to help develop "strategies for overcoming barriers to private infant adoptions."

The facilitator asked the room: *What are the barriers to birth parents considering domestic adoption? How can we overcome them?* They showed a chart on-screen documenting the decline of adoptions over the last many decades, presenting these data as an unfortunate pattern or grim harbinger. The government wanted to understand from where—and from whom—we can get more babies, and soon.

What is helpful in bringing birth parents to an adoption decision? the facilitator asked. The language here is important: it's not "the expectant parents who are still making a decision" but "the birth parents," as if relinquishment is already the preferred and inevitable outcome. It's not "the right decision for them," but "an adoption decision," because that is the goal. Other attendees responded: women need more information about adoption; they need better, adoption-positive options counseling; they need to be more comfortable having their children parented by people of a different racial background; they need to be taught about open adoption.

The next question we were to consider was: *What policies and strategies are working to promote adoption?* The responses were quick: educating students in the public schools about adoption; working to decrease the stigma around placing a child; requiring education about adoption for those working in the family regulation system and empowering women to have "options for adoption" within the foster system; calling birth mothers brave and selfless. Six different programs sponsored by various state anti-abortion organizations were cited as "successful" in promoting adoption.

What was never asked: *Why do we want to increase adoptions?* If the decrease in adoptions reflects a lowering birth rate because people have more tools to prevent unintended pregnancies, why is that a problem? If fewer relinquishments means that more people feel equipped to parent in the way they would like to, why do we want the number of adoptions to go up? Who is being served here?

Before *Dobbs*, the rate of domestic adoption relinquishment was low—dramatically low when compared to those who parent or have abortions. One of the largest adoption agencies in the country, Bethany Christian Services, stopped accepting applications from prospective adoptive parents for their domestic infant adoption program. Smaller adoption agencies were closing because of lack of available infants. Anthropologist Kathryn Mariner, in her ethnography of a nonprofit adoption agency, noted how one director of a recently closed agency was forced to conclude: "I don't think domestic adoption is going to economically recover. I really don't." Yet history has shown us that adoptable children will be obtained from *somewhere*.

Two years later, I was startled but not surprised to find Alito's footnote on the "virtually nonexistent" supply of adoptable infants in the *Dobbs* opinion that unraveled protections of abortion rights across the country. It is telling that, while the *Roe* decision that expanded access to abortion was premised on the decisions made by Norma McCorvey, a relinquishing mother, the *Dobbs* decision that overturned it was premised on figments of jurisprudential imagination about what adoption might mean in the lives of American women today. Yet, despite not being rooted in the realities of relinquishment, conservative leaders found the promotion of adoption to be a winning message. The National Senatorial Republican Committee released a statement saying, "We should do all we can to encourage more adoptions and fewer abortions," while Texas congressman Dan Crenshaw tweeted: "Less abortion, more adoption. Why is that controversial?"

Here's the question I wish I could have asked my fellow meeting attendees that day, two years before the *Dobbs* decision: What happens next? What other policies will be enacted in the interest of increasing the domestic supply of infants? How definitively will we preclude access to abortion? How closely will we police and punish birth parents in the interest of encouraging them to relinquish? Are we willing to withhold support for those families who are the most vulnerable? History has shown we are willing to go quite far in the name of supporting some families over others.

Cassie

"I would've needed maybe a thousand dollars for my life to change—just a very small amount of money would've probably changed my entire world. It's really weird to think of that now."

In 2012, Cassie (who is white) was a twenty-two-year-old college student living in the Rocky Mountain region when she found out she was pregnant. She relinquished her son, Miles, for infant adoption. At the time of our interview in 2020, she was parenting a three-year-old daughter, Amelia, with her boyfriend, John, who is also Miles's birth father.

I was twenty-two and in college when I got pregnant. I had a low-paying part-time job, making nine dollars an hour, and a studio apartment. I had been anorexic for a couple of years, and I was trying to recover from that. I was gaining a lot of weight and just getting bigger in my midsection, but I thought that was normal, healthy weight gain. I had stopped having my period because of the anorexia, so I really missed all of the signs. I noticed a lot of changes in myself and my body, but I didn't realize I was pregnant for a very long time, until about six months along.

I got a pregnancy test at Planned Parenthood, and I actually wanted to have an abortion right off the bat. But as soon as the person at the clinic saw me, she told me that I was just way too far along. She said I could go to Las Vegas to get an abortion, and I thought about that for maybe a day. I didn't feel right about that at all. It would have been a two- or three-day procedure. I mean, it's one thing to have an abortion, but I was kind of uncomfortable with having one at that point.

I never considered parenting. It felt impossible given my situation. I was just so poor at the time. I would've needed maybe a thousand dollars for my life to change—just a very small amount of money would've probably changed my entire world. It's really weird to think of that now.

But in addition to money, I really didn't have a lot of family support. I mean, I have family and they live in the same city as me, but I didn't feel like I could ask them for help. They might have helped me, but the price would be their scorn and disdain; they would look down on me and make me feel like I had failed them. Even though my family is politically liberal, they are not liberal or open-minded when it comes to me. To even consider parenting, I just felt like I would need their support, and I just knew I didn't have that. They were extremely supportive of the adoption, though. They were like, "It's such a smart, mature decision," which is pretty much what everyone told me. I think they were really happy and relieved that they wouldn't have to help me.

I immediately felt like adoption was my only choice. I went to an adoption agency—I wasn't super excited about adoption, but I went there. The agency has such a lovely, warm, welcoming performance that they put on. They say, "Oh, you're so smart and responsible, and you're doing, like, the most wonderful, best thing." They seemed so nice. The first time I was there, they talked to me for a couple of hours and ordered me lunch. I couldn't stop bawling. I didn't want to be there; I didn't want to be in that situation. I just felt like this is not my life. They just said, "This is just going to be such a wonderful, happy thing for you and for your baby."

They didn't talk to me about any other options. It was all adoption all the time. They say, "Oh, we can help you decide what you want to do. You know, if it's parenting, we'll help you find those resources and make that plan." But it was never a real conversation. There wasn't overt coercion, but there was still coercion. They gave me this work sheet divided into two columns, labeled "Things I can provide for my baby" and "Things adoptive parents can provide for my baby." They say, "You know, some things that adoptive parents might be able to provide are money or stability or marriage or a house." I wasn't 100 percent sold on adoption when I went to the agency, but to be confronted with that, how could I not be?

Sometimes I feel like the adoption was my fault because I reached out to them. I went there, and I didn't necessarily want to discuss parenting. But no one talked to me about it at all. No one said to me,

"You know, you can make this work. You can do this. It will be okay."
I was in a huge crisis and terrified. It's very possible that I wouldn't
have been open to that conversation about parenting. I do think it was
probably too big for me to consider. It was just really overwhelming.

Before even picking parents, the agency ladies talked to me about
openness, and I was able to just select from a few options. It didn't
feel like true openness was an actual option. They asked, "How long
do you want to stay in touch with your child and their parents?" The
options were one year, two years, five years, etc., and I just wrote until
age eighteen—you know, always. They said I could get some pictures
and a letter every six months or every year, and that's pretty much
what they offered me. I was like, "Oh, yeah, of course. I don't want to
bother the parents too much." I didn't really know what else to ask for.
I didn't feel like I was in some position to make a bunch of demands.
I felt really low about myself.

The adoption worker pushed me to pick out parents immediately.
My first visit to the agency, they sent me home with a big stack of
parent profiles. They even had me look at some while I was there. A
lot of the adoptive parents were just very different people than I am.
They were religious or extremely straitlaced. Because I'm not religious,
I didn't really want someone like that. I aspired to have someone who
was like me, but better. The parents I picked just seemed so cool to
me. For one thing, they were obviously very high profile. They're not
celebrities, but one is a journalist and the other is a fashion designer.
I was blown away that they had such cool jobs. How can you not be
impressed by that? Like I said, I felt pretty low about myself. I made
nine dollars an hour. They just had the cutest pictures, an amazing
house, an adorable dog. They lived in a big city. They never told me
where they lived, of course. I always thought I would find out eventually, but I never did. I just knew it was a big, diverse city.

I didn't meet the parents until I was pretty close to my due date.
We had a supervised brunch together with the agency ladies about a
week before he was born. It felt like the right fit at the time, but honestly, I was so in awe of them. I was a people pleaser. I just thought I
was making them so happy, and I really lived for that.

When I went into labor, I checked with them and let them know, and they knew that my plan was not to have the adoptive parents there during the birth. I did not want that. I didn't really want that many people there. I just wanted my boyfriend, John, my best friend, and my mom. That's not what happened at all. After he was born, the adoptive parents showed up right away.

I was having second thoughts. I was so crowded in the hospital. I never really got to even be alone. I felt like everything about me had just changed. Beforehand, everyone said, "Oh, the hormones. Like they're going to make you second-guess things." So I was prepared for that, and I just thought I was supposed to push through and ignore those feelings, and that's what I did. It's very hard to do that when you have a newborn that you're falling in love with. But I didn't have space for those thoughts and feelings. There were just so many people in my room at all times: doctors, nurses, the adoptive parents, my family, my boyfriend, four or five ladies from the agency.

I was discharged without him. I had to roll the bassinet down the hallway to where the adoptive parents were, and then I just walked away and went into an elevator. It was the worst moment of my life.

I did nothing but cry. It was just the darkest and most depressed I've ever been. I knew I would be sad, but I don't think I realized the depth of feeling, the depth of love. Every part of my body ached for him. I wished I was holding him or nursing him, and I couldn't believe he wasn't there. I would have nightmares all the time and I'd always think he was there, or I would hear crying but there was no baby there. I did whatever I could to numb myself. I'm not really a big substance user, but I would just drink a lot or smoke pot to shut my mind off. It never really worked.

I had no contact with him. Absolutely none. I knew they were in the same city, because they couldn't leave the state for a certain window of time. I'm sure it wasn't fun for them, taking care of a newborn in a hotel room. It was torture knowing they were in the same city, and not talking to me. They were right there. They could have reached out to get together or at least say goodbye. But they didn't, and that's okay. It would have been a lot to handle—but I went from having so much contact with the agency to none. I felt like I was dropped. The agency ladies texted a few times to tell me they had named him Miles, and to share one picture. That was pretty much it.

In the beginning, they would write an occasional letter. I usually felt like they were just copying all the, like, milestones from some website. Like, "Oh, here are his milestones. There you go." I never really felt like it was super personal, although I do think, especially in the early days, they did try. I would get letters every six months, with maybe eight to twelve pictures. When Miles was two and a half, they came back because they were adopting their second child. We had a visit then. It's the only visit we've ever had. After our visit, I was right back in the dark place for a really long time. It was just so intense for me. I think you have to be really strong to have an open adoption, because it's like you're confronted with that all the time. We haven't had any contact since his fifth birthday, and he's eight now.

I've never really known how I should act around Miles's parents. I've never really wanted to make more demands on them, and I think for their part, they only want a very surface, casual relationship. I think they feel like they're doing it as a favor to me, to help me heal. I do want to be closer. I wish I knew more about their lives. I enjoy knowing about his life. But I do wish—I don't know. I do kind of feel like what I want is something I couldn't really have, because I don't think they really want Miles to talk to me. I don't think they want personal closeness or connection between us, even though I would love that. I would love to be there for him in some way. I don't really think that's something they want. And it might not even be something he wants. Sometimes it's honestly better to distance myself from it as much as possible in my day-to-day life, and not always be in an emotionally heavy place.

I do feel differently about adoption. Before everything, I was like, "Oh, it's a great thing." The only thing I knew about adoption was from the media, and everyone says it's great, so that's what I thought, too. My experience completely changed that for me. Now I find most media stories pretty problematic. I really can't think of much that is true or positive to me. There are so many different experiences out there, and I'm sure that some of them are true for some people, but for me they're all very problematic. And I guess one of the biggest ones is that birth mothers move on and it's not a big deal to them. The greatest example of that is in *Juno*. She's off riding a bicycle and singing a song immediately, you know, and that's kind of what the agency told me, too. You'll move on. You'll grieve, but you'll move on and you'll be happy about it. It's a win-win situation. None of that has ever been true for me. I've never moved on. I guess I've moved on in that I've kept living my life and doing the best I can in some ways, but no, it's not like I just got over it. It's not like that.

And I guess the other thing that I find problematic is that it's always depicted as a choice, right? It's a choice you make. Yeah, it was my choice to go to the agency; it was my choice to choose adoption—but, like, it really wasn't. It felt like my only option. I was so naive. I had so many people telling me like, "This is what you should do." I was just very eager to please. I didn't know what I was doing. I really trusted the other adults in my life to tell me what to do, and I trusted that wholeheartedly. When I look back on so many things, I realize it wasn't a choice. Obviously, I was very culpable in the things I did and how I, like, went along with them, but it's not like I made an informed choice. I never got to make that choice again after birth, and that's the biggest thing to me. You can't make that choice when you're pregnant and it's such a crisis moment. In this state, you can sign your termination of parental rights twenty-four hours after birth, and the agency workers pretty much make you do it as soon as possible. They don't encourage you to wait. They don't encourage you to think about it after. They are in the hospital with you, having you sign those papers as soon as they legally can. If I could go back, I just wish I would've waited a couple days, because I wouldn't have made the same choice. That's not enough time. It's not okay to make that decision in a hospital. Because who is in their right mind after they give birth? Seriously, the emotions and the hormones are just overwhelming, and I couldn't even sit with that because of all the people around me.

After a few weeks, everyone was just like, "Why are you not over it?" I'm never going to be over it. I do have John. I do talk to him. I don't always feel like I can talk to him, but for the most part, he's who

I turn to and lean on if I need to. And I've kind of gotten to a point where I'm just very used to being on my own and self-sufficient in those feelings. If I'm having a really bad day, which isn't often anymore, thankfully—it used to be every day was pretty much a bad day, but now it's very rare. If I have a bad day, I know I can talk to him. I had a day like that—the thing that triggered me was seeing polka dots. I was wearing a polka-dot nightgown in the hospital after Miles was born, and for some reason, just seeing polka dots set me off. I just had, like, this epic panic attack. I couldn't talk. I couldn't, like, breathe for so long, and once I was able to talk, I did talk to him. I don't really feel like a therapist would help. I feel like most of them would just kind of believe the same things about adoption that most people believe, and I don't care to talk to someone like that and hear what they have to say.

Before Miles was born, I never really wanted to have children. I think becoming a mother changed everything about me, even though I wasn't raising him. I felt like my old self was dead, didn't exist any-more, and I was just a new person. All these beliefs and values I used to have were completely gone, thrown out the window, and I, like, suddenly did want to have kids, and you know, I didn't want the adop-tion to be my only experience with pregnancy. I didn't want that to be my only child. I really wanted to have another one. I didn't want to be trying to replace him, but I did want to have another child and, in a way, rewrite my experience before and to actually have a good one.

My daughter, Amelia, was born when Miles was four years old. Was it a planned pregnancy? Yes. Maybe no. We could have been more intentional about it. I had had an IUD, but I was having trou-ble with it and got it taken out and just . . . didn't get anything else. We were aware of what would happen. I wanted to be pregnant—I don't think my boyfriend did, as much, but he knew and was willing to let it happen. He was really happy when I did get pregnant. That pregnancy was completely different, because I was just aware and present the entire time. With Miles, I honestly was so busy with work and school that I never really, like, listened to my body or paid much attention to symptoms. This time was so different because it was happy. I was extremely happy the entire time. I was just doing all the normal mommy things, just really looking forward to it. It was just a completely different experience because I was happy.

When I had Amelia, I really realized just how hard it is to have a baby. It's not easy in any way, and especially in our society, which really doesn't have any support. And I was really prepared: I saved up a lot of money. I dreamed of it for so long. I was prepared in all these ways and it was still so hard. I would never say adoption was the right thing, but like it would've been incredibly hard for me to parent Miles at age twenty-three with, like, no preparation like that. I can't even imagine how hard that would've been. I could really never say adoption was the right decision for me, but I always considered him, first and foremost. As far as him, I don't know. Sometimes I do think it was the right thing for him. His parents are clearly amazing. They're very loving, warm people, very well off. He could have whatever he wanted, could have, like, the very best life possible, and he does. He has seriously had amazing opportunities and travel and life experiences. I don't feel like it was the wrong decision for him. I don't know if it was the right one. I honestly think that's something that should be left up to him to decide. You know, maybe someday, if I ever do talk to him, he can tell me what he feels.

Jordan

*"I took the pregnancy tests and I cried
because I was so happy."*

**When I interviewed her in 2020, Jordan had given up her son
less than a year earlier. She was twenty-three years old and living in a large city on the East Coast. She had grown up in foster
care, moving from home to home before ending up in a group
facility for several years and aging out of the system. She was not
connected to her family and wasn't even sure of her own racial
background.**

When I found out I was pregnant, I was homeless. I had just gotten
out of a relationship, and I was being harassed by the police a lot, all
the time, just because I didn't have anywhere to go. At the time, I just
felt super depressed, like, suicidal depressed. I was ready to die. And
then the morning sickness didn't help—I didn't realize it was morning
sickness at first. I just thought I was sick and it was making me misera-
ble. But then after a week of it, my friend said something and she was
like, "What if you're pregnant?" She went to the store and got me like
a bunch of pregnancy tests.

I took the pregnancy tests and I cried because I was so happy. It
just changed everything for me. I just felt . . . I have to do what I can
to make sure this baby has a good life. I was planning on spending
those nine months trying to prepare myself to parent. I was more motivated to do better things for myself, not specifically for me, but just for
the baby. I was getting prenatal care at the free clinic by the subway
station. I made sure to get on some housing lists, and then I was trying
to find a job. I was getting food stamps and other support, but that
was my only income.

But then I went to jail. I'd been in a relationship with this guy for a
while, and we'd broken up. We actually got back together after we
found out I was pregnant, but he'd been dating someone else in the

meantime, and she *hated* me. She tried to fight with me. I didn't want to fight, especially because of the baby, so I tried to defend myself. Everything I did was definitely in self-defense, but she called the cops first and played the victim, so I went to jail. I ended up in jail for a few months. I was just glad that I got prenatal care while I was in there, and I had my own cell, so I didn't get bothered too much. But that's why adoption ended up being what we went with, 'cause I didn't have enough time once I got out of jail to get things together.

I started thinking about adoption while I was in there. It had seemed like the best option, because there was no way I was going to get into housing by the time he was born. They had given me some adoption information at one of my prenatal appointments, so I went with that.

The only thing that I knew for sure that I wanted was an LGBTQ family. I am bisexual and my son is biracial—his father is Black and Middle Eastern, and I'm whatever I am. But I wanted my baby to grow up knowing that they could be whoever they wanted and that they wouldn't be judged for being who they are. That was important to me, and that was the only criteria I gave the social worker. She gave me the profile of all her LGBTQ families, and I picked from there. I just wanted my baby to grow up in an open-minded household.

*   *   *

Then COVID hit. I still didn't have housing, so the agency put me and my boyfriend up in an Airbnb for a few months, so that I would have a place to live. It also meant that I had to meet his adoptive parents via Zoom, and then just do a few socially distanced in-person meetups. It's a couple of dads. One of them is white and the other is biracial. They were just super friendly. After reading through all the other profiles, I was just like: these are the guys that I want. They seem really happy, and they've got this huge support system in, like, different places in the country, and they're both able to work from home. During COVID, that was a really big plus.

But COVID also meant that I was only allowed to have one support person with me when I was in labor, so I took my doula. After he was born, I spent like about an hour with him before they moved us to the maternity ward and brought the dads up. They had a private room for the adoptive fathers in the maternity ward, so they could bond with him. They would take him and then just bring him in every three hours for me to breastfeed and that was so relaxing—I could sleep for three hours between feedings, and I didn't have to do diaper changes. I couldn't believe I just pushed an eight-pound child out of myself, but other than that, like, I felt good. Every time I saw them bring him in, they were, like, so focused on learning from the nurses. I got to know them a little better and see, like, how they handled the parenting—just changing diapers and burping him, and just watching how excited they were. I don't know. It made me feel really good. It made me so happy to see them so whole, I guess.

We got discharged together and they drove me back to the Airbnb. It was the first time my boyfriend got to meet the baby, so that was cool. I did some breastfeeding, and it didn't feel too bad, just because I knew that it wasn't going to be the last time I'd see him. We set up a plan for me for the first few days to come over to their place for a few hours, do a couple of feedings. I got to spend a few days with them in their home to see, like, how they were in their home every day. That was also cool to get that little bit of insight. I feel like they're going to be really cool parents.

I stayed at the Airbnb for about a month after he was born. I was worried about the depression coming back, that I was going to go into a deep spiral afterwards because of postpartum depression, or depression because I didn't even have my baby there with me. And I was a little depressed, for sure. But I still have this feeling that I have to live for him, because he's going to grow up and have questions about me, and no one else is going to be able to answer. I still feel very motivated by that.

I just moved into transitional housing two days ago. I was homeless again for a few months after I left the Airbnb, and then I bought a van and was living in that for a few months. But I'm finally in housing now. It's basically kind of like dorm living or like a college co-op. They've got a lot of staff here. They've got staff who are, like, specifically here to help with education and employment, staff here to help get permanent housing. They have an on-site therapist that everybody sees once a week. There's a lot of support. I'm not working yet, though. I'm kind of trying to figure out like what I want to do. This program will help me like get into a job or into school, whatever I decide, and I'm still trying to decide. I'm hoping to get into trade school—I like hands-on work.

Right now, they send me a lot of pictures via text message, a few times a week. They also send me updates when they take him to the pediatricians, like his weigh-ins and how long he is. I've gotten a couple of videos of him being super adorable. We just had an in-person visit last month, and we're doing another one soon. I told them I want at least six visits a year, so probably his birthday, Thanksgiving, Christmas, and then, like, three other times in the year. I'm pretty happy with the amount of contact. I don't know. Once he gets older, if he decides that he wants more or less contact, I'll leave it up to him. But I had spoken with some birth mothers at the agency before he was born, and it was good to get their perspectives. I asked them what I should put in my openness agreement, and they mentioned stuff I hadn't been thinking about—like, if he gets involved in sports or drama or music when he's older, that I can come to his games or shows. All the stuff about breastfeeding at the hospital, and then nursing and pumping afterwards, because I really wanted to do that. The other birth moms told me to put in even more than I wanted, because it might get negotiated down. But his dads, they didn't negotiate it down. They totally agreed to all of it.

And I've talked with a lot of birth moms, and so many of them feel duped, and like the adoption agency was just out to take their baby and get the money from the adoptive family, and I don't feel like my agency did that to me. They made sure I knew my options, and then kept making sure I knew my options through the whole pregnancy. I am pro-choice. Abortion wasn't my choice—but if it had been, I know the agency would have said, "Okay, whatever is right." And my agency, they don't just do adoption service. They will also help you get resources if you do decide to parent. They will help you get to a place where you can do that. But I don't feel like I was duped.

I do want to have more children, though, when I'm in a more stable position and able to take care of a child, I would like to have one more, probably just one more. But first I want to have my own apartment and a steady job. That's why I did adoption this time, because I didn't have enough time to get into the place that I wanted to be at to parent. I was already six or seven months pregnant. It was just too late, after I got out of jail, to figure that out.

I would say that I don't think I'm feeling as much grief as people normally would, even though I do miss him. I've had people tell me, "Wait until the one-year mark and you'll really be feeling it." I guess I'll find that out next year. But I do feel like we're off to a strong start because I grew up in foster care and I know what it is to like have needs not met, and I did not want to do that to my son, and I'm glad that I could find a place and people that could do that for him.

2

Choosing Life

Emily and Sofia were both nineteen years old and pregnant. They were also both planning to have abortions—but they couldn't find a way.

Emily had lived a transient childhood, growing up as a white girl in Northern California. "It's always been just me and my mom," she shared, mentioning that she'd never met her father. But this image of a younger Emily and her mother as a duo wasn't quite the full picture. They'd spent much of Emily's childhood living with one or the other of her mother's parents, moving around to different small cities and rural areas, but always ending back up in the same touristy town where Emily's mother grew up. Her grandmother's household was a large, tight-knit family, with young uncles that Emily thought of as brothers, and a feeling of being "really close, with a sense of being there for each other."

Emily had graduated from high school—a school where "everyone had known each other since preschool"—a year early, when she was just seventeen. Her grandfather, the primary father figure in her life, had just died, leaving her with a sense of loss, confusion, and frustration:

> I was just really becoming my own person, and I decided it was a
> good idea to go ahead and move away [from my family]. I guess

a little bit of anger encouraged me to do that—and confusion, I think, all around. It was a combination of losing somebody at that time in my life, and also living somewhere where I didn't necessarily know that many people.

Emily moved just a few hours away to "the closest place that was far enough but still close to my family" and quickly became involved with a boyfriend that she described as "a little bit of a crutch to help me cope with everything, and help me step away from my family." She acknowledged it wasn't necessarily a healthy relationship, but her boyfriend had recently lost his mother and thus understood her grief. It also helped that he had grown up without a father—Emily felt they were coming from a similar place.

When she started feeling sick, Emily assumed she'd gotten the flu from her boyfriend. Her periods weren't regular anyway, so she didn't miss them when they didn't show up for a few months. It took a while for the idea to surface that she might be pregnant. She went to Planned Parenthood to confirm, and found she was over five months pregnant. She was referred from one clinic to another:

Each time they were like, "Oh, we think you're too far along." So I was sent to another place, and then they would say, "Oh, you're too far along, but this person can do it. You're too far along, but this person . . ." Finally I was sent to a clinic in San Francisco, and I find out that nobody should have sent me anywhere, because I was way too far along to begin with. At that last clinic, I did an ultrasound just to make sure. She did all the measurements. This nice lady tried to explain to me exactly: "Here's where the measurements should be if it was a possible procedure, and here's where you are. And I'm sorry to be the one to tell you, but there's no way you're going to be able to have an abortion. You're going to have this baby."

Sofia's story wasn't so different. Growing up in Los Angeles, she was very close with her Mexican-born, Spanish-speaking mother. Sofia's father was incarcerated for most of her childhood and then deported, so her mother relied on Sofia and her three siblings for support and translation after they were priced out of their Hispanic neighborhood and had to move to a mostly white neighborhood. Her mother worked multiple jobs, while her aunt would help with cooking and child care. "We're a really strong family," Sofia shared. "Whenever a situation happens, we really do have a lot of family that supports us." She spoke about how "not having anything is good for us," and how it helped her stay humble and learn a lot about life.

Sofia "practically raised" her younger siblings and felt she couldn't fail them, she said. She worked part time while in school to bring in much-needed income. She knew her new boyfriend (who was eight years older than she was) was distracting her from work, and she also resented his constant need for her time and attention. When she began to have some abnormal bleeding, she went to the emergency room while her boyfriend stayed on the couch. *Could she be pregnant?* the nurse in the ER asked her. She told them no, not that she knew of. But an ultrasound revealed that she was. And even though she recognized that she had no financial stability, a disengaged boyfriend, and a deep anxiety about increasing the burden on her mother, she met the moment with joy:

> Deep down inside I felt happy because I knew I was bringing something so beautiful into this world. And then when I stopped and thought about, well, you know, what happens if he doesn't want to be a part of the baby's life? What am I going to do? Everything's going to fall on me. I saw my mother struggle. Do I really want to go through this? Is this the right moment? So many questions popped into my head at that very moment, and I was just confused. My two minutes of happiness that I first felt drifted

away slowly when I started realizing that bringing a kid into this world was a lot harder than I thought it would be.

She was five months along. Her boyfriend reacted angrily and pushed her toward getting an abortion, and she conceded—but when she went to the clinic in Manhattan, there was nothing they could do. "Then they had me speak to a counselor about maybe putting the baby up for adoption. And I knew that was the best and only option that I had."

*   *   *

Emily and Sofia were interviewed by my colleague Heather Gould as part of the Turnaway Study, a ten-year project led by demographer Dr. Diana Greene Foster. The study followed 956 women who sought abortions across the United States, including over 160 women who gave birth after they were denied access to the abortions they wanted because they were over the gestational age limits of the clinics where they sought care. However, in my work with Foster, Gould, and our colleague epidemiologist Dr. Lauren Ralph, we found that only 15 of them, or 9 percent—including Emily and Sofia—relinquished their infants for adoption. That means that a full 91 percent of women denied abortions went on to parent the children to whom they gave birth as a consequence of that denial.

When we calculated this result, Foster was surprised: "Why do you think it's so low?" she asked me. After all, she was comparing the 9 percent to the 100 percent who had wanted to have an abortion and was surprised that the overwhelming majority were now parenting. I, on the other hand, compared the 9 percent to the estimated 0.5 percent of all American births that led to adoptions, and felt it was astronomical. These seemingly contradictory interpretations reflect an underlying truth about adoption relinquishment: it remains a rare experience when compared to the relatively common experiences of parenting and abortion, but it becomes meaningfully more frequent when women's choices are constrained. There are myriad ways that abortion is excluded as an option for women who might otherwise consider it. Indeed, for many relinquishing mothers who framed adoption as their "best" choice, abortion was never truly on the table. Some discovered their pregnancies quite late— perhaps when they went into labor or within mere days or weeks of giving birth. These women experienced the shock of learning they would soon be having a baby, perhaps even the next month, and lacked both the option of having an abortion (which some acknowledge they would have chosen had they discovered their pregnancies sooner) and the time to prepare to parent (which others acknowledged they might have preferred if they'd had time to get ready). Under these circumstances, adoption felt like the only immediate solution. Other women who were interested in abortion never pursued one, because they couldn't afford it or because there were no providers in their community. Even though these women never made it to a clinic, their stories were similar to Sofia's and Emily's: they could not or did not want to parent, but they never felt like abortion was available to them.

Relinquishment is never common, but when you remove other options, it occurs more frequently. These same constraints shaped the baby scoop era of the twentieth century: even as abortions were broadly illegal and single motherhood was deeply stigmatized and unsupported, every other available option was prevailed upon far more often than relinquishment. Indeed, before *Roe v. Wade,* the *most* common response to an unmarried pregnancy was marriage: about half of all pregnancies conceived outside of marriage ended in a birth to a married woman (and the proportion was even higher for white women). In 1970, the peak year for adoptions in the United States, there were an estimated 175,000 adoptions, including 89,000 adoptions to people unrelated to the infant. Yet in the same year, before abortion was even widely legal, there were an estimated 1.2 million abortions—nearly seven times as many abortions as there were adoptions. That year also saw 400,000 births to unmarried women, meaning that even if we assume all the infants who were relinquished for adoption were born to unmarried women, most unmarried mothers parented their children. Thus, even at adoption's highest point—a peak best attributed to the intense social pressure and coercive practices of the time—the relinquishment rate of infants born to unmarried American women was just under 9 percent, exactly mirroring the rate we found in the Turnaway Study five decades later. When abortion was legalized in the early 1970s, it led to a decline in the adoption rate and a reduction in the number of infants available for adoption. However, it also contributed to a social shift around unmarried pregnancy and motherhood. As abortion was legalized, women began to feel greater autonomy over *all* their choices, and more and more single women kept their children. When women have more options available to them, they are less likely to relinquish.

Most women seeking abortion are fundamentally uninterested in adoption. In a survey of over 5,000 abortion patients, they were asked a series of true/false questions including "I want to put the baby up for adoption instead of an abortion." In response, 99 percent of participants said that was "false," and exactly 0 percent said it was "true" (1 percent said "kind of"). Adoption was often ruled out—if it was considered at all—because women simply felt it was not right for them, either because they had health reasons for not wanting to continue their pregnancies, or because they felt there were already too many children in need of homes. Another study of interviews with seventy women who'd recently had abortions found that none of them seriously considered adoption, mostly because they believed it would be too emotionally traumatic. These feelings about adoption were equally held by focus groups of both "pro-choice" and "anti-abortion" women, all of whom considered adoption to be emotionally painful not just for mothers, but for the children who would be relinquished. In another study examining the decision-making of women who'd had an abortion, most of them were unequivocal in ruling out adoption, with one participant alluding to the flawed reasoning of anti-abortion advocates:

> I don't want to give my child away to nobody, and I'm not . . . and that's the part they don't understand. I can't just be bearing a child for 9 months, going through the sickness and then giving my child [away]. I can't.

A Turnaway Study participant who was able to get her abortion shared similar thoughts: "If I had given birth . . . no. I would never give it up for adoption. I wouldn't let it leave my sight."

Even among those denied abortions, interest in adoptions was low. Michelle, a Turnaway Study participant who was already parenting two children when she was denied her desired abortion, explained how she ruled out adoption:

> There's no way that I would be able to carry a baby that long and then give it away knowing that I have two other children at home and then have that kid maybe come back one day and say, "Why didn't you want to take care of me?" I couldn't do it.

Michelle is not unique. Only 25 percent of those denied abortions reported even *considering* adoption, and as detailed above, only 9 percent did relinquish.

Some adoption researchers and anti-abortion advocates see these enduringly low numbers of relinquishments in recent decades and posit that pregnant people just don't know enough about adoption to consider it or pursue it at higher rates, but this isn't true, either. One study of teen mothers—both those who parented and those who relinquished—found that knowledge of and positive attitudes about adoption did not correlate with relinquishment; the researchers concluded that "strengthening positive attitudes [toward adoption] alone may have little effect on pregnancy resolution decisions." In 2022, the Opt Institute, a conservative adoption-promotion think tank, commissioned a report from researchers at Arizona Christian University. The report, "Adoption and Its Competitors," surveyed American women of "prime childbearing age" and actually found high knowledge about adoption. According to the report's authors, all questions related to adoption knowledge were answered correctly by a majority of respondents. However, these participants did *not* report an inclination toward adoption relinquishment when asked about a hypothetical future pregnancy. The reasons were not complicated: the most common (56 percent) was that they "just didn't want to give up a child [they] gave birth to" and the second (39 percent) was that it was "emotionally too hard to give up [the] child."

This preference seems intuitive to pregnant people (or really, any parents). That relinquishment would be traumatic seems so self-evident that it was the premise of a *Saturday Night Live* sketch that aired soon after the leak of the *Dobbs* decision in May 2022, in which comedian Kate McKinnon played Supreme Court Justice Amy Coney Barrett. She quips: "What is more traumatic, safely ending an early pregnancy or giving full birth to a baby you can never see again?"

After the *Dobbs* decision came down, I spoke with many reporters who asked variations of the same question: *Why aren't women who are denied abortion more interested in adoption?* I would respond that women are generally not interested in giving away their children. *Can you explain more?* they would ask. I would try, but there comes a point at which I, as a researcher, cannot explain more. As a mother, though, I always wanted to ask them: *Under what circumstances would you give up your children?*

When Foster, the lead Turnaway Study researcher, asked me why the adoption rate was so low, she was expressing the premise that many women were seeking abortion because they could not or did not want to parent the child that would result from that pregnancy, which is certainly true. But what if some women were not just seeking abortions to avoid parenting that infant but specifically or intuitively *to avoid the pain of relinquishing an infant for adoption,* whether or not they think of it that way? This doesn't appear to be a conscious rejection: less than 1 percent of women seeking abortions specifically cite avoidance of adoption as a reason they are having an abortion. Instead, women simply do not consider adoption at all, even to reject it—it is irrelevant to their decision.

*   *   *

Emily and Sofia were making decisions according to a different framework, in which parenting was seen as the greater hardship of the options that remained available—and that's what put them in that 9 percent of women who were denied abortion and turned to adoption.

Emily thought if her grandfather had been alive, he would have encouraged her to raise her child, but he wasn't, and she didn't feel like she had an advocate at home. She had seen her cousins raise kids from unplanned pregnancies, but their boyfriends were involved in parenting—and hers wouldn't be.

Sofia's family was being evicted, again. She couldn't imagine telling her mother that she was pregnant; she couldn't imagine the two of them supporting her and her child. Both young women worried that adding another child to their families would be an impossible hardship on their own single mothers.

Emily fought against becoming attached to her pregnancy once she started planning for adoption, but it was a lost cause. "There was a certain bond that she and I developed . . . you just can't avoid that. But at that point, there was so much positivity and, like, joy around the whole [adoption] situation" that it was too late to change her mind.

Sofia was so worried about disappointing her family that she did not tell them anything—not about her pregnancy, not about the birth, not about the adoption. She told her boyfriend she'd had a miscarriage and kept the existence of her child a secret from everyone. Years later, she still had not told anyone.

The protesters outside of abortion clinics holding up posters that read WE WILL ADOPT YOUR BABY! or signs that say ABORTION in block letters with relevant consonants crossed out to instead read ADOPTION might be inclined to unfurl a MISSION ACCOMPLISHED! banner on hearing Sofia's and Emily's stories. But importantly, these young women didn't choose adoption *over* abortion. They considered adoption only *after* they were denied the abortions they wanted, and *after* they determined that parenting felt impossible. Adoption was all they had left. The thing about such constrained choices is that they aren't really choices at all—and coerced "choices" are even less so.

The repercussions for these denials of reproductive autonomy are profound. Such coercion and constraint are why so many first mothers from the baby scoop era faced compounding and enduring traumas: destruction of their self-worth, separation from their families and communities, grief and mourning, ambiguous loss, anxiety over their child's well-being, and a social inability to acknowledge these traumas. If abortion is illegal or inaccessible and parenting feels unaffordable, unsupported, unsafe, or otherwise untenable, then decisions around adoption are not being made from a place of reproductive autonomy and power. Such decisions will shape not just the lives of relinquishing mothers, but the lives of their children and of generations to come.

If the "choosing life" and "adoption instead of abortion" framing had little resonance for Sofia and Emily, it had even less for the many mothers who never considered abortion at all.

*   *   *

Taylor had taken several home pregnancy tests, and every one had come back positive. A white woman in her early twenties, she didn't have a reliable income or a reliable partner; she certainly wasn't planning a pregnancy. After all those positive tests, she wanted more confirmation, though, something definitive. She went to a Planned Parenthood for a pregnancy test, but they couldn't see her that day, so she was pleasantly surprised to find a clinic across the street offering free tests and ultrasounds. She went inside.

> At first, I didn't suspect anything. We did the pregnancy test, all of that. Then they started asking me really weird questions, like if I was going to get married. I was like, "No, that's dumb. I'm not going to get married. I would rather raise my child as a single parent than in an unhappy marriage." Then they gave me a pamphlet on how birth control will kill you. It had all of the birth controls laid out, and said "Oh, this causes stroke and this causes this side effect," and I was like, "That's false, but okay." Then I saw a poster on the wall with information about how abortion will definitely kill you. I remember clearly, because I took a picture of it with my phone, because it was so absurd; it said 75 percent of women die after having an abortion. Then I finally realized I was at an anti-abortion clinic and thought: "Great. I need to get out of here before they realized that I'm very opposed to everything that they're about." So I ended up getting the information that I needed—the confirmation of pregnancy—to get signed up for WIC and Medicaid and all of that, and then I left.

Taylor wasn't interested in having an abortion, anyway. Even though she described herself as "very pro-choice," and even though it was an unplanned pregnancy, she felt bonded to the pregnancy right away. She dreamt of her baby early on, and she "pictured going back to online school, and there was a little brown-haired, blue-eyed baby girl in a bouncer beside [her] while [she] did [her] schoolwork." But she knew that parenting would be a lot of work, especially without a steady income or a trustworthy boyfriend. When she googled "help for single moms" in her home state, she was flooded with ads for adoption agencies. "The first three or four search results were all for agencies. I was like, 'Huh, that's something I haven't really considered. Let me just look.'" Curious, she clicked on the ads for more details, and was soon mesmerized by the compelling profiles of waiting families with their suburban homes, stay-at-home moms, extended families, graduate degrees, and disposable income.

Things were getting harder and harder for Taylor. She was so desperately sick during her pregnancy that she had to quit her job. She sold her car to buy a plane ticket to move across the country to live with her mom, but then she'd spiral into anxiety about how her only available car was her stepfather's pickup truck, with no space for an infant's car seat: "I remember spending all night one night just throwing up, wishing that my pregnancy would just be over—which I thought made me a terrible mom—and obsessing over the fact that I had no way to even get a baby home from the hospital." Even though she still wished to parent, the idea of adoption became a lifeline for her.

*   *   *

Taylor wasn't the only mother I spoke with who was bombarded with similar ads while actually searching for parenting support. Adoption agencies pay for traffic to their sites, as do prospective adoptive parents who create their own websites to showcase their family profiles. They often specifically target terms that do not include adoption. A search of a keyword and digital advertising research platform revealed that adoption agencies routinely buy Google ads for practical search queries like "assistance for pregnant mothers in Nevada" or "housing programs pregnant DC," or seemingly generic searches like "college pregnancy stories" or even just "prenatal care." Many terms were related to unintended pregnancies but carried no sense of crisis: "unplanned baby announcement," or "how to tell your husband you're pregnant when you weren't trying." Then there were three agencies who bought ads on the desperate search string: "I'm scared I'm pregnant and I'm fifteen." Pregnant women searching any number of queries will have ads promoting adoption pop up—and if they click on any of these, the ads will follow them to Facebook, Instagram, YouTube, and other social media sites.

These ads are paid for by would-be adoptive parents who have been instructed by dozens of how-to articles in the art of search engine optimization and online advertising. These prospective parents are in turn sold a set of paid services in website design, Google and Facebook ad campaigns, and profile development (including photography packages and, in one case, an extra fee to have an advising birth mother provide feedback on their profile in advance of its going up online). As one service offers:

> Adoptimist is a great way for you to instantly expand your adoption outreach. We actively and constantly promote, market, and advocate for all our families on every major search engine and social network . . . Our outreach is second to none . . . Highly targeted Google banner ads, custom built just for your family. Social media—we promote our families on Facebook, Instagram, and YouTube . . . Profile statistics directly from Google analytics, so you always know what kind of impact your profile is making.

The cumulative costs of these services and campaigns are in the thousands of dollars, when most relinquishing mothers report that they would be parenting if they had that much additional money in their own bank account. And importantly, the costly bombardment of advertising is not always legal. Many states regulate the extent to which advertising for adoption is allowed, and by whom. But such restrictions are very difficult to enforce. One industry exploration found that unlicensed, for-profit adoption brokers frequently outspent regulated agencies on a massive scale, leaving pregnant people highly exposed to the least scrupulous players.

Women who seek abortions can face similar exposure. In

2016, I was inadvertently included on this email that was also being sent to adoption agency employees across the country:

> Copley Advertising can mobile geo-fence Planned Parenthood locations and other abortion clinics. We will geo-fence Planned Parenthood locations and other abortion clinics, tag all the smartphones in the clinic, drill down to demographic (women 18–24), place an ad in a mobile app (You Have Options). The ad will direct traffic to your landing page. When women leave the clinic they will continue to see your ad for 30 days. We just finished a large campaign with Bethany Christian Services. If you are not the appropriate person please forward the information of the correct contact. Thank you.

(I was not the appropriate person to contact.) The banner ads Copley offered would appear on the phones of anyone in—or near—healthcare facilities that provided abortions. Copley Advertising (a Boston-based firm) soon settled with then Massachusetts attorney general Maura Healey and, without admitting liability, agreed to stop geofencing clinics solely in that state— but only *after* they ran a campaign targeting 140 abortion clinics and methadone treatment centers for Bethany Christian Services, one of the largest adoption agencies in the country. This legal intervention in Massachusetts doesn't mean the geofencing has gone away. In 2022, Choose Life Marketing, a digital marketing firm that works primarily with anti-abortion crisis pregnancy centers and adoption agencies, was still promoting not just physical geofencing of clinics, but virtual geofencing. Virtual geofencing allows adoption agencies to advertise directly to people who have visited specific URLs, including abortion clinic sites or places to order abortion pills online.

The ability of these ads to appear in people's most innocuous searches or at their most vulnerable moments makes them especially invasive. It's difficult to overstate how captivated many mothers are by the adoptive family profiles they find online. While the profiles are designed to help prospective adoptive parents "match" with expectant mothers considering relinquishment, they also serve to spark interest in and increase commitment to the idea of adoption itself. Amy describes her experience:

> I was looking at the independent sites where hopeful parents can put up their profiles. And they write a letter: "Dear birthmother, we've been waiting so long." And I just got sucked into their need. And I started thinking, I have a way that I can help people.

For many expectant women considering adoption, who are often just getting by financially (if that), the comparative means of potential adoptive parents can be both intimidating and powerfully convincing. Cassie talked about considering her own paltry nine-dollar-an-hour job as she looked at the "impressive" profile with "an amazing house." Hannah, who was already raising a daughter on her tips as an exotic dancer, mentioned being "blown away" by the "really beautiful house, big land" and "good incomes" of her son's adoptive parents. It's not just the money, though. For expectant women who are lacking the support of their own families or the stable relationships with their partners that would help them parent, looking at the pictures of happy weddings, family vacations, and big holiday dinners have their own persuasive draw. Isn't this what a better life for a child looks like? Paige talked about keeping a printed profile under her bed and pulling it out every night, saying "it would feel right" to look at them again. Leah said after reading the profile of the parents she eventually chose for her son: "I just totally fell in love with them."

Women don't make relinquishment decisions based on a single advertisement, of course. But for many, the marketing of online profiles was a key step in their path toward relinquishment.

* * *

After exploring a few agencies online, Taylor connected with a large Christian adoption agency that sent her profile books of prospective adoptive families. She was immediately drawn to one family with a professorial father and stay-at-home mom who hand-made their older child's Halloween costumes. These two practiced gentle parenting and traveled around the world with their children. It seemed like just the sort of family Taylor wanted her child to have, and light-years away from where she sat, on the couch in her mother and stepfather's house in the rural Pacific Northwest, with no job, no boyfriend, no car, and no apartment to call her own. The family flew across the country to meet her for dinner at an Italian restaurant, where their older son drew pictures of his baby brother in Taylor's belly. She felt there was no way she could back out now.

In the spring of 2015, Taylor delivered her son. She spent about an hour with him before his adoptive parents came in the room. When Taylor had a postpartum medical emergency, the adoptive parents were given their own hospital room to bond with the baby while Taylor was in surgery. She remained groggy and heavily medicated for the next few days, and never got to be alone with her son again:

> I still cannot remember signing the termination [of parental rights] papers. It was either Monday evening or Tuesday evening that that happened, and I was still on a lot of pain meds. On Wednesday morning the agency worker came back, and I asked her when my termination papers were going to be filed, because at that point I was starting to feel unsure and I wasn't ready. She told me that they had been submitted and that my rights had been terminated at 8:31 that morning, exactly 48 hours after he was born. I sobbed. She never told me I had a revocation period, nothing. I remember my mom kicking her out of the room because I was crying so hard. Two hospital social workers

came down to talk to me. They tried to make sure I wasn't being coerced. It was right after I had just finished filling out a baby book with his adoptive parents, the first pages of his baby book with all the hopes and dreams that we all had for him. I just remember feeling so conflicted. I don't know why I was feeling so defensive, but I remember defending my choice on adoption and telling them like, "No, it was fine." So they left.

Taylor was adamant that if she hadn't been matched with that family during the adoption process, she would be parenting her son. Abortion consideration wasn't a factor in her story: "To me, adoption or parenting was a separate decision from abortion or keeping a pregnancy. Most birth moms I know feel the same way."

*   *   *

Stories from birth mothers who, like Taylor, desired to parent are more common than stories from birth mothers who had wanted to get abortions. One survey found that nearly 90 percent of relinquishing mothers also considered parenting, but only about 40 percent had considered having an abortion. This pattern might soon change as abortion becomes increasingly illegal or inaccessible in more places in the United States. The numbers of adoptions are so small that any constraint on abortion access could increase adoption numbers. Within a few years, we could find a larger proportion of women relinquishing because they couldn't get the abortions they wanted, instead of because they couldn't parent the way they wanted to.

Yet most of the women I interviewed clearly wanted to parent. Many of them went through most of their pregnancies intending that they *would* parent. For some, the crisis was a small accumulation of setbacks: Where would the car seat go in this pickup truck? How would they afford Wi-Fi to finish their schoolwork? For others, it was bigger: How would they come up with the money for a security deposit on a new apartment? How would they afford time off work for maternity leave? Could they count on the support of their family? And for a few, like Whitney, it was a singular crisis, sweeping and definitive.

* * *

Whitney was a white college student struggling with housing instability when she moved in with a friend of a friend. The man she was living with ended up effectively abducting her, moving her from city to city, and preventing her from leaving the house or having any contact with her family and friends. She eventually realized she was pregnant, but did not tell her abuser, telling him instead that she had a history of fibroids and doing her best to conceal her weight gain. (She's still not sure he ever believed her.) When she went into labor, she begged a neighbor to drive her to the hospital while her abuser was at work. She recounted:

> The baby was born healthy. She was only about five and a half pounds, but she was healthy. I told them at the hospital right away that I wanted an adoption. I didn't feel safe to parent, and I also had nothing to my name. He took everything from me. I wasn't really in contact with my parents at that time, so I really didn't have any other options. It was just me and her for two days before I signed the papers. I never let her go. It was really hard, because all my life I wanted to be a mother, and she was so beautiful and perfect. It was hard to hold her and know that I was going to have to let her go. They told me it was going to be an open adoption. I didn't want it at the time because I thought it would be very hard to watch her grow up with other people, so I figured that was going to be the last time that I saw her.

Whitney's abuser found her and "took [her] back" after she relinquished her baby. She became pregnant again and relinquished again (despite very much wanting to parent her second child). Only then, after the second adoption, could she get an order of protection that she felt would keep her safe. She was able to return to her parents' home to recover.

While Whitney's crisis was violence, other mothers faced challenges such as incarceration, acute mental illness, ongoing drug addiction, chronic homelessness—experiences that clearly would have made it difficult or impossible to safely parent their baby without meaningful intervention and prolonged support. Many of these mothers expressed their interest in parenting passingly, fleetingly, almost sheepishly; the idea of parenting seemed too remote, too impossible for them to consider. Weren't they *actually* giving their child a better life by allowing them to be parented by other people? Helping these mothers parent would have taken a sustained effort, and such efforts are scarce and scantily resourced in our country today. I will never argue that every parent is prepared to care for any child at any point in their lives. And given the positions they were in, some of the mothers I interviewed feared for the safety of their child if they had tried to parent—or they worried that they would lose custody of their baby to the foster care system, where they believed the child would be less likely to receive the love and care that they would from a private adoptive family, and where they, as mothers, would be less likely to have contact with their child. (This threat was especially true for Black mothers, who worried about losing custody not just of the baby, but of their older children, too.)

What is particularly sad about these stories is that, more often than not, little was done to support the mothers, even as they came into contact with social service workers, healthcare facilities, and adoption agencies. The only intervention offered to them was the opportunity to transfer their child to another family. They received little support accessing safe and affordable housing, medical treatment, or addiction services; they were almost never offered options like temporary guardianships, crisis nurseries, or other types of care that would allow them to retain their parental rights while navigating their own paths to safety and wellness. Does the mother's life, with her afflictions, her vulnerabilities, her flaws, mean so little that if the baby is ensconced in a stable middle-class home, we are able to convince ourselves that the crisis has been alleviated?

Most often, though, the reasons for relinquishment were less about acute crises and more about everyday survival. When I asked the women who wanted to parent what they would have needed to do so, it was simple: money. A survey of birth mothers found that over 80 percent cited financial reasons as a reason for relinquishing. The amount they felt they need to parent their child is less than you might think. As Cassie said: "I would've needed maybe a thousand dollars for my life to change." These women don't need enough money to pay for child care for five years or to buy a house. Most of them are used to scraping by and making do—they just need a little breathing room to make the transition to parenting feel a bit more tenable: to buy a car seat, move closer to family, afford a better apartment. Taylor mentioned how one adoption agency with which she spoke offered to help with housing and transportation costs during pregnancy. She laughed at the memory: "If I had an apartment and a car and all that, I wouldn't be choosing adoption. Then I would be fine!"

Stacy, a natural mother* herself, had worked in post-adoption peer counseling with other mothers. She reflected on the role that financial strain plays in adoption:

So many mothers, if you had put a roof over their heads, if you had offered them money and support, they would have parented. It's devastating to watch because they do not want to do it. What I tell people is, "The people I see who don't heal from this, who struggle with their decision, are the ones who felt like if you just helped them get financially stable or housing stable, that they could've parented. If that's where you're at, then stop exploring adoption. There are resources. We will figure out how

---

* "Natural mother" is Stacy's preferred phrase (instead of "birth mother" or other terms). Please see Appendix B, "A Note on Adoption Language."

to get a roof over your head. We'll figure out how to get food. You can get on WIC, whatever needs to happen."

In these cases, just a minimal investment in families—more affordable housing, easier options for public health insurance, better-paying jobs with parental and family leave, food security, affordable and reliable child care—would create an essential safety net that allows these mothers to raise the children they very much want to raise.* Importantly, this safety net needs to be made available without stigma. For Vanessa, that stigma was enough of a barrier. She knew about WIC, Medicaid, and other programs that would have made the difference for her, but she was too embarrassed to access them: "I guess my pride kind of factored in, because I know that there's government programs that you can get on like welfare, assistance to get you on your feet. I never really looked into those things. I should have checked out everything that I could, and I just didn't."

In addition to money, the other resources these mothers would have needed to make parenting feel possible was more support, both emotional and practical, from the people in their lives. A survey of birth mothers found that the majority felt they could not talk with their family about the problems in their life. Additionally, the potential *loss* of social support from family was the most common source of pressure that mothers felt when it came time to relinquish their children, followed by loss of financial support and then loss of housing. (They also had concerns that they would owe money to the adoption agency if they changed their mind and wanted to parent, or that they would face losing custody of their older children if they chose to keep the new baby.)

Later chapters will explore in more depth what these ideas of family support and preservation might mean, but it's critical to

---

* Given the number of women who have abortions because of financial reasons, this safety net could potentially decrease the number of abortions. But anti-abortion advocates rarely make the political alliances that would prioritize this work.

understand that—despite political rhetoric that juxtaposes the two—rarely are pregnant people deciding between abortion and adoption. Instead, most relinquishing parents had hopes of parenting, but could not find a way to make those dreams tenable.

* * *

Natalie had volunteered as a patient escort at Planned Parenthood and considered herself "very pro-choice," so when she found herself unexpectedly pregnant in 2012, she first reached out to the doctor she knew who performed abortions. But fairly quickly, she just felt it wasn't quite right for her: "Something didn't feel like that was what was meant to be." Her casual boyfriend wasn't someone she wanted to parent with, and it was a priority for her to make sure her child had a two-parent family. She started looking into adoption, which felt like it would be a beautiful, loving solution:

> I just wanted her to have a family. I didn't want her to be with me, single and miserable. I'd been in a loving relationship before, and I knew it could be different. I wanted it to be different for her. It only took me about a week to decide, and it felt right. I was super solid in my choice right from the start.

During her pregnancy, Natalie made scrapbooks for her daughter of their "special time together" doing prenatal yoga, running a half-marathon, traveling the world. "That was super important for me to have that time with her, and then I was okay with someone else having time with her. I knew my mind was made up and not changing."

But Natalie is the exception rather than the rule. Of the over 100 relinquishing mothers that I have interviewed, in adoptions going back to the early 1960s, I have heard very few stories in which their decisions were driven by the belief that adoption was truly the best way of giving their child the best possible life.

Much of the "better life" thinking is tied quite concretely to markers of financial stability: adoptive parents frequently use their prospective family profiles to showcase their large homes, expansive backyards or nearby city parks, exciting travels, reliable jobs, and comfortable lifestyles. As Natalie mentioned: "I was looking for people that would kind of give her a similar life to what I would have, but with more financial stability. I ended up choosing a couple that financially was really well off."

When we consider the cultural ideas that made adoption compelling to Natalie, it's not likely that she (a queer white woman who spent her pregnancy belly dancing and volunteering at an abortion clinic) was listening seriously to anti-abortion and religious ideals of adoption. Instead, her aspirations for her daughter were shaped by the "better life" argument for adoption that is rooted in what kind of parenting is most desirable for a child and which family makes the most opportunities available to them. These beliefs are the water in which we all swim.

Natalie had been certain about her adoption decision when she made it, and she thinks her confidence in her choice meant that the agency didn't feel she needed options counseling. No one ever really talked to her about parenting, but they also never really counseled her around what adoption might look like. Years later, she now speaks with other expectant parents who are considering adoption and offers them the advice she wishes she'd received:

> Sometimes I'll talk with other potential birth parents before they've made their decision. I just talked to one a couple months ago, and she was about the same age I was, and she was looking at adoption because she wanted to travel. That was her reason. And I was like, "Would your child be safe with the guy that you got pregnant with? Would you feel okay?" And she said yes. I was like, "Would your mom help?" and asking her all these questions about parenting. I didn't, like, tell her what to do one

way or the other, but I also shared how much pain I had, how much I missed my daughter, and how much I wished I did have her. Ultimately that mom decided to parent, and I think that I would've enjoyed receiving that phone call while I was pregnant. I think that hearing from a birth parent about how hard it is would have been important. All I got from my agency was "Yay, adoption. It's a great option. Yay." And of course, from an adoption agency, that's what you're going to get. I would've loved a little more counseling on the parenting piece. I wish I could tell my past self: this is going to cause you more heartbreak than you will ever, like, than you ever could have imagined. You are and will be a really good mom. I was so afraid that I wouldn't be a good enough mom, just me, and that there needed to be someone else, another parent, and I couldn't give her that.

Does she think the adoption was the right decision for her and her daughter? "It's so hard to know if it was the right decision. Would I be where I am in my life right now if I had kept her? Could I have the best of both worlds? Could I have my husband and all my children with me? That's the world I want."

* * *

None of the mothers discussed at length in this chapter reported that they had comprehensive options counseling during their pregnancies. The few relinquishing mothers that I interviewed who *had* received meaningful options counseling had all had adoptions via the same three small adoption facilitators (one of which is no longer in practice).

Different pregnant people want different things out of pregnancy options counseling, but most often they are seeking guidance that prioritizes their reproductive autonomy, avoids assumptions about their desired outcome, considers their broader life and individual circumstances, and—for those who are facing indecision—mentions all available options.

Prior research has found that when expectant parents receive good options counseling, fewer relinquish their infants. But only seven states require counseling prior to relinquishment; only thirteen require that a parent be given an explanation of the "legal effects of relinquishment."* One survey of birth parents found that only 22 percent reported that they had access to a licensed counselor who was unaffiliated with the adoption agency—but of those who had access to such counseling, the majority found it "very helpful." The same survey found that over half of birth parents felt they did not have enough opportunities to talk to someone about their decision, that they did not receive enough information about different options available to them and their child, and that they faced pressure toward adoption when making their decision. Most wanted more counseling about parenting support; they also frequently reported lacking information about how adoption would impact their child, what "open adoption" really meant, what their own options for independent legal counsel were, and what rights they had to reconsider their decision or change their mind at any point prior to legalization. Over 40 percent of survey respondents felt pressure from agency professionals, and 20 percent felt direct pressure from the prospective adoptive family (with many falsely believing they would owe money to the agency or prospective adoptive parents if they changed their mind).

In 2000, Congress passed legislation requiring the U.S. Department of Health and Human Services to fund nonprofit organizations to develop an Infant Adoption Awareness Training Program (IAATP) to train staff members at federally funded health centers in "nondirective options counseling." The bill received bipartisan support, as conservative congressman Jim

---

* This number contrasts with the thirty-two states that require counseling prior to abortion, including fifteen that require in-person counseling. In some states, this requires providing patients with medically inaccurate information that exaggerates the physical and psychological risks of abortion (Guttmacher Institute, "Counseling and Waiting Periods for Abortion," March 1, 2023, https://www.guttmacher.org/state-policy/explore/counseling-and-waiting-periods-abortion).

DeMint described: "As we worked it through the House and the Senate, we found virtually unanimous consent or agreement, and that hardly ever happens here, and I think that tells us something." Democratic senator Mary Landrieu concurred: "Adoption at any age . . . is a real option, is a better choice than many options out there." In theory, this effort seems good and reasonable: Isn't nondirective counseling a good thing? In practice, over $6 million of the original $8.6 million in original funding went to the National Council for Adoption (NCFA), a nonprofit organization that works to promote adoption, represent the interests of adoption facilitators, and shape legislation around the practice of adoption (including the bill that funded IAATP itself). The training developed by the NCFA led to the inadequate, adoption-promoting counseling that many relinquishing mothers experience today.

The NCFA's training materials describe adoption as "a good social institution with positive outcomes for birth mothers, birth fathers, birth families, individuals who were adopted, and, of course, adoptive families." It provides specific ways for counselors to override an expectant mother's concerns about adoption, including the barrier of regret—"the client feels she will regret making an adoption plan for the rest of her life"—the barrier of "parenting is bliss"—"the client has unrealistic expectations of what it means to be a parent, is likely ignorant of the huge responsibilities involved, and often believes (and is being told) that she will receive all the help and support she needs to raise a child and meet her life goals." To the hypothetical statement "I could never give my baby away," a suggested response is: "Adoption can be a courageous and unselfish decision because you are putting the child above yourself." In response to the worry of "What if my baby ends up in a bad home?" counselors are encouraged to respond: "Did you know that many famous and successful people are adopted: Faith Hill and Ray Liotta?" Healthcare providers at family planning clinics across the country reacted negatively to the program, one saying the training gave "tips and techniques . . . about how to work against [women's] resistance." Another noted that "counselors were encouraged 'to identify clients as deluded, not living in the real world, not being practical, participating in self-betrayal, being ignorant, and generally being unable to make good choices, unless . . . it's the choice the counselor would make for the client.'" The trainings were overtly religious, including opening with a prayer and promoting the adoption into "good Christian homes."

The religious overtones in adoption messaging are ubiquitous—even in purportedly secular spaces. Oftentimes, though, options counseling does not even purport to be secular or nondirective. Much of this outreach happens in the context of specifically anti-abortion crisis pregnancy centers, like the one Taylor first visited to take a pregnancy test. These centers are bastions of misinformation, sharing medically inaccurate information about abortion and misleading women about their available options, and are rooted in religious organizing. Of the approximately 4,000 centers across the country (over twice the decreasing number of abortion clinics), 2,300 of them are associated directly with the evangelical church.

Research has shown that most people who visit and use crisis pregnancy centers are *not* seeking options counseling—they, like Taylor, are more often seeking services to support parenting and recognize that the centers share misinformation about abortion. However, the largest crisis pregnancy center networks, Care Net and Heartbeat International, are closely affiliated with adoption providers and heavily promote adoption (or marriage) as the preferred alternative to unmarried parenting. Despite these affiliations, there's a gap between the organizational and movement-wide messaging about supporting women to parent and what happens in the crisis pregnancy centers, which all goes back to one core truth: women are generally not interested in adoption. As sociologist Kimberly Kelly, who has studied crisis pregnancy centers in depth, describes:

> Counselors' responses to queries about adoption . . . reveal that they value client rapport and well-being more than the opportunity to promote evangelical goals. . . . In contrast to training manuals instructing volunteers to discuss adoption repeatedly across multiple client visits, those counselors who did initially mention adoption in counseling sessions typically did not do so again once clients indicated they were not interested. Pushing the issue, especially before clients have decided about abortion, would destroy client-activist rapport and increase the chance that clients would abort. Since most clients ultimately choose single parenthood, counselors fear they will undermine the clients' sense of self-efficacy as parents or inadvertently insult clients by implying that they would be unfit mothers.

Anti-abortion messaging is developed by political and movement leaders with specific ideas about what adoption can accomplish, but with little or no experience working with expectant mothers weighing their options—a disconnect that some within their own movement recognize is unhelpful.

This disconnect doesn't stop them from cashing in, though. As of 2018, anti-abortion centers receive public funding in fourteen states, for a combined $40.5 million—with that number expected to increase dramatically with more restrictions on abortion access—for "Alternatives to Abortion" programs, including adoption promotion. In ten of these states, these resources explicitly come from dollars allocated for Temporary Assistance for Needy Families (TANF), a program aimed at providing support for families living in poverty. That means the public money that is intended to provide direct assistance for housing, food, and child care—the exact resources that could allow expectant mothers who want to parent to keep their children—are instead being spent on biased options counseling.* Legislators also use the public's general sense of adoption as a public good as a way to divert this funding, so as not to make their anti-abortion aims too overt: in 2021, Arizona, Maine, and New Hampshire all used the guise of adoption support to promote and route money to anti-abortion centers.

* * *

The reasons that Emily, Sofia, and Taylor relinquished their babies instead of having abortions were complex and varied. But none of them were, at any one point in their pregnancies, deciding between abortion and adoption in a way that the anti-abortion movement suggests.

All three women became pregnant again within two years of their first pregnancies—none of them intentionally.

Emily, who had very much wanted an abortion and gone to three clinics to try to get one, had an abortion right away. For her, the abortion was a much easier experience:

> With the adoption, there's always a little bit of doubt, because it's always ongoing. Forever. It's ongoing, and the process is still new to me, my daughter, her adoptive parents . . . And therefore, I always kind of doubt it, because any of us can make a bad decision that makes it turn to a negative experience. Whether it be us losing contact, or maybe them not explaining it the right way to her, or causing her to rebel, or go through a phase of not wanting to see me. Whereas having the abortion, I made the decision. This abortion that I had, there wasn't a baby . . . I think it's a little

---

* In 1996, conservative policy writer Frederica Mathewes-Green described the "pro-life dilemma" that crisis pregnancy centers must face: they must discourage abortion *and also* discourage welfare use, because "welfare causes more crisis pregnancies . . . [by] remov[ing] the stigma of sex and pregnancy outside marriage." The only solution in this conservative paradigm is adoption: "Counselors must strike a delicate balance: Encourage mothers-to-be to love their babies enough to give them life, yet still be willing to place them with two-parent homes."

bit different. It's ongoing as far as the reminder of what it could be, but it's never going to be like the adoption.

Sofia, who had felt joy and hoped to parent when she found out she was pregnant the first time, before resigning herself to abortion and then adoption, was parenting her daughter from her second pregnancy. Nothing in her life was much different the second time around: her boyfriend was still uninterested in parenting; she hadn't discovered she was pregnant much earlier; she still hadn't finished school; her income was neither higher nor more stable. The only difference was that she decided to tell her mother that she was pregnant the second time. While she'd been fearful that her family would reject her and her child the first time around (they still didn't know about the existence of her first child), she found instead that her mother was "ecstatic" and excited to be a grandmother:

> That made me realize that my mother is always going to have my back. At the end of the day I'm always going to be her daughter, and she's always going to love me no matter what I do or what I say . . . I knew with this child I wanted to have my son even if his father was not going to be around. This time around I had my mother there for me. I had my family there for me, so it was so much easier.

Taylor, who wanted to parent and felt coerced into relinquishing, was happy to find herself pregnant a second time, and didn't think twice about parenting her daughter.

None of these three women considered adoption during their second pregnancies.

Camille

"I was so scared about everything, about them taking my kids, because with my ex passing all of a sudden, there wasn't another parent for my older children. That's when the fear crept in that I could lose all three of the kids that were still at home with me. I didn't feel like anybody would help me."

Camille (who is Black) was a recently divorced mother of three children living in the Midwest when she became pregnant in 2017. An adoptee herself, she relinquished her son in early 2018, when he was about six months old.

When I found out I was pregnant, it wasn't planned, obviously, but it was a happy thing for me. I was excited when I found out. But I was facing single motherhood, and my kids' father had passed away, so it was a hard situation. I started having problems with depression around that time. I was just not well. I wasn't eating. I wasn't drinking. It was just not good. The doctor was aware. I told her and she just tried to encourage me—I don't know if she got me on medication then, or after. But they knew about the death of my ex-husband, and that we were pretty close. It just affected me really badly, and I just couldn't connect with the baby when he was born.

There were times when he was a newborn, and he would wake up and I would feed him and try to put him back to sleep right away, because I really couldn't handle him being awake. When I did take care of him, I did it really carefully, almost methodically. Really, really carefully—I didn't miss a beat, but I was doing it like I was watching someone else do something. Almost an out-of-body experience.

I thought everything would be okay, eventually. But it was a hard time. I was really isolated. I didn't have a job. I didn't have any support where I was living, and my family's not here. It was really rough. My thoughts, they progressed from just regular depression to having delusions, not understanding what was going on. Then those thoughts started to progress, and I would have thoughts of hurting my son. I knew it wasn't right, to have thoughts like that.

He was maybe two months, one or two months—I can't remember exactly when the thoughts started like getting really bad, because they didn't crowd my thoughts all at once. It would just be like a thought here or a thought there. Like, he'd be in the tub and I would have a thought of letting him drown. I was just like, "That's not right." At some point the thoughts got worse, and I felt hopeless in my situation. I didn't have anybody to talk to and I was scared. This is not normal. I can't talk to people about this. They will just take my kids. I just wasn't logical. Later on, obviously, I found out it was postpartum psychosis, but at the time I didn't know at all what was going on. I just was like, "What is wrong with me?"

I was so scared about everything, about them taking my kids, because with my ex passing all of a sudden, there wasn't another parent for my older children. That's when the fear crept in that I could lose all three of the kids that were still at home with me. I didn't feel like anybody would help me. For me, as an adoptee myself, this is all I have—my children. I couldn't lose them, and I didn't feel like child protective services would work with me, so I didn't tell anybody. If I could do it over, I would tell someone and believe that hopefully they would help me get counseling. But at the time, I was just so scared I didn't tell anybody.

I started reaching out to people to maybe take him for a while, but my family really wasn't in a position to. My oldest daughter—she's raising her two kids—she took him for a little while, but it was too much. So I just said to bring him back and then I just continued to call around. I got pretty connected to a church and they were supportive, but they didn't do much. They just said: "Oh, you'll be fine. Oh, the baby's cute. Let's pass the baby around at church." But the other six days of the week, I was isolated and desperate and nobody knew, because I put on a smile. I finally decided that no one would help me except the adoption agency.

I hadn't planned on adoption at all. I've raised three other kids, so it wasn't easy to just give up. But I finally placed him in January 2018—he had been born the summer before. I remember all that fall, I was calling around to different agencies, just to get information, to start getting profiles sent to me. I hinted to some friends what I was doing, and they were just like, "Oh, it'll get better." They didn't know exactly what I was going through. They just thought I was overwhelmed in having a new baby, which I was, but it was more than that. I had a lot of fear, not just of hurting me, but I would go out in public and think people were judging me and watching me. I wasn't normal, that anxiety. It was overwhelming.

But when I started looking into adoption online, it felt unreal because the adoptive parent profiles looked so perfect. It didn't feel real. I started learning more and more about it, and things got more and more desperate. I called the agency and started to talk to someone, and she was really nice and made me feel like I could talk to someone. She set up an appointment to meet with an adoption specialist, who came out to my house. We talked and she was wonderful, and she said that she had the perfect family for what I wanted. They lived just a few hours away, and they just had another baby.

I had been looking for a Black family, and I said that if I couldn't find a Black family for him, I wouldn't do it. But not a lot of Black families do private adoptions, I guess, maybe because it's so expensive, or it's just our beliefs. And it was also hard because he was a few months old; he wasn't a newborn. People want to go to the hospital and come home with a baby, even if they didn't give birth. They want you to have the baby, spend a few hours, and then give them their baby. They don't want a baby that's six months old, used to some other mother, which is, I guess, pretty understandable. It's so sad just to think about it, but I realized at the time that it was like going to the store: do you want a brand-new object, or do you want a used one, you know? The bidding goes down because he wasn't brand-new. I don't know if that's the right way to say it, but that's what I learned. That was my truth about it.

The family the agency lady found, though, wasn't a Black family. They were white, and they'd already adopted one Black baby. And

I was so worried that I wouldn't be able to keep him safe and so worried that we wouldn't find another family that I thought: at least he would grow up with a brother or sister of his own race. So we started communicating with that family, and even though it was still iffy, I just kind of jumped in.

They started visiting a lot, and they even came with me to a lot of his doctor appointments. They would drive hours to come to his appointments, and they even helped drive me to some of his specialist appointments that were farther away. I felt like they were pretty dedicated, and at this point, I felt a little obligated. I felt like I couldn't go back and forth. I pushed myself to just keep going. That's what I did.

The adoption was supposed to be open. That was really the only way I would do it, if it was very open. They even wanted more openness than I thought was possible—they were saying we could visit several times a year. They said maybe I could move closer to them, saying, "That would be awesome. You could see him even more. You'd be like an extended family and could help him and their other son kind of figure out their race." *They* were saying all that stuff.

But once the adoption was finalized, I also still didn't know what the heck was wrong with me, and with the idea of not having to care for him every day, I felt like I had the courage to find out. I thought, *Okay, if I don't have him, at least I can get well, so that when I see him again I can be better and he can be proud of me.* I started going to the hospital for mental health reasons, and I told them that. I started telling them everything I'd been through. And it scared them.

We had decent communication for those first months that they had custody, but pretty much as soon as the adoption was finalized, the communication was cut off. I didn't know that open adoption wasn't a legal thing. They started ghosting me, and I just got frustrated and I kind of went off a little bit, and I said, "This is not what it was supposed to be." And that conflict severed the relationship. I haven't seen him now in over a year, so that was not part of the deal at all. I wish that it had been more like the picture that was painted, like an extended family and stuff like that. I just feel like I was kind of lied to. I feel like it was all these fluffy things to get me to do it, and then when it was done, then I was thrown out. I was cast out. I'm not saying I wanted them to call me every day or anything like that. I just wanted more planned meetings, something I can plan my life around. Now I feel like are they going to ice me out if I ask them, maybe email them, say, "Hey, am I ever going to see him again?" I'm scared to even ask that because then maybe they won't even send me a picture anymore.

I continue to get counseling, and I talk to somebody three or four times a week, so it's pretty intense.

I feel like it was very brave for me to do what I did. I feel like it was the best I could do with what I had. I did the best thing that I could've done for all my kids at the time. I feel like I wish that I picked a different family. I know that's really harsh to say. At the same time, I get pictures through the agency and he's happy, he's clean, he's doing well, he has horses and dogs, he's happy. That's all that matters, you know.

I think my story really needs to be told because women end up in prison for thoughts like I had, and I'm glad I found the right thing to do, no matter what. Because the other part of me thought to just deal with it, like everybody said: "You'll get through it." No, sometimes you won't get through it. Although it didn't go as I planned it, maybe it'll change. Maybe it'll get better. I still have hope that the story's not over and that I'll be able to see him and everything will be okay and it'll be all worth it.

I am pregnant again now, due in March. This pregnancy wasn't planned, but I was happy about it. I did get married again last year, and my husband knows everything that happened, and of course he's like, "I'll take the baby if anything goes like that." When I found out I was pregnant, the anxiety came right away; we have to make sure this doesn't go down that road again. So I came clean to my doctor, about like putting the actual horrible name on it: postpartum psychosis. This is what it is. We have to really watch that. I just committed myself: if anything gets bad, I'm going to the hospital. I'm not going to hide it. I'm just going to depend on my support system to help me and have faith. And I have way more support now. I have so much more support.

Stephanie

"It's hard to say, because I love my daughter just as she is, and I know she wouldn't be the person she is now if I had raised her . . . I'm grateful for what she has, but I look at the system that got us here, and I think that there's a lot of flaws in it, and they're flaws that get glossed over."

Stephanie (who is white) was twenty-nine and living in a large city on the West Coast when, in 2010, she found out she was pregnant by her on-again/off-again boyfriend, Mike. Mike is Black; their relinquished daughter, Emma, is biracial.

I'm fiercely independent, is how I think I would describe myself. I had been living on my own, working full-time on movie sets. My parents and my family are all in the Midwest, so I was fairly far from any sort of family members or support system. I lived with a roommate and had been working at this job, which I did like, but which didn't pay very much. I had been dating Mike casually on and off for about three years when I got pregnant.

Life was sort of stable, but I didn't have a good support system. I had friends but no family close by, no kind of other people. I didn't talk to a lot of people, and I never told my family I was pregnant. I mostly talked to people at work—I had a second job at the time, too, so my work friends became my support a lot. But honestly, I avoided talking with everyone as much as I could. I very much isolated myself. Mike had two older kids with his ex, and he was not a super present father. He wasn't great on paying child support. He would see his kids occasionally, but not regularly. He wasn't a full-time parent to them, not by any measure. So even when he said, "Oh, I'm here for you," I knew he wasn't.

* * *

Financially, I wasn't in a great place. I was still underwater on my student loans. Then I was put on furlough at work thanks to the recession, and I was making the least amount I had ever made since leaving grad school.

So it wasn't really a great time for me. I was in a little bit of denial, in shock that I was pregnant. I think that I put myself in a position where I couldn't consider abortion, if that made sense. I was raised Catholic. I still consider myself Catholic. I come from parents who are extremely pro-life. Before I got pregnant, I would have told anyone I would never get an abortion, period. . . . I think if I really sat down and weighed it as an option, I don't know whether I would have stuck to not getting one, so I tried to avoid facing it.

I think my denial kept me from taking a pregnancy test and kept me from seeking prenatal care, because even though I didn't want to be pregnant, I didn't want to have to make a decision about an abortion. I finally took a pregnancy test at thirteen weeks, and I finally saw a doctor at seventeen weeks, and then I was just like, "Okay, abortion isn't even an option because I'm too far along." But I think the fact that I got to seventeen weeks before I went to the doctor was part of my not wanting to have to make that decision. I just wanted the decision to be made for me, if that makes sense. I don't know that I was aware that that's what I was doing at the time, but I think it was.

I just didn't see any good choices. I didn't kind of know a path through where I felt like I could get to the other side and be able to parent and support my child in the way I wanted to, or in the way I thought was necessary.

I am not a person who easily knows how to ask for help. Before my pregnancy, I never asked for help from anyone for anything. When I was about six months pregnant, I went to visit a friend on the East Coast, someone I'd been friends with for a long time. It was my way of sort of seeing if I might have more support somewhere else. I guess I was hoping I would reach out, and somebody would say: "Oh, let me create this support for you; let me help you," but that trip went pretty poorly and I never really found that. I was in a weird space. I was sort of waiting for something to happen that would change my circumstances, but I wasn't doing anything to actually change them myself. I talked to Mike a little bit about it and said, "I'm thinking about adoption, because I need help to do this. If I were to parent, I would need a support system." It was my way, basically, of telling him I didn't think I could count on him. And I was right. He disappeared. And that sort of made me decide on adoption. I just didn't feel like I had other options.

And I really believed that adoption would be best for my child. But I think somebody who knew me and cared about me could have sat me down and talked to me about it and moved me in a different direction. I do think that if somebody had said, "Here, let me help you," things could have been different.

You have to understand, it is really hard to see long distances when you're in that kind of time-sensitive crisis, right? I had no money in my bank account. I remember thinking that I couldn't even bring her home from the hospital. I didn't even have enough money for a car seat. It was like, "I can't clear this huge obstacle right in front of me, the obstacle of not having a car seat, let alone the whole path after that." Maybe I could have asked my boss to fire me? And then I could have qualified for Medicaid and more support. I guess there were routes to take if I really, really wanted to make it work. But I don't have the car seat; I don't have an apartment that's safe to bring a child home to. I don't have any of those things. I just needed someone to really like talk me through these obstacles to get to the long-term planning.

* * *

I started googling "adoption," and a bunch of adoption websites came up. I started looking for someplace in my city and then honestly just found one that had expectant parents that weren't all white. Mike is Black, so I knew my daughter would be biracial and would be half Black, so I was thinking about that. I looked a little bit for, like, some diversity and inclusion within the website. So I found one agency and started meeting with them around seven months.

I'd never talked to like a therapist or a social worker or anything like that prior to that, and it's interesting I did feel like I finally had a place where I could talk about where my head was and get things out. I was feeling guilty because I hadn't told my parents I was pregnant, but at the same time, I didn't think I could. I was frustrated because Mike wasn't there, but I didn't want to keep reaching out to him over and over, because I didn't want him to show up just because I was nagging him. I wanted him to be there because he wanted to be there. It felt like a relief to have someone to talk to about all that. After the adoption, though, I felt less great about it, because I know that some of what I said in those sessions was shared with the adoptive parents and their attorney. I thought I was getting real counseling, but I guess it was just all going in my file. There's no ill will, I guess, but I don't think I fully understood what was happening at the time.

During those appointments, I was extremely closed off to the idea of having an open adoption, and the social worker really talked me through it and honestly changed my mind about it. I still don't think I fully understood what the end result would be. I think she said all the things she was supposed to say, but whether or not I fully understood and heard them is a different story. She did encourage me to talk to my parents or my brother, and she did always say it was my pregnancy, my child, my decision. But she never, like, helped me imagine what it would be like to parent or offered to help with logistics like getting on WIC on something like that.

She gave me hundreds of profiles to look at, big books of two-sided pages that had a bunch of information like religion, age, whether they had other kids, all those kinds of things on the front, and then the second page was like a letter. From those profiles I could narrow it down and get these actual books that the families made, these picture books about their life. I think I picked four or five to look at. I wanted someone I thought would parent similarly to how I would have if I could have. The couple that I picked was a gay couple, and I think [the approach to life of] one of the dads reminded me of me at my best, like, what I want life to be, so that's where I ended up. I liked that they were Catholic but not dogmatic; I felt like that represented to me my complex views about religion. I did look at some biracial families as well; that was one of the factors I was thinking about. The parents I chose for her understood that part of Emma comes from somebody who grew up in a different class, in a different race, and they said it was on them to do the education to understand where that comes from, and to really try to, like, integrate it into a part of her identity. I felt like they were very realistic about it. It wasn't like, "Oh, we don't see color," or anything like that. They said all of the things I believed and thought. Her parents, they're two very different people. They're kind of the opposite of each other, but in a very complementary way that appealed to me. I remember having a conversation with them where they talked about letting her find her own path, and how to adjust their life for what she cared about and liked to do. That appealed to me a lot as a kid that had gone into the arts from a family who wasn't really excited about my choices, but also because this child would have different genes from them. I wanted to make sure that if she had really different interests than they did, that they'd let her have those. If she loved swimming like I did, I wanted her parents to support that.

I started having contact with her dads, which the agency didn't love. My social worker was like, "Normally that doesn't happen." But if these people are gonna raise my kid, I wanted to get to know them and feel comfortable. I did reach out to them. I would send them ultrasound pictures. When she was born, they came to the hospital to meet her. I needed to feel like I knew them and understood them a little bit.

And I guess I did feel as good as I could have? I mean . . . I felt as good as you can when you're giving your child to people that you've met for about three hours, total. You know, thinking about the way that adoption works feels a little bit crazy to me now. I mean, it did feel crazy then, too. But I am extraordinarily lucky because they're pretty amazing parents.

After she was born, I had the option to do cradle care, which the agency actually encouraged. Their belief was they wanted the child to stay with a third party, so that the mother could recover and make a decision once she was out of the hospital, once her hormones balanced out, all of that. But I felt like I wasn't going to change my mind, and I didn't want Emma to leave me, go home with someone else through cradle care, and then have to transition again. It just felt overly dramatic for me, and like it would be harder on her. And if I had wanted to visit her in cradle care, we would have just met at the agency or an office or whatever—it's not like she would have been with me, living with me. So if she wasn't living with me, I just wanted her home with her parents as soon as possible.

*   *   *

When I was with her in the hospital, there was a moment the last night where I just lost it. I had been pretty positive the whole time, but that was really hard. I didn't really understand—I didn't understand before, before she was born, just how connected I would feel to her and how much that would mean to me. I don't know. It wasn't until she was born that I realized really what I would go through, like, what it would mean to me, how much loss I would feel. No matter how much people told me, no matter how much it was laid out, until I felt that connection, the idea of severing it—I mean, it was really hard. It wasn't that I was doubting it—logistically, I still felt the same way. I just felt so heartbroken, knowing that I would have three days as her mom, without a qualifier, that was all I had.

When I was pregnant, I was like, "Oh, open adoption. Sure. Maybe I'll see her." But then I remember signing the papers and knowing that the openness agreement really meant nothing if they didn't follow through. But it still felt valuable to have it on paper, and I asked for more. It said that we'd visit once a year, and I asked, "Can we put twice a year?" The social worker said, "Okay." As we were talking about the visits, I was finally realizing like what it meant and what it felt like for me, and it really wasn't until later that I really understood what it did to Emma, too. I was just a mess. I was a person who probably hadn't cried for years before that, and I was just in tears for like hours. Oh, and this is terrible, but I don't really love her name, but I can't exactly say anything, can I? We'd had a conversation and I thought we'd agreed on a name together and that's the one I gave her on her original birth certificate, but then they changed it. That was another loss. I guess in the scheme of losses, it's a small one, though.

*   *   *

After I left the hospital, I didn't get any maternity leave, and that ended up being my biggest worry—like, I had to put my sadness aside a bit, because I was worried that I wouldn't be able to pay rent or whatever.

But I remember going to dinner with people from work or like going out with people, trying to be social a little bit, and just sitting at tables crying while they tried to talk to me about how I was doing. I was just a mess. I wrote her parents this nutso email, maybe three days after I was back from the hospital, about how hard it was and how much connection I felt with her. I said I wanted as much contact as they were comfortable with and like anything they were willing to do, I would be happy to do. I'm pretty sure I offered to babysit. It was wild. Her dad is a lawyer, and I think he was freaking out, because he knew legally I could change my mind completely. But I don't think I was really saying I wanted to parent—I couldn't make that happen—but they invited me over for dinner and we had our first visit and it felt a little more normal after that.

The agency wasn't supportive then, really. That's when I found out that they had shared things that I'd said during the counseling sessions, things I thought were mostly private. And after I found that out, it felt like the agency wasn't really a safe place to talk. I wanted a support system, and I didn't really find it there. I mean, they're always sort of there and they're always willing. But it's on their terms. At the beginning I was like, "Do you have a support group I could join?" and they're like, "Oh, it's really for mothers from the closed era of adoptions, and new mothers don't really join." But they didn't have anything else to offer me, so I joined anyway. And it was great! But then they kind of changed the group, and suddenly it disappeared and wasn't happening anyway. And then it's back again, but the schedule is different. They're a nonprofit agency, and we're not their main mission, right? I mean, I understand it.

* * *

Since then, my social worker has sent some mothers to me who have recently relinquished and who were looking for someone to talk to. One of them, in particular, I became really good friends with, and I appreciated that. But all of them, I'd go out for coffee with and try to make a connection. I encouraged this, I appreciated that she sent them my way. I think there is a sisterhood in a way, where regardless of your story, there's things about other women who relinquish that—you can have a shorthand with them that you just can't with other people. There are things about it that you can know, implicitly. Those sorts of connections, like, I really appreciated. That's really the only thing I do for the agency now. I've never done any fundraising, and I won't talk to potential mothers. One time I was on a panel, and I would say I wasn't super pro-adoption when I was talking about it. I haven't done that again.

They've moved pretty far away now, out of the country. And I was really anxious it would hurt our relationship, because I used to visit about once a month, for shorter visits. Now I see her less often, but for longer visits. I get to stay with them and put her to bed, longer things like that. During COVID, I think she was driving them a bit nuts at home, so we started FaceTiming every day to give them a bit of a break, and I would play board games with her online a lot. Now she's getting older, and she can say, "Hey, I want to talk to Stephanie," and get out her iPad and call me. She has a little more ability to do that.

After they moved, I stayed in the same city just in case they moved back. I didn't want to risk them coming back to the country and the same city she was born in, and I wouldn't be there. I didn't want to move away from her. But now that I see how it's working, I felt more comfortable moving to another city that's more affordable, because I know we can make the distance work. If they hadn't moved first, I never would have moved. I think it's always a hard relationship to have because Emma will always be my top priority in my life, and I will never be hers. And that's okay. It's okay that her family is the center of her life, and that's fine. It's just hard to be that person, because you're always kind of like waiting or hoping or whatever.

Even though her parents have always been awesome, I always worried that one day something would change and they would just disappear and I would have no ability to change that. I felt like I could never ruffle their feathers, I could never ask for things. Now Emma is driving some communication on their side, so it feels a little more balanced. I will say there are times where I have to have really hard conversations with Emma, and those started pretty early, when she was two and three. She'd be like, "Why do you have to go back home? Why can't you live at my house?" And I'm like, "I don't have a good answer for you other than I have my own house." Watching her struggle to understand has been really hard, but I'm not sure it would be any better if our relationship was any different. I think her having this relationship with me and being able to talk to me about it is like the best I could hope for.

If you look at me, if you look at who I am, you would not assume that I relinquished. I am not the, like, stereotype of a sixteen-year-old or someone on drugs, you know, what people assume. But the idea that I had when I was pregnant was: if I do this, I will hurt, I will have pain, but Emma will have a better life and that will make it all worth it. And it's more complicated than that, and I think that it wasn't really until long after that I began to realize all of this. It's hard to say, because I love my daughter just as she is, and I know she wouldn't be the person she is now if I had raised her. And, you know, even like when she was like, "Oh, I wish you would come live with me," she never said, "I wish I hadn't been adopted." She can't imagine a world where she doesn't know her dads. That's her family, right? It's all very complicated. I'm grateful for what she has, but I look at the system that got us here, and I think that there's a lot of flaws in it, and they're flaws that get glossed over because the people who are benefiting are the adoptive parents, and those are the people with the money. And the other parties, the birth parents and the adoptees, are sort of left behind.

I think there are systematic problems in adoption. There's too much money in adoption. In my case I think I lucked out, but that doesn't negate that it was all luck. As a culture, we say adoption is a way of saving a child who's unwanted. I've met too many women who've relinquished to believe that. I feel like if we want to help kids, we would be fixing that system, and we would be having paid maternity leave. I used to joke that if I had been pregnant in Canada, I probably would've parented, and it's kind of true. If I'd had help and better health insurance, maybe things would have been different.*

---

* This observation is possibly true. In 2017, Canada had fewer than 1,000 private domestic adoptions, which means—when controlled for population—the rate in the United States is 2.5 to 3 times higher.

But more than how I feel, I don't know what it's like to be adopted. No one ever talked to me about what it meant to be adopted. No one ever talked about higher suicide rates in adoptees. No one ever talked about how adoptees might experience their own sort of trauma, of feeling isolated or feeling like they don't fit in with their family. It wasn't until after I relinquished that I started actually reading about adult adoptees and their conversations. I know that I'm watching a ten-year-old who already, like, struggles with some of this. She struggles with the fact her skin color is a different one than her parents. She struggles with the fact that she doesn't live with me. She'll ask me questions that I am sure everyone who has been adopted has in their head, though whether or not they feel free to ask them or not is another question.

I remember talking to Emma's dad about abortion and he's like, "I'm so much more pro-life than I was before, because Emma exists because you made that choice." For him, that's what the adoption represented. But for me, knowing what I know now about what I went through, what Emma goes through, what we're continuing to go through, it's not that easy. Today, I have a really hard time with pro-life and pro-choice being, like, the two options. I think I would never put that on anyone else, even though at the time of the adoption I was pro-life for myself, probably. I would say that now, I'm much closer to pro-choice than pro-life. I feel like it's a much more complicated question than I used to believe. Once you are pregnant, there's no alternative that doesn't cause some hardship. If you parent, you're living through that and you have to parent without a proper support system. If you choose abortion, I do think that you have to go through grief. And adoption, it's going to affect generations of people; it changes families forever, for generations to come.

It's just all very complicated. Too often, birth mothers don't talk about it, and when adoptees talk about it, they get relegated to like, "Oh, you must have had a bad experience." And people don't want to talk about it because they don't want to hurt someone else's feelings, so it's like a weird taboo subject that people aren't honest about and then society just keeps going, believing these things that aren't true. I hope that there's a world where adoption isn't like it is now, where we understand the connection between mothers and children and work for family preservation. I think I can work toward that world, while still living my own life with my daughter and her parents.

3

The Family My Heartbreak
Made Possible

In every private adoption, there is one shared moment. Most frequently it's at the hospital, within hours after giving birth. Sometimes it's at the adoption agency or perhaps in the back room of a church. This is the moment when a lawyer or social worker hands the mother a legal document to begin the process of terminating her parental rights, and—whatever brought her to that moment—she takes a pen and signs it.

A surprising number of the mothers I interviewed could *not remember* signing their papers. They know they did, but the moment was so fleeting, so wrapped up in the other paperwork of birth certificates and medical consents, and for several, so traumatizing that their otherwise sharp recall becomes hazy when describing the act of signing. But that is the moment on which the adoption hinges.*

---

* In fact, what these papers *are* varies meaningfully by state. As adoption legal scholar Malinda Seymore described to me, these papers might include: a release of custody to the agency (or merely permission for the agency or adoptive parents to remove the infant from the hospital), which, in most states, can be signed immediately after birth and does not require notarization; a waiver of their right to be notified of future court proceedings around the termination of their parental rights, so they are not an active, present part of the ongoing legal finalization of the adoption; or an affidavit affirming their intent to relinquish. (In some states, these affidavits or nonbinding "matching contracts" can even be signed prior to birth.) All of these measures—whether legally binding and final, or not—can alternately serve to remove the child from the mother's custody, remove the child from the jurisdiction in which the mother lives or gave birth, remove the mother's involvement from the legal process, and increase the mother's sense of obligation in completing the adoption.

The course of what happens next diverges. Some mothers see their babies discharged with the adoptive parents while they stay in the hospital a bit longer to recover from a cesarean section. Some leave to go home first, while their newborn stays in the neonatal intensive care unit under the care of their soon-to-be legal parents. Some go home to empty apartments, others to older children. Some are pumping breast milk to be bottle-fed to their baby; others are doing everything they can to suppress lactation. They are all recovering from pregnancy and birth, and they are all starting a lifelong process of understanding what adoption will mean for them and their child. To begin, they are mourning.

* * *

The intense sense of loss and sadness immediately after the adoption came up in nearly every interview. One woman described it as a "black hole of depression"; to several, it was an "out-of-body experience." Rebecca, who relinquished her daughter in 2009, shared:

> When I left the hospital, we went home. But I couldn't bear, like, even looking at the apartment. When I looked at it, I could see where I could make a baby work. Coming back home, my belly was empty and so were my arms. So was my heart. I just felt like my whole world was just shattering around me and I couldn't stay there. We ended up packing up some stuff and then we got in the car and we went and we got drugs and drove up to this lake town in the middle of winter and got a hotel super cheap— because it was outside of tourist season. We just drank and did drugs to try to forget it. I don't know that he really felt anything, but I know that I didn't want to. I was constantly crying. There were many moments I would just burst out in tears and scream, "I want my baby back."

Rebecca's emotional collapse was a refrain shared by so many mothers, but for Phoenix (who relinquished in 2012), the collapse was quite literal: "I was starting to feel like the ground was falling out from under me. . . . When my son left, I just fell to the floor. I just folded in half. It was like the muscles in my body stopped working."

These mothers were newly postpartum: hormonal and bleeding, just starting to heal, still leaking breast milk, and mourning their missing child. For some, this grief translated into immediate regret, but for most it didn't. "Even while I was crying harder than I've ever cried in my life, I remember saying, 'I still think I'm going to do it,'" Phoenix shared. "The way I was thinking of it at the time, all I had to offer was my love. But since it was an open adoption, he's still going to have my love. He'll have even *more* love because this couple who paid the adoption agency my yearly salary to adopt him were going to love him." Even Rebecca, screaming in a cheap hotel room that she wanted her baby back, did not try to revoke the adoption:

> It was such a conflicting thing because I did indeed want my baby back. But I knew that she deserved better than what I was going to be able to give her, and that made it hurt even more. Every time I would consider revoking the adoption, I would talk myself out of it because her parents had already had her for so long. You know, how could I do that to them?

Nearly 70 percent of relinquishing mothers say they wish they'd known more about their legal options for revocation after signing their papers, and even more wish they'd known more about their rights *prior* to signing the papers. But without that knowledge, very few considered regaining custody, even in these early days when they were in the depths of their grief.

*   *   *

In late 2019, Olivia, who is white, was living in the rural Midwest, working two jobs as a medical assistant and raising her ten-year-old son, Dylan, by herself. She sometimes struggled to make ends meet, but she took pride in never needing "funding from the government." Her on-again, off-again boyfriend, Josh, was newly off again when she found out she was pregnant. It was a shock to her core. At least when she'd had her son at eighteen, she was "young, dumb, and in love," but she knew her current relationship with Josh was not one to which she wanted to add a child. She'd made single motherhood work somehow, but it was a constant struggle, and she was "terrified" of doing it again. She thought of her friend Cori, who had been struggling to get pregnant, and offered her the baby.

I interviewed Olivia less than a year after the adoption. When we spoke, she was hesitant and halting in her speech and often swallowed tears; it was clear she was still in very intense mourning. She'd had second thoughts about the adoption immediately after giving birth to her son, Lucas, but felt like she couldn't talk to anyone about them. She also felt beholden to Cori, who had been with her throughout her labor and her time in the hospital: "I felt like that was a terrible thing to do to them, if I changed my mind. The adoptive mom had just been involved so much, like she was—the way she was just so excited. She came to all my appointments. She was there for everything." Despite their friendship, Olivia kept her second-guessing quiet. "I don't know that I ever told them. I do know that I cried the whole time." Everyone cried in the car on the way home from the hospital: Olivia, Josh, her older son. "I think Josh regrets his decision a lot, actually," she told me.

Cori shared pictures of the baby occasionally via text and on Facebook, but oftentimes seeing the pictures was hard for Olivia. "It's nice," she said hesitantly, and then started crying. "I mean, sometimes, depending on the mood, it makes you sad. Because I regret my decision."

Olivia's family didn't know how to support her. She felt like they were "walking around on eggshells" all the time, and nervous about talking about Lucas. She felt like she had no one to talk to, and when she did mention the adoption "everybody would always tell me how strong I was or how amazing it is. I don't know. I guess hearing that helps, even though I didn't feel that way."

When we spoke, Olivia had just broken up with Josh again. Was that a good thing this time? I asked her. "It will be in the long run. It has to be." But that meant even one less person in her life with whom she could talk about the adoption. "When I heard about this study, I was, like, maybe she could shed some light on what I'm feeling. Everything is kept so hush-hush. I'm not sure . . ." she said, her voice breaking as she started crying again, "that I understand, really."

*   *   *

The interview with Olivia was a hard one to do (for both of us) because her grief was new and terribly raw. But mothers in adoptions as recent as hers were often the most adamant about being interviewed. They needed someone, anyone, to listen to their stories—even just a stranger on the other side of the country.

The emotional trajectories of relinquishing mothers and their feelings about their adoptions are complicated, sometimes contradictory, and often vary over time. Within the complexity is a great deal of evidence that for most birth mothers, relinquishment is fraught with grief, ambiguous loss, mourning, shame, regret, and isolation—most overwhelmingly in the early days after the adoption. Certain practices make that emotional trajectory worse, in ways that are quite predictable: mothers who felt pressure from their agency or attorney or mothers who knew their babies went to foster care rather than directly to an adoptive home were more likely to experience grief and regret. Mothers who were isolated and had poor social support or few people with whom to talk about their adoption also coped more poorly. Most of these findings are intuitive: giving away your child is emotionally hard, and the less support you have in that loss, the harder it is.

* * *

For relinquishing mothers of previous generations, this sense of immediate acute grief endured. During the baby scoop era and through the early 1980s, adoptions were closed, and mothers were forced to cope with the loss in secret isolation, and without any ongoing knowledge of or contact with their child. Mothers in closed and in the few semi-open adoptions that occurred in that period were often clearly traumatized by these losses and the absolute severing of a connection between them and their children. Birth mothers in closed adoptions (compared with those in open adoptions) report more traumatic dreams, sleep disruption, and a surrealistic sense disconnection; they consistently report that they are unable to "get on with their life." Even early "open" adoptions in the late eighties and early nineties usually just meant the relinquishing mother got to choose the adoptive parents for her child, but the profiles were often without identifying information, and contact post-adoption was very minimal or nonexistent. The ability to choose the adoptive family and continue very limited contact was *not* found to reduce grief and may indeed have increased it, as it required mothers to revisit their loss continually in a way that did not offer a real connection to their child.

Adoptions today, however, are usually quite different. Open adoption is much more common, meaning that mothers often have some degree of contact with their child as they grow. Openness gives space for relinquishing mothers to have a greater range of feelings as they emerge from the immediate emotional aftermath of the adoption. Many studies have shown that openness *does* significantly increase satisfaction with the adoption process and improves mothers' post-adoption adjustment and grief resolution. These studies include my own research looking at the experiences of women who relinquished infants after being denied an abortion. My colleagues and I found that most birth mothers felt the adoption was the right decision for them and were either "somewhat" or "very happy" with their decision. However, most of these studies collected data from within a few years post-adoption, and little research has examined how durable these feelings are over time. Many birth mothers referred to these early years—after the immediate grief subsided, when they were often still living in circumstances similar to the ones they had been living in when they relinquished, and when they felt very optimistic about their open adoptions and their relationships with their child and their adoptive family—as a "honeymoon" period.

"There was still a lot of sadness in the beginning," Tiffany, who relinquished in 2015, told me. "But you can't let your emotions take over your thinking, you know? I know my baby's in a good place, and she's well taken care of and she's thriving. She's got the life I wanted for her." When her daughter was born, Tiffany had already raised eight other children, and she was physically and financially exhausted by the prospect of raising another baby. Her happiness with the adoption was rooted in the relief of knowing her child was well cared for in a family that could buy her new clothes for her first day of kindergarten, and that they wouldn't "have no issues with the lights getting cut off."

For many mothers, these honeymoons are real. They feel optimism about their own life and their child's; they feel a real connection to their child *and* to their child's adoptive parents. This openness is crucial; their ongoing relationship with their child is at the core of their satisfaction with the adoption. After Mallory relinquished in 2011, she was able to form a meaningful relationship with her son's adoptive parents, and she still felt very present in his life:

> Usually when I come across other birth moms, I tell them I don't regret my adoption because I'm still able to be in his life. I feel very strongly about open adoption, not closed adoption. Open adoption is what I hone in on when I talk to other birth moms because, I mean, I'm still able to see him. I'm still able to talk to

him. He knows who I am and he's going to grow up knowing me all of his life.

Kate Livingston, a birth mother who is also the founder and director of the Ohio Birthparent Group, was among the first mothers I spoke with to describe this period as a "honeymoon." Critically, this word conveys two reliable assessments: that the adoption itself will last forever, but that the period of heady optimism probably will not. As Kate describes:

> I've been talking to a girl who has an open adoption right now. She's definitely in an adoption honeymoon, and I hope it lasts forever. I hope what is going on now with her adoption really does work. I don't think it's inevitable that adoptions fail or turn sour. I *do* think it's common. I can't speak to people with closed adoptions, because they probably never had a honeymoon period at all.

Kate's assessment resonated with what I heard from other mothers: in closed adoptions, there is no honeymoon. In open adoptions, there might be—and it's a question of how long it lasts. However, openness in adoption is not a single consistent idea, either practically or legally. In some adoptions, openness means occasional letters, either sent directly or via the agency; in other cases, it means going on family vacations together. For some, it means limited contact for the first few years; for others, it means a lifelong kinship-like relationship. In many states, open adoption agreements are legally unenforceable, and in some states where they are enforceable, it's only for certain types of adoptions and specific types of contact. But even in states with some degree of enforceability, the recourses available to relinquishing mothers if post-adoption contact agreements are violated are few, and they require the relinquishing mother to hire an attorney (at her own expense) for breach of contract. Disputes over these agreements are never grounds for setting aside an adoption or undoing the termination of parental rights. Once parental rights are relinquished, they are gone, and with them any real guarantee of contact.

As openness varies, so do mothers' feelings about their adoptions. A 2014 study found that approximately 75 percent of birth mothers with some degree of contact with their child viewed their emotional health as "very poor," "poor," or "neutral" in the first year post-placement. Another recent survey found that about a third of birth mothers were "very satisfied" with their decision, a third were "very dissatisfied," and the final third were somewhere in the middle. Roughly as many birth mothers reported that the adoption had had an "overall negative" impact on their life as said it had had an "overall positive" one, with the plurality maintaining that the impact was "mixed." Birth mothers in open adoptions do report thinking about their child more. Adopted children in open adoptions have an increased "psychological presence" in their birth mothers' lives, and mothers in open adoptions think of their child more positively. However, it's not clear that an increased psychological presence is always protective of the mother's mental and emotional well-being.

*   *   *

After Kristen relinquished her son Benjamin in 2003, she was at first hesitant to visit with him and his adoptive family; she believed it would be too painful. But soon after his first birthday, she tentatively reached out about having a visit and they agreed. She met Benjamin's family at a playground for a few hours.

> I think the actual visit was really good, but beforehand I cried for weeks and afterwards I cried for weeks. But I was still really glad that I saw him, because then I had a small picture of who he was and what his life was like, and how he moves reminds me of how my brother used to be when he was little.

When Kristen and I first spoke in 2010, their visits had turned into annual meetups, often at a park or a McDonald's near their home, where Benjamin and Kristen's younger daughter (whom she is raising) enjoyed a Happy Meal together. Kristen was frustrated that the burden of initiating and planning visits fell to her, but the hardest part of being in an open adoption was that Benjamin's adoptive parents *had not told him* that Kristen was his birth mother—he just assumed she was a friend of his adoptive mother's that he saw occasionally, someone who sent him birthday presents and Christmas cards. Kristen, who was white, felt that Benjamin, who was biracial, was unlikely to recognize their biological connection at a young age because of their racial difference. This secrecy was especially hard as Kristen's daughter got older, because *she* knew Benjamin was her brother and, as a chatty preschooler, couldn't be relied upon to keep the secret imposed by Benjamin's adoptive family. All of this led Kristen to ask: What's the point of this openness?

> The visits aren't really beneficial to me, they're more like emotional trauma. I would love to show him that I care about him and I love him and I want to be a part of his life and I want to know him. I want this relationship to be benefiting him. I'm not doing these visits for me. I'm doing it for him, and I'm doing it for my daughter, so she can know her brother. So I don't know this summer if we'll visit or not, because I don't really know if it's fair to him to be coming and not knowing who I am. Because if he doesn't even know, then the purpose of the visit is not for his benefit, right?

As another mother told me, choosing open adoption was like choosing to "continually dive headfirst into [her] own pain" to protect her son as much as possible. This reasoning reflects why most birth mothers engage in open adoptions: it's not primarily that it will be easier for them, but because they believe it's better for their child.

Most relinquishing mothers do not learn until *after* the adoption is completed that adoption carries risks for the adopted person, but that awareness often increases their commitment to openness. Research has found adopted people experience increased rates of depression, attention deficit and hyperactivity disorders, obsessive-compulsive disorders, anxiety disorders, eating disorders, substance use disorders, and suicide attempts—and these findings were especially common among adopted people in international and transracial adoptions. Adopted people are about twice as likely to seek out counseling, and issues around adoption are the most common reasons that they seek therapy. With regard to their physical health, adopted people have less access to their own personal biological medical histories, which can lead to misdiagnoses or delays in treatment. We should not overly pathologize adopted people: while they are at significantly greater risk on all of these measures, the differences are relatively small, and a majority of adopted people show healthy adjustment. But the risks are there, and they exist for all adopted people, even those who have the resiliency and support to avoid poorer outcomes. Many adopted activists draw on key texts like Betty Jean Lifton's *Lost and Found: The Adoption Experience* and Nancy Newton Verrier's *The Primal Wound: Understanding the Adopted Child* to describe issues around abandonment and trust, loss and connection, guilt and shame, power and control, approval and perfectionism, intimacy and loyalty, and identity with which so many adopted people struggle throughout their lives.*

---

* Many birth mothers are surprised to learn about these risks, as they—like so many— believe adoption to serve the best interests of children. And who can blame them, when this is the common narrative? In 2009, NPR ran a story with the headline "Most Adopted Children Are Happy, Healthy." While acknowledging the increased likelihood of psychological diagnoses, the article describes how adopted children do well in school and receive more attention from their parents. The source of these findings? A survey

As it does with relinquishing mothers, openness mitigates some of these risks, increases satisfaction, and improves outcomes for adopted people. Yet many of the mothers I spoke with felt that their child's adoptive parents were engaging in openness as a "favor" to the birth mother, more than as a real investment in what was best for their child. This idea of openness overlooks the ways that ongoing connection is valuable and protective for everyone involved, and often means that adoptive families have less of a commitment to making the open adoption work than the birth parents do. Often the burden falls on relinquishing mothers to initiate visits, stay in the adoptive family's good graces, and accommodate the adoptive parents' conception of an open adoption over their own desires—or risk having contact cease altogether.

Soon after my first conversation with Kristen, Benjamin's adoptive parents decided they were not comfortable doing any more in-person visits, because "it was getting too hard to explain things to him." Kristen said she respected their decision, but that she'd still like to get pictures and letters from them. They did not oblige, and when we spoke in 2020, she had not heard from them in ten years. As she awaited his upcoming eighteenth birthday, she was planning on sending him a card with all her contact information, should he choose to reach out as an adult.

* * *

There are many stories like Kristen's (and so many other mothers whose adoptions are closed) because open adoptions, while increasingly common in the adoption world, are still a cultural anomaly. Americans are acculturated to the ideal of nuclear families with two married (usually straight) parents and two or

---

of adoptive parents, reporting on their own children. Yet other academic research has shown that adoptive parents are not the best predictors of the mental and emotional well-being of their adopted child (and particularly, of their adopted teen). When the popular press relies on the reports of adoptive parents to conclude "The kids are all right. At least, the adopted kids are doing okay," they are leaning into a cultural belief of adoption as what's best for children, and not critically considering the best evidence.

three children, with other branches of the family tree—aunts, uncles, cousins, and grandparents—dropping by for Sunday dinners or holiday celebrations. But open adoption introduces an entangled, sprawling root system to the child's family tree: more parents, more grandparents, other siblings, a full biological heritage. Furthermore, the child often has a racial identity, a social privilege, and a set of values that do not always match one or both of their families. The work of openness is the work of a lifetime.

Even in the best possible circumstances, openness can be a big logistical ask, as relinquishing mothers and adoptive families follow the trajectories of their lives: birth mothers get married and have more children; adoptive parents get divorced; birth mothers go to college on the other side of the country; adoptive families take jobs outside the country. Adoptive families might adopt more children, with their own birth families and sets of relationships to be negotiated. Some families adjust to any challenge. When Stephanie's daughter's family moved out of the country, they just flew her out for long visits and added weekly Zoom calls to their routine. When Shelby's daughter's family moved across the country, she followed them a few years later.

But many challenges are deeper and prove truly disruptive. Vanessa's daughter's adoptive mother died while she was still rather young, and her stepmother (who felt no obligation to fulfill the promises of openness to Vanessa) dramatically changed the circumstances of their relationship. Erica was so distraught after the adoption that she immediately had another child, and decided to keep the adoption a secret from the daughter she was raising, effectively cutting off contact with the son she relinquished. Few of these challenges reflect a disregard for or lack of interest in openness. However, they do suggest just a few of the ways that a tentative, nonbinding agreement—sketched out between a pregnant person and a set of hopeful parents-to-be—can feel remote or irrelevant to the now-parents of a ten-year-old, who are juggling soccer practices and ballet classes and summer vacations while living hundreds of miles away from the woman who gave birth to their child. And on the other side of the stalled text thread, there might be a birth mother who is herself working a job or two, parenting, and not especially eager to revisit that very sad and still painful decision she made a decade earlier. The constant work of showing up, making the trip, fitting in the phone call, shifting priorities, being vulnerable, and holding space for a real, ongoing open adoption might feel like a lot to ask, and it is. But it's also a lot to ask someone to give you her baby, and it's a lot to ask for an adopted person (especially as a child) to navigate their adoption without their birth family.

Many of these challenges are exacerbated by the differences between adoptive and birth families, especially at the outset. The most practicable of these differences is also the one that most contributes to the adoption in the first place: money. Most adopted children are growing up in households with more financial stability than those of their families of origin. For Tiffany, this meant that her daughter's family didn't have to worry about the lights getting cut off; for Jordan, it meant her son wouldn't face immediate housing instability. For others, it meant their children were growing up with wealth that far exceeded what the birth family could provide. One survey found that nearly half of adoptive parents were characterized as affluent, with household incomes over $100,000 per year. (Remember that most birth mothers report personal income below $5,000 per year.) Many birth mothers relinquished specifically because they wanted this financial comfort for their child. In looking at the adoptive parent profiles, they are drawn to the suburban homes, yearly ski trips, safe neighborhoods, and good schools that the adoptive families can offer. But once they are living in an open adoption, they need to form a meaningful relationship across that economic and social class divide.

Phoenix, a white nonbinary person, relinquished their son, Aiden, in 2012. The gulf between their income and the income of Aiden's adoptive parents was one they felt acutely. During our interview, they mentioned several times that the cost of the adoption was more than their annual salary, and that they wanted to consider parenting but couldn't even afford food or diapers. Phoenix actually ruled out several prospective adoptive parents because they felt that wealth was the defining characteristic for some aspiring parents, and "money makes people *so boring*." Yet the gulf between their financial status and Aiden's adoptive parents' wealth was one that they continued to feel:

> The grief is still there. It's just changed form. I think there's probably a way in which I'm not letting myself fully feel the grief, because I want our relationship to be fun and easy and positive for Aiden. And I don't want to resent that his parents have so much more money than me and were in a position to parent when I wasn't, and that their family was possible because of my heartbreak. I have a feeling that someday I will have to excavate all those feelings. It just doesn't feel possible to do that right now, in the middle of watching him grow up, and just wanting to be excited and proud of him and have fun with him and make him laugh.

Birth mothers aren't the only people who notice these financial divides. Brandi, who is Black, is the mother of two boys, Xavier and Jaden. She relinquished Jaden in 2006 because she could not afford to care for both sons. But Jaden's adoptive parents lived in the same town, and the boys attended the same schools. They knew they were brothers and remained very close. Occasionally the boys would each suggest to their mothers that they go to a certain restaurant for dinner, only to "coincidentally" end up in the same spot at the same time. As they got older, Brandi often had to explain to Xavier why Jaden had bigger birthday parties, newer sneakers, and more frequent vacations. Jaden's adoptive family was close to and generous with Brandi's family—throwing her a baby shower for her third pregnancy and passing along hand-me-downs—but the difference in financial comfort was clearly felt by the children that Brandi was raising, who watched as their brother had access to objects and experiences that were unobtainable for them. As a teenager, Jaden decided to stop having contact with Brandi even as he continued to spend time with Xavier. In this small decision, it seemed to me that the challenges went both ways: Xavier had to struggle with his envy over his brother's financial ease, and Jaden needed to come to terms with his mother's choice to raise his brother and relinquish him.

Some of these differences around affluence and stability can lead to relinquishing mothers feeling starstruck or infatuated with their child's adoptive parents. Earlier studies have shown that open adoption arrangements can lead to birth mothers becoming almost "childlike in their dependence on the adopting parents, only to feel discarded and betrayed by them once the baby is born." Among the mothers I interviewed, this feeling was particularly true for those who were teenagers when they relinquished their children. Readers will recall Haley, who spoke about her son's adoptive mom as "like a sister," who she felt cared about her independent of the adoption. Years later, when I spoke with Haley, who had been nineteen years old at the time of the adoption, there were no mentions of sisterhood or daily phone calls—she hadn't seen her son (or his adoptive parents) in about two years, and she texted with Rachel every few months. She knew which state they lived in, but not exactly where. "I don't ever initiate, just because I don't want to bother them," Haley said. "But it's a nice little surprise whenever Elijah sends me a text message. He recently sent me a picture of his birthday cake."

*   *   *

In 2006, Jaime was living in rural Vermont when she was sexually assaulted. A self-described shy person and white evangelical Christian, Jaime had spent her life within a narrow radius in New England and had never had a consensual sexual relationship. She was shocked months later to discover that she was not only pregnant but already into her second trimester. Despite growing up in the anti-abortion movement, she tried to get an abortion, but she could not afford one even after receiving support from the local abortion fund. Eventually, her boss referred her to a local crisis pregnancy center. "I went over to talk to them because I thought maybe they could help me with the money I needed," Jaime shared. "But that was the first time anyone talked to me about adoption. And I had been nervous about flying and traveling that far on my own, anyway, so I just decided that's what I wanted to do."

Through a Christian agency, Jaime soon found Pamela and Rob, and felt very connected with them. After she relinquished her daughter Esther, she joined their church and saw them there nearly every week. In our early conversation, Jaime focused more on her relationship with Pamela than her relationship with Esther. "I was at such a low point in my life, and Pamela and Rob made me feel like I belonged somewhere. I know they really care about me, and it's not just about Esther." This relationship seemed, at least by Jaime's sharing, to reflect Pamela's perspective as well:

Pamela told me: "We didn't do this to get a baby. We're doing this because we want to reach out to birth mothers." Her focus was never ever the child. She has a real love for birth mothers, and that's, like, her big thing. So, talking about openness, she's like, "I really want you to be—I mean, even if Esther turns seventeen and she decides that she hates you and won't talk to you, we still want a relationship with you. Our relationship is separate from anything that goes on with Esther."

Jaime spoke calmly, almost serenely about her adoption. "Ultimately," she said, "we've realized that Esther isn't mine, and she's not Pamela's. She belongs to God."

A decade later, Jaime and Pamela's connection had frayed. Jaime now described their formerly shared church as "a cult." Pamela and Rob were desperately worried about Jaime's lack of church attendance, and Jaime was grappling with her own beliefs—both political and religious. "I'm still a Christian," she told me. "But, after the [2020 presidential] election, I am not sure what I believe." She became tentative, her voice halting.

> After I learned about Ruth Bader Ginsberg and everything that she did, I kind of—it just kind of changed how I felt. I may still identify as pro-life but—well, I can't say that I'm always going to. Because I would now consider myself a Democrat? As opposed to when I was a Republican.

The tipping point for her went back not just to the adoption but to her having been raped and the resulting pregnancy. The reality of the sexual assault also contributed to her strain with Pamela. Jaime had always wanted Esther to know the truth about her conception, but Pamela and Rob were averse to sharing that with her. It took a political moment to surface this conflict again:

> Whenever Justice [Brett] Kavanaugh was being considered for the Supreme Court, I had put something on my Facebook about sexual assault, and how I was very upset that they were putting Dr. [Christine Blasey] Ford through all of this, and how they automatically didn't believe her. Pamela commented on the post, and she just totally ripped me a new one. She was like, "You should be excited to have him. He's a Christian, and your sexual assault has nothing to do with any of this." You know, she was just really mean to me. We didn't talk for almost a year. Now we're talking again, but I haven't seen Esther since then.

Jaime wanted to talk directly with her daughter, to text her on her own phone. "I would love to be able to just talk to Esther by herself, not because I'm going to go against Pamela's wishes, not because I'm going to tell her things she shouldn't hear, but just because I want a relationship with her. I would like that." She sighed. "I just feel like we're so far apart, as far as their ideals."

Jaime wasn't the only mother who felt that their open adoption was burdened by differing religious and political views. Many adoptive families pursue adoption *because* of their conservative religious and political ideals, and it's not surprising that many will continue to hew to those paradigms as time goes on. In contrast, many of the mothers I interviewed shifted in their belief systems—sometimes because of the adoption, sometimes simply because the circumstances of their lives changed.

This divergence extended not just to adoptive parents, but to the adopted people who, as they grew, often adhered to the conservative perspectives in which they were raised. For Alison and her daughter, this difference in views was a hurdle in their relationship.

I wish that our relationship was different. I had wanted an open adoption, and I was told we would have an open adoption, and her parents did not continue with that. Then when she was a teenager, they let her find me. I think she wanted someone who was identical to her, and we're very, very different. She's lived a much more sheltered life. She's been in the same city for her whole life. She's much more conservative than I am. So I think it's been a challenge for her to find someone who didn't share her insights to the world. It sounds weird to say that, but she holds these beliefs that are so strong that she's very judgmental. I find that to be, in my opinion, a bit immature. I mean, I love her. She's so great in so many ways, but this political difference is a challenge for us.

Toni grappled with similar issues and acknowledged that her son was raised with these beliefs, precisely because he was raised in the family she chose for him. While she acknowledged there are "plenty of adoptive families with way better politics," a conservative belief system was the driving force behind her adoption: "It was my religion and politics that led us to adoption, and that picked out the family that I picked out for Noah." As her own worldview changed, this shift created a divide between them:

> Noah grew up in a very conservative—not just conservative, but straight-up right-wing family thanks to me and my poor decision-making. At the time that I chose them, and even in some years after, I hadn't come to an understanding of my own beliefs. What were my political and religious beliefs? I didn't know. When I looked at their profile, I didn't see a belief system. Because it doesn't say their political or religious affiliations, I just saw a big Catholic family that looked like mine. I don't actually believe we talked about anything as deep as values, other than "Oh, yeah, he would be raised Catholic." For practical purposes, there are a lot of iterations of what it means to be a Catholic, so there was no guarantee that they would be essentially a fundamentalist Catholic or whatever, but they are. It wasn't until later that I realized what that meant for my kid. I am sad that he grew up in and is very much invested in an all-white, racist, middle-class community that's super anti-choice and that's, in a lot of ways, misogynistic. I did that to him by virtue of making a decision to do an adoption and by choosing this family for him.

In the years since the adoption, Toni's political, religious, and social views had shifted profoundly, largely because the adoption had led her to recognize the gendered systems of power that shaped her own relinquishment. It was this divergence that made the gulf between their worldviews feel so significant: "Honestly, had I not had my own personal and political transformation, I would probably be very content with where he's at right now," Toni said. "But I'm not."

*   *   *

As with money and politics, yet another difference that complicates most relationships in American culture—including open adoption—is race. Most of the mothers that I interviewed were white, as are most mothers who relinquish in the private adoption system. (In the 1990s and early 2000s—the earliest part of my sample—over 90 percent of relinquishing mothers were white. Today it's about 55 percent—still a majority, but much less of one.) Similarly, most adoptive parents in the private adoption system (a full 91 percent) are white. However, just because relinquishing mothers are white does not mean their children are. About 20 percent of the mothers that I interviewed had children with a racial or an ethnic background that differed from their own. This includes not just white mothers relinquishing biracial children, but Latina or Black mothers relinquishing children that were part Native, a Chinese American mother relinquishing a biracial white son, and a few mothers who—because of a one-night stand or a sexual assault—had limited or no specific information about their child's birth father's background, but assumed that their child was multiracial.

The overwhelming whiteness of adoptive parents means that more children of color who are relinquished are placed in transracial adoptions with white families. The whiteness of adoptive parents is not incidental. Critical adoption scholar Kimberly McKee has written about the ways that white supremacy, white saviorism, and American colonialism have shaped adoption into an institution that directly works to involve and appeal to white prospective parents. Additionally, as detailed in Chapter 1, transracial adoptions are often a reflection of the oppression of adopted people's original families and communities (and, in the case of international adoptions, countries). This book is not about the experiences of adopted people, and it is not possible to explore fully the complexities of transracial adoption here. But it's essential to recognize that the needs of transracial adoptees extend beyond the challenges and separation traumas that all adopted people face. As social work scholar JaeRan Kim has examined, the unique work of transracially adopted people includes an ongoing reckoning with compounding losses around their own racial, ethnic, cultural, and national identities. These patterns are why the National Association of Black Social Workers released a strong statement *against* transracial adoption in 1972, arguing that Black children should be kept in Black families. They are why the Indian Child Welfare Act of 1978 was viewed by tribal leaders and advocates as essential policy to keep Native children within Native families. And they are why the Hague Convention on Intercountry Adoption—working to ensure more ethical practices around international adoptions—argued that "each State should take, as a matter of priority, appropriate measures to enable the child to remain in the care of his or her family of origin."

The accounts of transracially adopted people are of course as diverse as the people who live them: from those struck with overtly racist abuse and harm at the hands of white adoptive parents, to those who recognized the love, support, and self-awareness of their adoptive families, but still struggled with how to understand themselves as people of color while growing up in white families, schools, and communities. Nicole Chung, a domestically adopted person of Korean heritage, wrote in her memoir *All You Can Ever Know* about the intertwined understandings of herself as both an adopted person and a non-white person in her mostly white town:

> The truth was that being Korean and being adopted were things I had loved and hated in equal measure. . . . Sometimes the adoption—the abandonment, as I could not help but think of

it when I was very young—upset me more; sometimes my differences did; but mostly, it was both at once, race and adoption, linked parts of my identity that set me apart from everyone else in my orbit.

Many transracially adopted people carry the burden of navigating their racial identities on their own. In her memoir, *"You Should Be Grateful": Stories of Race, Identity, and Transracial Adoption,* Black adoptee Angela Tucker writes about the enduring tension between loving her white parents and wishing she had not been adopted. She must carry the burden of often being the sole Black person in white spaces, while also working to have her Blackness validated within Black ones. After speaking at a conference, Tucker was once approached by a former member of the National Association of Black Social Workers. "You are my worst fear realized," the stranger told her. "You aren't a true Black person . . . I'm sorry the system erased you from our culture." Tucker felt flabbergasted and numb—she had found the NABSW's 1972 statement to be "a powerful reclamation of Blackness," and having her Blackness rejected by this woman felt like "the core of [her] being [had] just been sliced open." These complexities and the potential for harm should make us more highly attuned to how adopted people of color are situated with the private adoption system. Yet, as I found, very few of the relinquishing mothers of children of color were immediately cognizant of these challenges, or if they were aware, they were unable to shape their adoptions in a way that would mitigate these hardships for their children.

Sometimes the racial difference between a white mother and a child of color was a contributing reason to the relinquishment. Readers will remember Haley at the opening of this book, who seemed puzzled and hurt by her family's seemingly collective decision to withhold support for her during her pregnancy with her second son, even though they had supported her during an earlier pregnancy. It wasn't until the end of our interview, when I prodded this further, that she mentioned maybe it was because this baby was partially Black. Similarly, Kristen overtly worried that her family wouldn't accept a biracial Latino child. Neither of these mothers explicitly said they didn't want to parent a child of color, but their access to family support that might have been available for a white child was limited or denied to them, and thus led them to their relinquishment. Both Haley's and Kristen's sons ended up with white adoptive families. In fact, none of the white mothers who relinquished children of color placed their infants with families of color, and very few of them really considered it an important factor in choosing a family. Said one:

> I knew he would be half Hispanic. But when you look at him now, he looks like a normal kid. He has brown hair, he's tanned usually, and he has brown eyes, but he's not super dark or anything. He actually looks a lot like his adopted mom. Race wasn't really a factor for me in picking parents.

Few of these white mothers really thought much about what it would mean to have a child of color raised by white parents, which may have been because they didn't feel they really had other options. Even those mothers—both white women and women of color—who *did* want adoptive parents of color for their children often had to let go of that idea, because there were so few available. Caroline, who is white and relinquished her biracial Black daughter in 2019, shared:

> I really wanted her to have a parent of color. That is something that was important to me and that I really wanted. This agency had one Black couple, basically, and they were one of the couples that kind of declined to move forward. So, unfortunately, that didn't happen. I think if I'd had more time, that would've been something that I definitely would've looked for specifically. But

I am part of the queer community, and that's a community I've always identified with and been around. So I chose a white gay couple.

Many women of color made the same concession when their agencies failed to offer them diverse prospective parents from which to choose. As Camille mentioned, she was at least able to take consolation in the fact that her son's adoptive parents had already adopted a Black child, so at least he wouldn't be the only Black person in the household. But the fact that the adoption was open—that she could still give her child a connection to his Black family—was also important to her, which made it all the more crushing when the adoptive parents cut off contact.

Because many of these adopted people of color were relinquished by white mothers, and because birth fathers are—for myriad reasons—far less likely to engage in post-adoption contact, these adoptees of color often have connections only to their white adoptive families and their white birth families. In her memoir, *Surviving the White Gaze,* biracial adopted person Rebecca Carroll explores this exact dynamic: as a Black child in a white adoptive family, Carroll has a tenuous and fraught relationship with her white birth mother, Tess. When she meets Tess for the first time and asks about Joe, her birth father, Tess replies: "Basically, he was a dog . . . he was a jive-ass black man." Tess's racism extends overtly toward Carroll's father, and in a more complex (but no less harmful) way toward her own daughter, who is left to grapple with and find meaning in her own racial identity without the context and support of her Black family. When Carroll meets Joe as an adult, she finds him kind, vulnerable, and eager to be involved in her life. Joe tells Carroll he wanted to raise her, but that Tess's mother was racist and refused to entertain such an idea: "Just like slave times . . . they shut me out and stole you away from me." Reading Carroll's story, I thought of the white birth mothers I had interviewed who were anxious about how their families would fail to accept a biracial child and who relinquished instead. It does seem likely that race is a bigger factor in their relinquishment than these few birth mothers are capable of acknowledging, either to themselves or to me. It is also clear that openness, when it means continued connection between the adopted person of color and a white birth mother, does little to create connection and reconciliation across these racial divides. Rebecca Carroll writes: "After meeting Joe, I wanted to show him that I had found the blackness I'd been robbed of while growing up in the white family that adopted me."

Even as the birth mothers I interviewed often faced a lack of power when it came to making decisions for themselves and their family, most of them were white and thus still had white privilege. Their racial privilege made it possible for them not to consider or to overlook the complicated and precarious ways that their biracial children's lives would be shaped by transracial adoption and by the racialized and racist power structures within American society.*

While white relinquishing mothers thought little about their child's race—even if it differed from their own—mothers of color often thought about their child's race or ethnicity in complicated and counterintuitive ways. If a Black mother couldn't find Black parents for her child, at least she could choose white

---

* These mothers' white privilege contributes not only to how their lives take shape and their adoptions are lived, but to how they understand them and how they choose to share them with me. Tess's real name is Jan Waldron. In 1995, Waldron published *Giving Away Simone*, her own memoir about relinquishing Carroll. A review of her book in *The New York Times* described it thus: "In *Giving Away Simone*, Ms. Waldron argues by example that 'mistake' means surrendering a child, not conceiving it. Her life is a cautionary tale in a new maternal order in which anti-abortion activism 'sells adoption as an adorable idea,' haunted 'by that awful spirit that presided over the day I walked away,' and by the words of a hospital roommate, an older, motherly woman. 'Don't do it,' Ms. Waldron remembers her warning. 'You'll regret it for as long as you live.'" Waldron's account would not be out of place in this book, and reading her thoughts, in contrast to Carroll's own understanding of her adoption, is an important reminder that I am presenting only one perspective of complicated, evolving stories.

parents living in an urban area, where their communities and schools would be more diverse. If a Latina mother couldn't find a family with one Hispanic parent and one white one, maybe she could choose a queer couple who she felt would be more accepting of difference than a white evangelical household. These mothers thought about race a great deal and sought to put their children in homes that would support them in understanding their own identities.

One troublesome pattern that I observed, however, was the erasure of Native heritage by adoption agencies. None of the women that I interviewed were members of a Native American tribe, though some mentioned Native lineage. Their absence was not surprising; as mentioned in Chapter 1, less than 1 percent of mothers relinquishing in private adoptions are identified by their agencies as Native. Whenever a child is relinquished or removed from a Native parent, social workers or adoption agencies are required to notify the parent's tribe to see if the Indian Child Welfare Act applies to the adoption. If it does, the tribe has the opportunity to place the infant in a kinship or intratribal adoption or, failing that, with a Native family of another tribe. This practice means that these adoptions occur, for the most part, outside of the private adoption system. From my interviews, I have observed that when Native adoptions *do* occur within the private system, they are intentionally, carefully, and illegally hidden.

Three of the mothers that I interviewed reported that their child's father was Native American. *Did ICWA apply to this adoption?* I asked each time. According to their adoption agencies, it never did.

Savannah's agency told her that ICWA meant she needed to fill out a "special form" to avoid having her partner's tribe notified. Natasha's agency told her that ICWA existed because her home state of South Dakota "was very strict about babies who are Native American," so it would be better for her to say she wasn't sure who the baby's father was. When they told me these stories, I had to swallow my fury toward their deceptive agencies.

What both Savannah and Natasha described seemed to be violations of federal law. Specifically, they were violations of a law designed to correct generations of coercive, abusive child-taking from Native families. Their agencies lied to them, and how could they—young women, neither of them Native American themselves—know anything about a relatively obscure fifty-year-old adoption law?

Madison, who relinquished her son in 2017, was already suspicious when she spoke with me:

There was some drama about the Indian Child Welfare Act very, very late in the pregnancy. I had been lied to pretty extensively by the social worker about what the law actually means and entails. I reported my boyfriend's affiliation, and one of the Nations said there was enough blood to count, which meant the adoptive parents I had chosen dropped out immediately. They didn't want to move forward with the adoption, because ICWA would complicate it so much. The agency immediately flooded us with profiles of white people that they really wanted us to choose. They were pushing very, very hard, but I didn't like anyone. Then, at the hospital, right after my C-section, I'm on morphine and the social worker says that we got a call that the Indian tribe had messed it all up. This wasn't an ICWA adoption. The adoption was back on with the couple we had chosen. As I've been able to talk about it and think about it and have the freedom to do that, I started realizing that little things weren't quite right, especially the thing with ICWA. As I was reading online, there was this one person who is a Native adoptee who was adopted before ICWA, and I learned a lot from them. I realized everything I thought I knew about the law that the agency had told me was wrong and pretty racist. That just kind of rocked my whole understanding of everything, and I started looking into things more. I looked at the paperwork, the original, wet-ink signature papers, the legal ICWA paperwork, and only two of the fifteen pages are filled out. So that raised some red flags with me, and I started doubting if they'd even sent those papers out properly. I started looking into that, getting DNA tests, researching family history, just because I felt that it was very important, that if that should have applied, then at the very least, my son should know that. He should have that information.

ICWA has faced numerous existential threats from the federal judiciary, most critically in *Adoptive Couple v. Baby Girl* (known as the "Baby Veronica" case) in 2013 and *Haaland v. Brackeen* in 2022. In the *Haaland* case, white adoptive parents asked the court to rule on the constitutionality of ICWA, arguing that ICWA constitutes racial discrimination against non-Native prospective adoptive parents. The tribes, in response, argued that ICWA operates based on tribal membership—a political designation, not a racial one. In this, the *Haaland* case represents a threat to all tribal sovereignty, with adoption being used to potentially upend all of federal Indian law. While the Supreme Court ultimately upheld ICWA in its 2023 decision in *Haaland v. Brackeen,* the law is likely to face ongoing legal challenges. It's also clear from the stories shared with me that, for some agencies, ICWA might as well be a legal relic.

* * *

Alyssa grew up in a quaint, picturesque town in New York, where Manhattanites would frequently visit to escape the city in the summer or view the changing leaves and go apple picking in the autumn. A transracial and transnational adoptee from Central America, she was raised by white parents and was one of the only children of color in her small community. Her adoption was the defining experience of her childhood:

Being a transracial adoptee has been the hardest thing I've ever faced, I would say, besides my own daughter's adoption. It was really tricky growing up to feel like I fit in. I never really felt like I belonged anywhere, because my parents were older and they were white and I wasn't. Just to paint a picture, I was one of four kids of color at my elementary school, and that really took a toll on me. It was really hard for me growing up being racially isolated. That's kind of the basis of everything in my childhood. I never really fit in or belonged. I definitely feel like it played the biggest role in my life, me being adopted. I know other adopted people that don't feel that way, and I also know a lot of adopted people that *do* feel that way.

Despite these critical feelings about her own experience, when Alyssa found out she was pregnant, she immediately thought about adoption. "Adoption was just so central in my life that it was almost obvious that that was what I would do with my daughter if I didn't choose to terminate the pregnancy, which I had considered because I was young."

Alyssa briefly entertained the idea of parenting and acknowledged that her adoptive parents were financially comfortable and could have supported her, but she also felt that they would be disappointed in her if she did decide to raise her daughter. When she told them she was pregnant, her adoptive mother cried and "compared it to a death in the family." Faced with her adoptive parents' tears, Alyssa immediately told them she was considering adoption: "I think that gave them the confidence to just chill out a little bit. They thought that was good, obviously. They adopted me and they didn't see anything hard about that at all, in their experience."

Alyssa then began the adoption process and was soon connected with the adoption facilitator who had managed her own adoption. She still had mixed feelings, though. "I really wish someone had been like, 'All right, well, we're on your team. We want you to make an informed decision.' No one did that at all. No one," she said. "I think it's so messed up. I think if someone had expressed that they were on my team and they supported me no matter what . . . I don't know what I would have chosen. And I'm mad that I don't know." But without that supportive team and with her parents' enthusiasm for adoption driving her forward, the process unfolded quickly.

On one point, though, she did hold her ground: Alyssa was firm that her daughter would not have white adoptive parents. Her lawyers didn't have any prospective adoptive parents that matched Alyssa's own Latina background. They did, however, have an Asian American couple, so Alyssa chose them.

> When it came to my daughter, I knew for a fact: she's not having white parents. I'm not doing this to her. Growing up, I wanted white skin. I didn't like myself, all because I wasn't white, and I was surrounded by white people all the time. There was no way in hell I was going to do that to her. I refused to interview white parents. I was just very set on finding someone that might resemble her. I didn't find any Latino adoptive parents, but I found an Asian couple and I interviewed them both, and then I chose the second couple to be her parents. They're not white, at least.

Yet having her daughter raised in yet another culture—one that didn't match either the one Alyssa was born into nor the one she was raised in—left a disconnect between Alyssa and her daughter, Layla.

> They acknowledge that Layla is Latina, but it doesn't really feel like it's a thing for them. But honestly? I don't know what that would look like if it was part of their life. I wasn't even raised Latina, if that makes sense. I was raised in a white family. If I wanted her to have that connection, I would have to learn it

along with her. It's not like I have this entire culture that I want to show her and make her a part of, because I just—I don't have that, either. I've done a lot of soul-searching, going to therapy, and trying to make sense of things in my own head to understand what happened after I placed my daughter. It made me wake up to the reality of what adoption is, and how loss and grief are the central themes of what adoption is, even if there can be healthy and happy parts. I believe that I have a healthy relationship with both my adoptions, both as adoptee and birth mom. But I did a lot of the "coming out of the fog"—that's what many birth moms call it. It's when you wake up to the reality of what adoption is, and it's really challenging sometimes. I did a lot of that after I placed my daughter.

Even though Alyssa was optimistic about her ongoing relationship with her daughter, she acknowledged: "I'm not sure, in hindsight, if I would choose adoption again for my daughter, truly understanding like the complexities that I do now."

* * *

When we talk about the differences between adoptive families and birth families (money, religion, politics, race) and the challenges these differences present, it's important to remember that for many, including Alyssa, that's a false dichotomy. Adoptive families often *are* birth families: many relinquishing mothers are adopted themselves.

While there are no good large-scale data, it was clear to me that adopted people are meaningfully overrepresented among relinquishing mothers. About 20 percent of the women I interviewed were adopted themselves, either from foster care or in private adoptions. Many more had adopted siblings with whom they were raised, and thus grew up in adoptive families even if they were not themselves adopted. Part of this pattern is likely about the salience of adoption: by being adopted or growing up in adoptive families, they are more likely to consider it at all.

One study found that teen mothers are heavily influenced in the decisions to relinquish by having personal experiences with adoption—either by knowing someone who was adopted, or by being adopted themselves. But there were also far more complicated dynamics at play.

Some adopted people felt obligated to give birth and choose adoption simply because their own birth mothers had done so.* They felt that their existence was owed to adoption, and thus they owed that to their child. For the relinquishing mothers that grappled with this, their stories were largely about guilt and obligation and not a persistent joyful belief that they had been so well served by adoption that it was clearly the best choice for them and their child. Importantly, though, adopted people (like all groups of people) are still more likely to have an abortion or choose to parent, rather than relinquishing.

Adopted people who face pregnancy decisions were also making those choices in the context of the belief systems in which they were raised and the support available to them from their own families. Because of the religious and anti-abortion forces that shape who pursues adopting children, many adopted people grew up in conservative households that not only made abortion feel less accessible but also promoted adoption. They were also raised by parents *who had been served well by adoption* and thus encouraged it as a solution when their own daughters faced unplanned pregnancies. Many times, adoptee relinquishing

---

* In an essay entitled "My Adoption, My Abortion: Getting Clear About What Counts as Reproductive Choice," philosopher Michele Merritt has written about her decision to have an abortion in the same context: "I had internalized the idea that I should be grateful for the choices my birthmother made, but never could shake the sense of sadness I felt for her, having to make those decisions. The older I got, the more strongly I believed she should have had the right to have an abortion, even if that meant I never existed. One day, I blurted this out to my adoptive mom and immediately regretted it. Despite having a wonderful relationship with my adoptive parents, to this day, abortion is not safe to discuss. . . . Nevertheless, the more I matured, the less I kept silent around my family. That day, I blurted out: 'Well, I would have an abortion if I got pregnant and didn't want to be!'" (*Adoption & Culture* 10, no. 2 (2022): 203–9).

mothers said their adoptive parents were strongly encouraging of adoption and were unlikely to offer support for them if they expressed an interest in parenting.

* * *

Fundamentally, adoption is premised on the permanent legal separation of one set of family relationships to accommodate another, which means that maintaining a true connection between birth families and adopted people is counter to what the system is working to accomplish. Maintaining that true connection requires a new concept of not just what adoption could be, but what *families* could be. It often falls short of what everyone hopes. I believe that openness can help protect both relinquishing mothers and adopted people from some (not all) of the deepest traumas that we know are characteristic of closed adoption. I also believe that openness creates a relationship that is fraught with an imbalance of power, lets grief and anxiety linger, and requires hard logistical and emotional work for families that are deeply committed to making it work.

For many relinquishing mothers, then, openness is a failed promise—but it's a promise that's intentionally made. They would not relinquish without it. "I wouldn't have done an adoption if I couldn't have done an open adoption," Kate told me. Yet the way that adoption is practiced rarely fulfills relinquishing mothers' hopes and expectations in the long term. One adoption marketing site that helps prospective adoptive parents promote their profile to expectant mothers suggests: "Many of our birthmothers like the idea of open adoption. If your client can honestly offer this kind of relationship to a birth mother, it will increase their odds of finding a birth mother." Yet there's no discussion of what openness means, why it's important, the support it requires, and what it will look like in the long term—it's mentioned here purely as a selling point to increase the chances of finding a baby. Legal scholar Malinda Seymore has written about how openness is used in adoption agency marketing, even in states where openness agreements are not legally binding. She describes how an agency in North Carolina offers "different levels of openness with the adoptive family"; an agency in Missouri includes a glowing open adoption testimony from a birth mother; an agency in Ohio tells expectant mothers that "arrangements can be made . . . to stay in touch with your child's adoptive parents through his/her lifetime." None of these agencies can offer legally binding open adoption agreements.

Private agencies also rely on the offer of openness when marketing adoption toward women who have already lost children to foster care. The threat of family regulation services removing their children was particularly salient for mothers of color. Camille, a Black mother suffering from postpartum psychosis, relinquished her son because she was worried the state might take custody of all her children. Yet many other mothers grapple with this Solomonic decision-making even without the mental health crisis that Camille was experiencing; sometimes it was just because they were poor. Sociologist Elizabeth Raleigh has noted that in moments of economic recession, "impoverished mothers struggling to feed their children were attempting to place their toddlers for private adoption, rather than have the state take them away and put them in foster care for neglect . . . [one adoption] attorney discussed this trend: 'They [birth mothers] can't afford to have foster care come in and take custody of their children. So they want to plan a plan for their children, because they think it is a better plan than to have them in foster care.'" Several attorneys interviewed by Raleigh confirmed that this was happening with greater and greater frequency.

Jasmine, a Latina woman, was incarcerated when she found out she was pregnant. She'd already lost two older children to foster care because of her drug addiction, and open adoption seemed like a better option:

> I wasn't interested in adoption at all, but the people at the jail mentioned it. I knew that I wasn't ready for a baby, but giving

up a baby . . . I couldn't do that. But I was scared, because I already lost custody of my two oldest. I don't know where they're
at. At the time, it had already been, what, three or four years,
and I haven't heard from them at all. But as the weeks went
by, I started thinking about my daughter that I still hadn't lost
completely. I'm going through CPS [Child Protective Services]
with her, and I hadn't lost her completely. And I just decided—I
needed to focus on her. So I decided to do the open adoption,
so at least I could see the baby. I told the person in the jail to call
the agency, and they did. I talked to them, and within a day or
two—I was actually surprised how fast, because usually it's really
hard to get mail there!—I got a package from them with profiles
to read in my cell.

Because mothers like Jasmine are already involved with the
family regulation system, they face increased scrutiny of their
parenting and intense policing of their families. When they are
expecting a new child, they may know it's possible or even likely
that they will lose custody of that child to the state and choose
open adoption instead.

This pattern of offering incarcerated women open adoptions
to relinquish does not seem to be an anomaly. As reported by Rebecca Nagle on her podcast *This Land,* an offer of open adoption
is also how Jennifer and Chad Brackeen gained standing in the
child custody case that would become *Haaland v. Brackeen*—the
case that challenged the legality of the Indian Child Welfare Act
before the Supreme Court in November 2022. The case involved
custody of Yoselyn (a pseudonym), the biological sister of the
Brackeens' adopted son. As Nagle reports:

After crying at the news of Yoselyn's birth, Jennifer [Brackeen]
decided she had to fight for custody of a child that she had not
fostered, and over that child's blood relative. At first, Chad and
Jennifer Brackeen contacted the Texas Department of Family

and Protective Services [DFPS], but social workers wouldn't give them information about the baby. So their lawyer . . . sent a letter to the Deputy Commissioner of Texas DFPS. But the department wouldn't budge. They wouldn't place Yoselyn with the Brackeens. So, Jennifer tracked down Yoselyn's mother in jail and got her to sign an affidavit that she wanted the Brackeens to adopt Yoselyn. Yoselyn's caseworker would later testify the Brackeens got that affidavit by promising Yoselyn's mom an open adoption, meaning she could always have contact with the baby. The caseworker said that was concerning . . . Chad and Jennifer used that affidavit to help get standing in Yoselyn's case, in other words, to have a say in what happened.

The practice of offering open adoption as a way of averting foster care is also practiced in more progressive adoption spaces. Open Adoption and Family Services, a private agency in Portland, Oregon, offered a webinar for Oregon's Health Authority, Public Health Division, entitled *Empowering Expectant Parents: Pregnancy Options Counseling and Open Adoption as an Alternative to State Adoption.* OAFS is one of the foremost agencies promoting open adoption in the country; they do not facilitate closed adoptions, and they provide long-term services to help relinquishing and adoptive parents manage their open adoption arrangement. However, through this webinar, OAFS argued that "proactively planning an open adoption gives [mothers] a voice in their adoption plan and an ongoing relationship with their child," in contrast to the foster care system, where a birth mother has effectively no control over what happens to their child. The many benefits that OAFS outlines for their private adoption include: "child avoids possible trauma of the foster care system. . . . saves [the mother] the humiliation of having her parenting rights terminated in court . . . the open adoption process is healing and empowering for her. . . . If adoption is likely to be in her future, she deserves choices as to what that adoption looks like." It is true that private adoption *may have the potential* to offer more control and openness to relinquishing mothers than the public foster care system *as foster care is currently practiced*. However, it's not clear that all of the women targeted by this program would inevitably have their parental rights terminated if they did not engage with private adoption. Giving parents the opportunity to terminate their own rights preemptively, when the loss of such rights is not a foregone conclusion, is merely a way of selling private adoption within the context of an abusive system, under the false promise that it can offer contact, dignity, or empowerment. The messaging in the OAFS webinar begs the question of why we allow a traumatizing foster care system or a humiliating family court system or a violent family policing system to continue their work under the guise of child welfare for *any* families. If these systems were actually about supporting families and caring for children, they would be fundamentally different. OAFS seems to at least intuitively understand this. The agency's materials share: "Birthparents say they wouldn't choose adoption under any other circumstances."

There's another insidious dynamic that emerges from open adoption: it prevents many relinquishing mothers from speaking critically about adoption, out of anxiety that they would alienate their child's adoptive parents and have their contact with their child limited or ended. I have participated on conference panels with first mothers who use pseudonyms to share their stories, and connected mothers with reporters only once the condition of anonymity has been agreed upon. These mothers want to share their stories—they believe the stories are important—but they are unwilling to jeopardize their contact with their child to do so. I don't blame them. This dynamic, however, does mean that publicly shared stories (or even research based on focus group data) often paint a rosier picture than the one I am sharing. Kristen, whose adoption had been closed when her child was seven, was awaiting her son's eighteenth birthday so that she could reach out to him directly. Similarly, many relinquishing mothers count down to their child's adulthood, when their relationship with them is no longer contingent on their adoptive parents' permission. I once asked a first mother how old her daughter was. "Nine," she replied. "I am halfway through my sentence. Then I can speak openly."

Sarah

"How long that trauma lasts, how quickly you get over it or accept it, it varies depending on the person."

Sarah (who is Chinese American) was in her mid-thirties, recently divorced, raising her two daughters, and living in the Pacific Northwest when she became pregnant in 2016.

I was adjusting to that single-parenting life at the time. I was dating Nick—casually, long distance—for a couple of months, but we had ended things a few weeks earlier because the distance was just a pain. Then I found out I was pregnant about two weeks after ending the relationship. I was in shock, complete and utter shock, and somewhat panicked.

I considered abortion very briefly, but I am Christian, so I don't really believe in abortion for me. I did consider it for a minute, though. I'm definitely pro-choice—I believe it's up to people to choose. It's not my place to choose for somebody. I just don't believe in abortion for myself. I do feel like the baby is a life even early on.

Parenting was an option, but I had such a hard time with it. It was a scary option. I wasn't really comfortable with it. I had just gotten out of a really long marriage, a really complicated relationship, and I didn't really want to get into another one. In hindsight, I was really afraid that that relationship wouldn't work out and I'd have another child that I would be single-parenting and the kids I was raising would suffer. I brought up adoption out of fear more than anything.

I started searching online and ended up on the "waiting families" page for the adoption agency nearby. I just scrolled through really quickly, and I just saw their profile and I don't know, something just clicked. I ended up sending the link to their profile and a few other profiles to Nick, and he actually picked the same couple. I liked them because they were a mixed-race couple—the dad is Chinese and the mom is white. And I liked that they were both Christian, and family is very important to them. I've always said since the adoption that they are the family that I never knew that I always wanted. They are just really great people. Nick and I were in alignment on choosing them *if* we did an adoption, but I wasn't ready to make a decision, because I was still considering parenting. Honestly, that was primarily the reason I was thinking about parenting, because he was a boy and I've always wanted a boy—both the kids I'm raising are girls. That was part of the reason I was thinking about parenting so much.

I probably flip-flopped back and forth about parenting and adoption through the entire pregnancy, but we did decide to move forward with the adoption when I was about halfway through, even though I wasn't 100 percent sure. Nick came out for a visit and came with me to meet the adoptive parents. We spent, like, a full day with them, getting lunch, going hiking. I was very comfortable right away, and so we felt like they were the right people. I was thinking we'd have a closed adoption, which was probably part of the reason I wasn't fully settled on adoption. I didn't even know that there were open adoptions. It was Maggie, the adoptive mom, who said: "Hey, would you be willing to have an open adoption?" She actually has a sibling who was adopted, and she said, "You know, I saw what my sister went through with having a closed adoption and how much it impacted her. I think it's really important to have an open adoption." That's when the decision was made. In the back of my mind, I knew I could change my mind, right? But that was when I'd say most of me had decided to go through with adoption.

*   *   *

I had to explain to my daughters, because they were old enough to understand what was going on. I didn't end up telling them that I was pregnant until after we made the adoption decision. I told them that I was pregnant and I was going to have a baby, but that this baby was going to live with a different family. I was saying "this isn't our baby" from the start and setting those expectations. They . . . sort of understood.

I was definitely having second thoughts after Ethan was born, but I think that was more hormonal than anything. I had prepared myself for the adoption the entire pregnancy, training myself to think that he wasn't mine. And then he's born and that overwhelming love, all the oxytocin kicks in, and then I'm bonding with him while I'm breast-feeding. It was a lot harder on me than I had anticipated. That is one thing that I will say, is even with all my preparations, even with all my compartmentalization and everything else, it was probably the hardest thing I've ever done.

The first weeks were just a living nightmare. It was absolute hell because I couldn't exercise, I couldn't really do anything. It was bad. The milk coming in, and then having to get rid of it—it was hard. I ended up signing the papers within a week or so. The social worker came over to our house. And I just couldn't stop crying. I could not stop crying. And my friend pulled me aside and said, "You don't have to do this." I was just an emotional wreck. She's like, "You can still change your mind. You don't have to do this. If you want to keep him, parent him, whatever, I'll help." Through tears I'm like, "But I made this decision when I was not an emotional wreck, when my hormones weren't like all over the place and my emotions weren't all over the place. It's the right decision, right? Like analytically, it's the right decision." But emotionally it was terrible, and Nick was hesitating, too. And then he finally was just like, "You know what, we made this decision together when we were both in a sound state of mind, so we should go through with it." He went ahead and signed, and then so did I, and that was the end.

Maggie and David were texting me updates and pictures. After I did the research about open adoption, I wondered what was best for Ethan, too, right? It wasn't just about the kids I was parenting. It's hard for adopted children to not have contact. I was committed to the open adoption, and we were going to keep it very open. So the text messages from them, I was comfortable with it. They made me sad, sure, but at the same time it made me happy to see him happy. It was just an emotional roller coaster.

We were texting almost constantly for the first year, not every day but probably every other day. I mean, we were in a lot of contact early on. And I had a few visits with him, too. I was nervous to start the visits because I wasn't sure how well I was going to keep it together. It actually went really well. I'd say the first year we probably saw them three or four times, and then slowed down. Work got really crazy for me, and then they moved pretty far away, so obviously we didn't have the option to see them as often. I used to be able to text them and ask if we could just meet up for an hour so I could see him, but then that obviously couldn't happen anymore.

The contact has really dwindled down now, and I'm not thrilled about that. We are connected on social media, so I see what they're up to, but it's actually really infrequent that we text or talk. When I reach out, they usually respond, and vice versa, but we don't actively talk that much anymore. It's probably once every other month that we might exchange messages.

But my daughters love him, and Ethan loves them, too. When we're together, it's very sweet. He sticks to them like glue—especially my youngest daughter, he's just always just holding her hand. They love him and they are sad. They ask me all the time, why did I give him up for adoption? They wish that I would've kept him. That is heartbreaking and that is probably—well, I don't know if it's regret. But it's guilt. The guilt always follows. I didn't realize how it would shape their views on child and families, and I'm seeing those impacts now. Both of my daughters have told me they don't want to have kids, or if they do, they just want to adopt. Because they see adoption as . . . I don't know. They view the adoptive family as having more of whatever they want. More of their brother. At some point, I will have to have a conversation with them about why that's not a good idea, why I just don't want them to adopt.

It's complicated and it's a lot of emotions and a lot of—just a lot. I am very blessed that we have such a great relationship with his parents, and I recognize that. I recognize that I probably have the most ideal situation out of any relationship you could build. I know that there's a lot of hurt and anger on both sides in a lot of cases. And from what I've read in studies since, there is still trauma to the child who is adopted. Regardless of how loving, how well it's done, there are studies that show there is trauma because there's that separation.

Those are the things I never considered when I made the decision for adoption. Learning that, knowing that now, it's shifted my opinion of adoption. I think it's still necessary and I think it's still a good thing, but I think people should go into it with a much more wide-open lens and understand the implications and really the complex emotions and relationship. I mean, you have to be really good at relationships to sustain this kind of relationship. You just can't grasp it until you go through it. I thought I would understand it because I already had kids, but I was totally wrong.

I think I had a lot of things working in my favor that made this adoption go decently okay, so far. I'm older than his adoptive parents, but we're all about the same age. None of us are really young; we have an emotional maturity. The fact that I already have kids and understand parenting, I think that helps. And they are very communicative, and very, very committed to open adoption. It was very important to them for the health of Ethan. But I would also say that I went into this decision with eyes wide open, or at least as open as they could be—and even then it was traumatic for me. I think that a lot of people wouldn't be able to handle that. It would take a lot longer to process. I also was already in therapy before I had him, and I continued therapy through. I still see that therapist, knowing I have things to work on. Honestly, those are some of the reasons why I think it worked out decently well for all of us: we are very open with each other, and we're committed to working on our own feelings.

I do feel like a lot should be different about adoption. I think that there need to be more conversations between birth mothers and prospective birth mothers. I think that should be a requirement. And there need to be far, far more support services. There are just a few organizations—really, one organization that I found, and they really helped pull me through at the very beginning. I went to a retreat with them about six weeks after Ethan was born. It was very emotional and it was very difficult, but having women who actually understood and had been there and could tell me their stories actually made me very thankful for what I had. I think that that should definitely be a requirement to have those discussions and have that available to prospective birth mothers. I think counseling should be a requirement, not an option. It should be a requirement, and it should start prior to the birth and extend for at least a year after the birth. I would also love to see open adoption being the only way to go, but I know that's not reasonable or feasible. Because today, once those adoption papers are signed, the adoptive parents really have the say. If they want to close the adoption, they can, and that's not fair. Contractually, I feel like there should be more of an obligation to keep it open. Birth parents should have their rights protected even after they sign off, if there was an agreement made at the time of the adoption. I feel like the system could definitely do a better job of monitoring and managing those relationships for people who aren't good at it on their own.

If I were the one having those conversations with a prospective birth mother, I think the biggest thing I would tell her is to consider the impact that it will have on her existing children—that's probably the biggest one for me, if she already has a kid. They were my number one concern when I was making the decision, but I didn't understand what it would be like for them. The reality of that decision and the reality of how it impacted them is very different from what I had in my head.

But I would definitely tell her that it's going to be harder than she thinks it's going to be, and that it's traumatic for everyone involved. How long that trauma lasts, how quickly you get over it or accept it, it varies depending on the person. No matter what, this child's always going to be a part of her in some way. They'll be someone that you think about regardless of time or distance or space.

Erica

*"I just wish that adoptive families would understand
that their happiness and their joy, and their life and this
child—there is another woman who has grief in that.
How do you balance that juxtaposition?"*

Erica (who is white) grew up in the northern Midwest and relinquished her daughter, Ava, during her senior year of high school in 2000. I spoke with her in 2010 and again in 2020, soon after Ava had become a legal adult and they no longer relied on her adoptive parents to facilitate a relationship between them.

2010

I think I'm going to take you back to when I was in middle school—not because I got pregnant in middle school, but because it's important to understand who I was. I was a really good child; I was popular, and I got great grades and had really strict parents. I was going to a private Catholic school at the time, and I had a lot of pressure on me.

Then in middle school, I flipped the bill and tried alcohol. I was starting to rebel, for sure. My dad came down really hard on me. When I was a sophomore in high school, I started smoking pot, and they came down even harder. We started family counseling; I stopped using drugs. Then, beginning my junior year, I met a boy. He was an incredibly charming person, incredibly charming, and I got sucked in right away—and my rebellious streak really blew up. I was still clean when we started dating, but then we started dropping acid and everything started spiraling. I was getting in trouble at school, getting suspended. When you were suspended, you had to go plead your case to the school to be let back in. So I refused to go beg publicly in front of everyone. And I got kicked out.

I was still in this very turbulent relationship. It was abusive emotionally, for sure, and somewhat physically. That summer, between my junior and senior year, I was committed to getting back on track. I got clean and wasn't using any drugs, and I was ready to refocus on school to graduate with my class on time. And then I got pregnant.

My mom came to me because I was having morning sickness. She was like, "Why are you missing school?" She thought it was because I was back on drugs, but I was just sick because of the pregnancy. And I was struggling because I'd stopped taking my antidepressants, because I wasn't sure if I should take them while I was pregnant.

I told the psychiatrist that I was pregnant and afraid of that medicine. He really, really was angry. I think I hit a chord with him. He treated me really, really badly after that and made some crude remarks to my mom, which I think made her suspicious. So during our next family counseling session, I had the counselor tell them. They are both crying, but my dad was like, "We love you and we will support you in any decision that you choose." I really believed them when they said that. I realized soon that "any decision you choose" meant adoption to them.

I was thinking about getting an abortion, but then my mom had me go with one of her friends who had an abortion and sit down and talk with her. Her friend said how it was the worst thing in her life and she regrets it. And then I went to a crisis pregnancy center, too. They really give you a lot of propaganda about abortion. And so abortion was out. Parenting never really came into the frame, because my dad said: "If you are going to keep the child, you are out of the house when you turn eighteen." And my eighteenth birthday was just two months away, and still in the middle of my senior year of high school. I didn't have any time to get a parenting plan in place.

They were not truly supporting me in any decision. They wanted me to do an adoption. I do think they really believed that they were doing the best for me—that's what I have to come back to. I have a lot of compassion around that, because I really believe they thought they were doing the best thing. Then it was the worst thing in the world. My parents were well known in our town; it's a really small city in a really rural state, but they did very well for themselves. And my pregnancy was incredibly embarrassing for them. It brought a lot of shame, especially being a Catholic family. They had me drop out of school to do a home-school program, so that no one would see I was pregnant.

So my mom called the adoption agency, one of the biggest agencies in the country, and I went in. I met this social worker, who was also an adoptive parent, who also was in the process of adopting. It's not like I got an unbiased perspective. She always told me that it was a win-win. She told me, and I remember this very distinctly: "I never met a girl who has regretted her adoption decision."

When you go into this Christian agency, you have to understand that the worst possible thing is a girl who gets pregnant. So adoption is a way to reconcile your sin, to still have that secret, no one will know. And the baby will be born. It will be perfect. It will be some sort of redemption.

I decided early on in my pregnancy that I would detach myself from the pregnancy, and the social worker told me, well, no, Erica, you can actually love that little baby growing inside of you. I really took that to heart. And I loved her. And I would talk to her, and I was kind of amazed at what was happening to my body at the time.

* * *

I wanted the baby to be the only child in their family, the first child. I wanted an open adoption. And I just thought that I would know the parents. Because I was Christian, I thought that it was important her parents be Christians, but I didn't have, really, a checklist. I went through many, many, many profiles, and I couldn't find anyone that felt right. Then I finally found Brenda and Scott, and they offered to have an open adoption. They were about ten hours away from where I was living, and I really liked them. They seemed to be involved in the church, they had just a lot of fun together, they were a very active couple.

The conversations about openness were very, very vague. Brenda was just like, "Whatever you want." It was vague, but, "We're happy, we're happy to send pictures, we're happy to send updates, and we're happy for you to see him, to have visits whenever you want." I said: "Yes, I want to visit. Yes, I want pictures. That's part of the reason I chose you." But we never had a plan. I wish that we would have set up some sort of schedule, and not just for her first year. I learned later that the agency actually requires parents to send pictures and videos for the first year, so I would have gotten that from anyone. It wasn't out of the goodness of their hearts. They were just fulfilling a contract. And I wished we'd set up an agreement, at least, rather than thinking it would develop organically. That just didn't happen with us. We were forming this relationship based on false intimacy. It wasn't an organic connection. But I have something they want, and they were a solution I needed.

After she was born, I just . . . looked at her. I can't believe that this is my child. I remember looking at her face, just this beautiful child. And I talked to her and she would look over at me. I was so bonded to her right away. It was really hard when I realized what I was about ready to do. You have this love and this connection with this baby. But right away—seriously, like five minutes after being sewn up—I called them. She's here. Her parents. So they drove out the next day.

I lost it. Like, lost it. I was bawling, sobbing. I think the person in the room next to me must have called the suicide nurse. But I was still going to follow through with this plan, because I owed it to them. I didn't have another plan in place. I would have been out of my house.

But it was also for Ava, she was my first allegiance. Intermeshed with everything I was dealing with, I was thinking about what's best for her. They will be able to give her everything that I will not.

This is where . . . I don't know about God. But if there is a God, this is where I think there might have been some divine intervention. Because of the insurance regulations, I was only able to stay in the hospital for, I think, three days. Well, because I just knew, God, I need, I need, I need, I need another day with this child. I asked my mom and dad if they would pay for another night, and they said maybe, but then there was this huge, huge, huge snowstorm and it shut down the entire city. The hospital workers were unable to leave. They shut down the interstate, so Brenda and Scott had to stay in a little farmhouse off of the interstate. And I was able to spend an extra day with my daughter by myself. I really see that as a great gift. I talked with her; I took a video of her. Everything was just shut down. It was quiet and just the two of us.

Then that night—I don't know if it's that night or the next day—we had our placement ceremony. And my social worker mentioned to me that I was disassociating myself, that I would kind of zone out and wasn't even there. She was a little concerned about that. She was like, "Erica, Erica, stay with me." I think it was so hard for me to understand what was happening. We had it in the hospital room, and I read a Bible verse and just sobbed. And I held her as long as I could until the social worker came and said, "You know, Erica, it's time. You need to hand her over." I stood up. I handed her to her mom, and said, "Take care of her," and physically collapsed when they left.

Supposedly, life went back to normal. The court date came, and they left to go back home. I went back to my high school to graduate on time. I walked with my class, and my whole family came to watch. Six months later, I was having this party and no one at least said anything to me or my family. Life supposedly went on like normal.

They had been sending me a few messages, but I cut off contact. On Mother's Day, Brenda texted me and said, "I'm so thankful that I was finally able to get a rose on Mother's Day. And I'm so thankful to be a mom." I just couldn't hear that. I had been sort of hoping they'd send me a card, acknowledging my part. But when I just heard from Brenda how proud she was to be a mom, and not recognizing my place at all, that's when I knew I needed to stop talking to them for a while. That's the last time I talked to her for about a year. I just couldn't hear that.

I went to college pretty far away and just started using drugs again. I found a boyfriend who was a drug dealer, which was great, because, wow, if you need something to numb your pain, it's great if you have a drug dealer there. I was in this pain. I was in this turmoil. I tried to get some counseling, my parents would pay for that, but I was really heavily medicated. I dropped out of school. I was enrolled in school, but I wasn't going to classes.

I think about two years after I gave birth, I did some real soul-searching. I started praying, asking God what my role in life was. I got clean, slowly, and moved to another part of the country. I started working with kids, which I loved. I just flourished, and I found life again. It was like me rekindling my mothering instincts through teaching these children, and it was at a high needs school, so a lot of underprivileged children. It was like they needed me, but I needed them even more, and it really built up my self-esteem and self-confidence.

But at the same time, my relationship with Scott and Brenda was deteriorating. They promised visits, and I did see her when she was eighteen months old, and again when she was two or three, but then not for a while. They stopped writing letters, they stopped reaching out, and I never did a whole lot of pursuing via phone, because I always wanted to put it in their court. I knew that they had all the power and control, and that if I did anything wrong, they would take the contact that I do have—which was pictures at Christmas—away from me. I wish we could have gotten to a better place. If there was a schedule, some sort of facilitation, maybe it could have been better. The contact they have with me now, it's not because they value me as a person or think of me as family. They're just fulfilling an obligation. What I wouldn't give to have a relationship with Brenda where, if Ava did something really well in school, she'd give me a call, because I would rejoice with her. I would absolutely rejoice.

Looking back, it's so clear that the social worker had an agenda and was so out of touch with how birth mothers feel. I don't think she should have called me a "birth mother" before Ava was born—I wasn't a birth mother while I was still pregnant, I was just an expectant mother. I wish that I would have had all my options laid out to me and I wish, I wish, I wish I would have known some of what would happen. The grief, the loss, the PTSD, the symptoms that I have, the nightmares—ten years later, I'm still experiencing all that. I sometimes wonder what it would be like if I never had to be working with this pain that happens in my life. It would have been nice if I'd had good information about abortion. I believe that abortion is such a personal choice, and I would support someone getting an abortion 100 percent because it's such a personal choice. But I was told I would regret that, for sure, and that I would absolutely not regret the adoption. I'm not bitter. I hope I don't sound bitter, but . . . I guess I don't want to label myself a bitter person, but I do hold some animosity. Toward my parents for not really giving me the choice, still toward the agency, and still toward Scott and Brenda. And toward society as a whole. But, what does bitterness do? It's way too easy to be angry.

It has affected every iota of my being, this decision I made ten years ago. I wish someone had told me: Don't take it lightly. Don't look at this like you will be able to go back to your life because you won't be able to. You will now be a mother without a child. I just wish that adoptive families would understand that their happiness and their joy, and their life and this child—there is another woman who has grief in that. How do you balance that juxtaposition? How do you balance those feelings while honoring her loss and still rejoicing in the gifts that you have?

I'm not shy when it comes to other types of advocacy work. But when it comes to this adoption, I just can't even talk about it. My own past is too raw. It's too tough to talk about. I don't think I'd be an activist if I hadn't gone through this. I'm very much aware that everyone has a story, and I'm slow to judge people and I have a lot of compassion. There's something in me, there's this passion and this drive to create social justice, to create change. I don't think I would have that drive, if I didn't experience this, if I didn't see how society works.

It's part of the grip that adoption has on you. It's not ending, there's no end in sight. You just have to learn how to find your voice. That's what the oppressed need to do: find their voice.

*   *   *

2020

On Ava's eighteenth birthday, I sent her a text message, a really heartfelt one about her birth and how I honor her every year on her birthday by going out into nature. And she wrote back right away to say that she was going to be nearby—her parents were taking her on a trip for her birthday. I just said, "If this is something that you're comfortable with, you know, no pressure whatsoever, but if you'd like to meet for breakfast or lunch, I would be delighted to see you." And she did and brought her parents along with her. We just happened to be traveling in the same place at the same time. We started asking each other all these questions. It was awkward, but we were just trying to get to know each other. And her parents were really kind.

Brenda, she knew I wasn't happy with how things had gone. She took me aside and she apologized and she just said, "Life got really busy for us and it's kind of why we didn't really include you in it." It was a little shallow, because like, "Life got busy"? Really? But she did not have to acknowledge it at all, and she did. I told her that there's not a "how to do this" guide for this relationship. So I forgave her. We made those amends.

That was the last time I saw Ava, but she actually just texted me this week. That was really profound; she just texted me to ask for a book recommendation, but she initiated the contact. Whenever I text her and reach out, my friend encourages me: "You've got to text her, go text her." I do that and she responds right away, always. She's super cordial. She's great. We're building something. I don't know what that is, but I have hope, I do have hope because she seems interested in my life, and you know, I'm always quick to respond to her. I think it's because she's an adult now, legally, she's more independent and not under her parents' thumb, and more comfortable contacting me.

I would love to be in her life more so because I've learned in the last few years that she's an incredible human being. I'm not even exaggerating. Everybody that's met her, my mom and my best friend, they're like, "We're all blown away by this kid." I'm not even saying this because I gave birth to her. We're all just incredibly taken by this child, or this woman, now. I would just love to be in her life to have another really great person in my world. She's kind and she's thoughtful and she thinks things through and she has her goals and she's silly. I'm not happy with the contact we have right now because I will always love to have more, but I think this needs to be paced, too.

My mom went with me to see her graduate, but my dad will not speak about her. But my parents did send her $500 for her high school graduation. That's not nothing. But he won't speak about her. And he won't speak to me about what happened. My mom will go there and just say, "We didn't know how hard it was going to be on you. We did the best that we could."

Looking at adoption more broadly: some people would tell me that I'm their hero. It's so hurtful. I've never had any support when I was pregnant. I got kicked out of school; I wasn't treated well. And now I'm a saint, a hero? It's bypassing the fact that there was a tremendous loss here, that this is a very nuanced story. It's still unfolding, but it's based on someone's loss. People are really uncomfortable holding space for others who have experienced trauma, and I consider this a trauma, what happened to me. And so they try to make it better. They try to make themselves feel better because I think sitting with the reality that this is a loss of a human—it's too much to bear, and so they just try to make it better because they want to feel better.

That's why adoption has just given me more compassion for others' choices. I'm so pro-choice. I am *so* pro-choice. I have a very close friend who's an abortion doctor. I have a sticker right here that says "I Support Planned Parenthood." If I was to get pregnant right now, I would have an abortion. Absolutely, 100 percent, those beliefs are because of the adoption. When you're given no choice, you have lifelong repercussions.

I never once had a choice. My counselor was an adoptive mother, someone employed and paid to convince girls to give up their babies. The adoptive parents? They came out, took me out to dinner, and bought me ice cream. The openness was bullshit. It is a corrupt industry that preys on people who are highly emotional because of hormones, highly vulnerable, scared shitless, and then you say, "Come here, we'll save you; we will take care of it. Meet these wonderful people who are infertile, and you're going to just make their life better." The only time anyone was really looking out for me was when they put me on suicide watch in the hospital because I was crying so much, and so the nurse came in. What if someone actually said, "Hey, you don't have to do this"? Never once was I even given the option. Then they gave me antidepressants immediately, that same night after I gave birth. They filled me up with pills to stop my grief. It was so cruel and traumatic.

But here's the thing: the adoption is absolutely the defining moment in my life, and it happened when I was still so young; to have a trauma like that at age seventeen, eighteen, it literally changed the course of my life. But I don't know if I would change it, in hindsight, because she turned out to be such a wonderful person. That's a hard statement to say because my own life, if I would've kept her, would have looked so much different. I just can't even imagine it. There was so much loss around this incident, so much loss, and yet I see how she turned out and I'm like, "Could she have been this much of a phenomenal person if I would've kept her?" That's the craziest thing about all this. I donate to Planned Parenthood. I'm fully in support of having a parenting plan in place. I would not recommend adoption to anybody, ever. And yet I don't know if I would've changed it because of how she turned out. She has so much love around her. Her parents love her. You can just tell she's adored by her parents, and I adore her in my own way. And we can never know what else could have been.

4

Ten Years Later

I first interviewed Leah in a Starbucks in South Carolina in 2010, leaning closely over our drinks—black tea for me, mocha latte for her—so that my recorder would catch our voices over the whir of the coffee grinder. Leah was a young, bubbly white woman who gesticulated with her hands while talking, as if overflowing with enthusiasm.

Yet, two years earlier, when Leah found out she was pregnant, this optimism was out of reach. After her parents' divorce, she had grown up with a single mom and a "disinterested" father, and she didn't want that for her child—but she also, very much, did not want to co-parent with her "crappy" boyfriend. The church where she worked fired her for getting pregnant, saying that the physical proof of unmarried sex was "un-Christlike." She had no real plan, and, with the loss of her job, no health insurance to get prenatal care.

Unsure what to do, Leah connected with an adoption agency. She was initially somewhat hesitant, but was thrilled to learn that the agency really expected their adoptive families to agree to open adoptions, and that they worked to diminish adoptive parents' fears around ongoing contact. She was even more de-lighted when she received this family profile:

> When I first got prospective parent profiles, I fell in love. The
> dad, Ryan, was a neurologist, and I was like: she gave me a brain

surgeon! I just totally fell in love with them. I think a lot of birth parents look for a couple who will parent the way you would if you were in your ideal situation, and they definitely fit into that. We met, like, four days later and hit it off really well. It was kind of awkward for ten minutes or so, but then we sat and talked for an hour, and it all just flowed really easily. We were talking about four visits a year or so, and they were like, "Whatever. You know, if you want to increase it, just let us know." They specifically said that they would never agree to something that they didn't fully intend to follow through on, but that they knew that life got busy and things happen and they asked me just to hold them accountable if they ever weren't following through on something, which is huge, having that permission.

Leah signed an agreement with them quickly to say that they were "officially" matched, and, at the agency's instructions, tracked down the absentee boyfriend to have him waive his parental rights. The prospective adoptive mother, Jacqueline, began attending all of Leah's doctor appointments. Together, they watched the ultrasound in rapt silence, listening to the amplified heartbeat through the office's speakers.

But still, Leah said she "really wanted to parent." She believed that adoption was the best thing for her son, but that parenting would have been the best thing for her. She was once again reassured by the supportive agency that encouraged her to think about parenting and develop a plan for what raising her son might look like. After giving birth to her son, Caleb, Leah did have second thoughts. However, her affection for Ryan and Jacqueline and her sense that she had been "empowered" through the process made her confident when signing her papers. That didn't mean it was easy: she cried ceaselessly right afterward, and it was hard work—physically and emotionally—for her to pump breast milk, around the clock, to be picked up by Ryan once a week and delivered to Caleb.

It's a decision I'm really glad that I made, but it was really hard. I mean, it was every three hours, being reminded of this huge loss. You know, you've got blisters on your boobs and soreness from birth and from the pump. When you're pumping every three hours—there's no room for denial there. That's good and bad. I think that a few weeks of denial, even a few months, is maybe healthy in a lot of cases. But it gave our relationship a really good time to grow, because I was seeing so much of them. I saw Caleb for the first time after the hospital at about two and a half weeks, and then again at about six weeks, and then his baptism a few weeks after that. Pumping was a way for me to be there for him, even if I wasn't physically there. It was evidence to me that I had something unique to offer him, so it gave me more confidence in our relationship. And it was also proof—not so much to Ryan and Jacqueline, but to their families—that I wasn't just doing this for me. I didn't go after open adoption so that I could feel better about it. I really was doing it because I thought it was what was best for him. I think that they were more easily open to accepting me.

When we first spoke—just over a year after the adoption—Leah was candid that she was still grieving, but she did feel that the intensity of her mourning was starting to ease up a bit. Other birth mothers had prepared her by saying that the first year would be the worst, so she'd expected it, and it felt like she was emerging on the other side. Leah's candid feelings about her adoption were complicated, but she focused on how hard life would have been if she'd been parenting, and how much better she believed the adoption was for her son. Her hopefulness was earnest, and when I asked her what she thought adoption *should* look like, she said:

Mine! I think every adoption should look like mine. You know, mine wouldn't work for everybody, and not every birth mom would be comfortable. It's very hard for birth parents to feel confident in that relationship and to feel like they're bringing something to the table. I think society still considers open adoption as something that's done for the birth parents. I think it's really important if the birth mom starts to pull away, for adoptive parents to remind her that they want her involved, that they think that she brings something to the table, that they value her, all of those things. Caleb's one now. He recognizes me. He is very comfortable with me. There are times when he won't go to his grandparents, but he'll come to me. He's aware of who I am. And they talk to him about me. They say "birth mom." When Jacqueline tucks him in at night, it's, "Mommy loves you, Daddy loves you, Leah loves you." There are pictures of me in their house. It's like I'm part of the family. It feels like a natural relationship. We never really wrote out a contract—it wasn't like that. The relationship will go as it is, but it's never going to be less than this. I feel like we've put a lot of work into it. When I have other children, when I get married, all of those things, they change any family relationship. But I feel like the base level of love and respect for one another will kind of help carry us through the times when there's not so much contact.

Leah's excitement about adoption was sincere and buoyant, so it was no surprise that she was eagerly working as a peer counselor at the agency that has facilitated her adoption. They couldn't have asked for a better ambassador.

*   *   *

When I started doing interviews in 2010, it was clear to me that the relinquishing mothers in more recent adoptions were happier than those in older adoptions: the mothers who placed from 2000 and on were *generally* more optimistic and content than mothers in adoption from the 1980s and '90s (and certainly were faring far better than the mothers in the closed, coercive adoptions from the 1960s and early '70s). However, it was impossible to know why this pattern was true, due to the intertwining of both personal timelines, in which mothers' feelings about their adoptions changed over time, and historical timelines, in which the practice of adoption changed dramatically. Were mothers in more recent adoptions happier and less critical because they truly had better experiences, or because the honeymoon had not passed?

The research on long-term emotional outcomes for relinquishing mothers is ambiguous. One study found that earlier in their adoptions, a majority of mothers reported "moderate to high degrees of grief," with this proportion decreasing over time. However, another study found that over a quarter of relinquishing mothers reported below-average adjustment, and half reported an *increasing* sense of loss over time, stating that they experienced a "strong and persistent sense of loss." Another onetime survey of mothers who relinquished between 1989 and 2016 found that satisfaction was lower for mothers in older adoptions, and concluded that satisfaction decreases over time. This dissatisfaction was particularly true for birth parents who reported higher levels of income over time, perhaps because they had made the decision because of lack of financial resources and, now having achieved some stability, believe that they could have given their children the life they wanted for them. Beyond finances, relinquishing mothers' experience of grief and satisfaction is shaped by the general course their life takes after the adoption. Mothers who are satisfied with their careers, marital status, and personal achievements also feel better about the adoptions. Most of this research, though, is older, and none studied the same group of women over longer periods of time. The question remained: Was this the historical timeline making adoption "better," and thus contributing to better outcomes for more recent adoptions? Or was this the personal timeline, with satisfaction inevitably declining as relinquishing mothers gained more temporal distance from their adoptions?

The only way to understand was to ask the same mothers how they felt, a decade later.

* * *

I spoke with Leah again in 2020. She was still living in the same city, with Ryan, Jacqueline, and Caleb just a short thirty-minute drive away. She hadn't had any more children, but she'd been happily married for just over seven years. She was working at a job she seemed to like and had a fair amount of stability and comfort in her own life.

"When I interviewed you in 2010," I began, "you told me that you thought every adoption should look like yours." She sighed. "Oh yeah, that sounds like something I would have said." She continued: "I personally feel a whole lot different about the adoption. With the benefit of hindsight and some time and space and counseling and all of that, I realize how much of my own trauma led to the adoption. I see it now as really unnecessary, unfortunately. But, you know, we are where we are and have been making the most of it where we are and where we stand."

Reflecting back on her relinquishment, Leah felt during her pregnancy that she had nothing to offer Caleb, so he wouldn't suffer from losing her—he could only gain. "The biggest thing that was never discussed anywhere in any space I was in while I was pregnant—and I tried to do a lot of research, like, I really tried to—was adoption trauma for adoptees." She now felt like she had failed her son by the choices she'd made.

Unlike other relinquishing mothers whose feelings about adoption turned dark when the adoptive family cut off or severely limited contact, Leah still saw Caleb regularly. A couple of times a year he would even come spend the week with Leah and her husband, Alex. Much of this was at Caleb's encouragement: he would call Leah, ask to spend more time with her, and Jacqueline and Ryan would oblige. As far as contact, she acknowledged, Jacqueline and Ryan had kept their word—Jacqueline with more comfort, Ryan with more reluctance. But they saw their shared son wanted it, and they accommodated.

Even though Leah always wanted more contact, the visits were hard for her. They were easier when they were more frequent, but after one long stretch during which she didn't see Caleb for five months, she described being catatonic for two days and crying for two more—she needed to take the entire week off to recover emotionally. The pain of repeatedly saying goodbye to him was acute, both because she saw how well he would have fit into her and Alex's life, and because she disagreed with many of the parenting choices Jacqueline and Ryan were making.

Those things that Leah had wanted for Caleb that she thought adoption would give him, she now had in her life—specifically, a reliable co-parent and financial stability—and she'd had that life since he turned three. Could she have gotten through those first few years as a single mother? Would the life she has now have been possible if she'd been parenting? It's impossible to know. All Leah knows is that she has a life now in which Caleb would easily fit, possibly better than in his adoptive family.

This disillusionment is not just with adoption, but with her own faith. "I grew up in an evangelical world," she told me. She attended a Baptist school, and that's where she got her sex ed, where she absorbed her ideas of right and wrong, and the evangelical church is where she spent her Sundays.

> But adoption has absolutely changed my relationship to the church. . . . The church leadership was so dismissive of me and just assumed that my pregnancy meant something horrible. I had to make a public apology in front of all of the staff. Growing up, the way that adoption was talked about, it was about scriptural and spiritual adoption, which is nothing like the practices of domestic infant adoption. All that doctrine, it says adoption

is redemption always and everything's beautiful. And I *needed* redemption. I would have done anything for it. I didn't feel like Caleb was losing anything by adoption, so it was all gain. I knew I would grieve, but I was a mom. I would've done anything for my child to have a better life, so it felt like adoption was the answer.

This background impacted not only how Leah understood her adoption, but how she was able to seek support after the adoption. Many of the mental health providers that she sought out for counseling also came from the church and brought those beliefs with them in caring for their clients. "I tried a couple of therapists, but it was all this, like, the combination of 'Adoption's beautiful. What are you talking about?' and 'It's so nice that they let you see your child!' and they saw my grief as ingratitude, which it's not." She also struggled with theological understandings of adoption in reconciling her own faith:

The church is really crappy about adoption if you're a birth mom, because they cling to this idea that it's got to be all beautiful because they conflate domestic infant adoption in America with God's adoption of his children, whatever. It makes it really difficult for them to see any other perspective of the reality of it. It puts a lot of crap on adoptees, because they can't deal with their own grief over their separation because adoption's wonderful and everything's beautiful and whatever. When you think about it, if the adoptive parents are playing God in that scenario, which that's kind of what they're doing, then the birth parents are . . . what? Saved in death? That's what they're talking about. And so it's really easy for them to put that on the birth parents. So much of adoption is adoptive parent centered, and if you think that adoption is a beautiful thing from that side, then you can't really accept how dark it is from the losing side.

Because her adoption agency was also religiously affiliated, the ongoing supports there were not especially helpful for Leah. Her days as a peer counselor were long past. When the agency started an online support group, the woman that facilitated it was "very 'sunshine and rainbows,'" Leah told me. But the idea of adoption as a "shiny happy thing" no longer fit for her. One week, the new facilitator asked the group of relinquishing mothers: If you could give any advice to a pregnant person considering adoption, what would it be? Leah and all the other mothers said, "Don't." "I don't think any of us got asked back," Leah commented dryly.

As we wrapped up our interview, she sighed. "Will you call me again in ten more years?" I laughed and said maybe I would, so I could hear what her relationship with Caleb looked like with him as an adult. That allusion to the future was the only time Leah's former optimism returned. Caleb was increasingly driving their communications, and eventually he would have the independence to reconnect with Leah without the direct involvement of his adoptive parents—that was something to look forward to. I asked her if she had any inkling during our first conversation of how things would turn out:

> There was a time, probably not long after our first interview, that I woke up in the middle of the night in a cold sweat, just thinking, *I could regret this someday.* It was the first time I had really thought that. That went away for a while, whatever, but it kept coming back. I definitely, at the time, didn't think there was any chance that I would truly regret it in the future.

Leah's story reflects how the failed promises of open adoption accumulate to give relinquishing mothers an entirely more critical understanding of their adoption. The transition is often described by both relinquishing mothers and adopted people as "coming out of the fog." (The phrase most likely is drawn from

Betty Jean Lifton's book *Lost and Found: The Adoption Experience*.) For many, this shift is rooted in an emerging political consciousness; adoption-critical scholars have described how coming out of the fog "allows adoptees the opportunity to critically explore adoption-related dominant narratives that may no longer be held true." The dominant narratives that make up the fog represent adoption as a "win-win" scenario, frame adoption as an empowered position, pay no attention to the traumas and losses core to many adoptions.

Taylor describes her process of coming out of the fog:

> Usually, birth moms start coming out of the fog around like five years or so, is what I've seen. I started coming out of it within months. During my pregnancy, I had tried to get on housing assistance, and there was a two-year wait list. I just could not find housing, and that's part of the reason I went with adoption. But then, after the adoption, I had a friend in a different part of the state, and I found out she got housing within six weeks. Six weeks! I was devastated. I sobbed for days, because if I'd known keeping the baby could have been possible if I'd just been able to get a place to live a few hours away, I would've parented. Finding out that there were options that I didn't know about was really hard for me.

Whatever the metaphor—waking up, emerging from the fog, seeing past the rainbows and butterflies (or sunshine and unicorns), ending the honeymoon—for relinquishing mothers, this transition represents the end of an idealized idea of what adoption means for their lives and the lives of their children.

Some mothers are shoved out of the fog abruptly and sharply when the agreements around openness are ignored, negated, or just fundamentally differently understood by their child's adoptive parents. For others, it's a gradual disillusionment rooted in a lack of support and a slower deterioration of openness. Openness is most protective of relinquishing mothers' well-being if they are satisfied with the level of contact, regardless of what the level of contact is. However, most mothers aren't satisfied. In a survey of birth mothers who had some contact with their child, 70 percent wanted increased contact, and only 20 percent wanted it to stay the same. (Only 2 percent wanted less.) For mothers who were not in contact with their child, 97 percent wanted to have contact, and most of them had tried to find their child. Negotiating openness in an ongoing way thus requires an intense amount of logistical work, emotional vulnerability, and empathy. The social supports and skills that often make greater openness possible—grief therapy, conflict resolution, flexibility, and clear interpersonal communication—could be facilitated by agencies and adoption providers. But these types of ongoing support are rare and inadequate, and over 40 percent of birth mothers—a plurality—are "not at all satisfied" with the level of post-adoption support. For example, Hannah's agency provided her with two counseling sessions, but when she called them again because she was severely depressed, they told her she'd used up her allotted visits.

Many relinquishing mothers found that agencies talked extensively about their post-adoption support services while they were expecting, but those services seemed to evaporate soon after the adoption was completed. Caroline described this disconnect:

> During my pregnancy, the agency always said: "We are here to take care of you." Not once did I actually feel taken care of, reflecting back on it. The social worker actually had the balls to say to me that once the adoption is final, "We don't provide services to birth mothers." And that's when I was like, "Well, then everything you've been telling me has been a lie, hasn't it?" That was the moment where I was like, "Wow. You want my baby and that's about it." That's what it felt like; it just became that business, that was very clear to me. My daughter's dads, they actually reached out

to the agency, because a big reason they chose that agency was because the agency markets itself as treating birth mothers really well. And I said, "That's not the case." They were upset.

Because so many agencies fail to deliver on promises of meaningful support, relinquishing mothers must look elsewhere. Sydney shared: "The agency promised lifelong support post-adoption, and then they told me they're really not used to women needing support that late. Ha! I was only a year post-adoption. They just don't hear from women. We find each other instead." They find each other online—on message boards, in Facebook groups, on Twitter. Alicia had been very active on these message boards when we first spoke:

On the message board, we referred to new birth mothers—you know, the ones who thought that everything was all positive and cheery and "Oh, it's wonderful, the adoptive parents are wonderful!"—they were drinking the Kool-Aid. Inevitably, every single one of them had that moment or gradual time frame in which the realities sink in. And that's when we were all like, "All right, we're here. Let's talk." That's a huge purpose the message board served, for the women who all of a sudden they fell off the edge of the cliff. But it happened with just about everybody I talked with who was a birth parent. Sometimes it was early on, something triggered it; sometimes it was much later. For me, it was somewhere around six months to a year or so. I mean, I was never, like, happy-go-lucky about it, but I had a good positive view of it. And then I don't know what happened. I think it was a gradual thing. I was processing things and I was just like, "Oh! This is terrible."

Interactions within these groups were not always easy, either, as mothers struggled to find common terms to share their experiences. Taylor shared this challenge:

Now it's very hard for me to interact with birth moms who still feel—I refer to it as the "unicorns and rainbows" phase of adoption. I was there. I have watched friends come out of the fog. I'm always very gentle with them. They know my story and they think it's horrible what happened to me, and when they're in that place, they can't see the parallels with their own story. I will never push someone out of the fog, because the very first thing that happens is you get pretty suicidal.

For many of these relinquishing mothers, coming out of the fog gave them a political frame for understanding what happened to them, particularly the ways in which their own lack of power and resources and, for some, their conservative ideals limited the options they felt were available at the time. Most of the mothers I spoke with became more personally compassionate and more politically progressive over time, wanting other pregnant people to have access to more resources and options than they felt they had had.

But not all of them.

A few of the relinquishing mothers I interviewed found support in the anti-abortion movement. These mothers represented a small but vocal minority. Whether or not they held anti-abortion beliefs during their pregnancies, they came to that movement because it celebrates adoption as selfless, beautiful, and life-affirming. For Alyssa, the support was buoying during her darker days of depression: "They say: 'You're so selfless. You made their lives better,' all those things just kept flowing in, flowing in. And that validation kept me afloat for months."

In 2014, the theme of the March for Life was "Adoption: A Noble Decision." On a sunny Saturday morning in San Francisco, I watched as anti-abortion marchers streamed down Market Street, carrying signs that read: "Birthmoms: Thank you for choosing life!" emblazoned above a chubby-cheeked, smiling baby. Another poster read: "There's strong—and then there's birthmom strong!" with an image of a woman posed like Rosie the Riveter: bicep curled, red bandanna in her hair, and a gingham crop top tied over her prominently displayed baby bump. A child toddled by wearing a placard: "My first mommy chose adoption!" Another: "I was unplanned, and I was adopted!" And another: "My birthmom walked out of the clinic and chose life! 60 million weren't so brave." For relinquishing mothers, it quite literally felt like a parade held in their honor.

Many mothers will ultimately move away from the anti-abortion movement. Savannah, along with many others, rejected having her story used: "The really radical pro-life is just using us to their advantage and using us in their propaganda. I wouldn't recommend placing for adoption in the current climate that we live in, because I don't like being used in someone's agenda." This rejection of anti-abortion messaging didn't mean all relinquishing mothers were in support of abortion—many continued to identify as "pro-life." But they also did not like how their stories were co-opted by a political movement that, they felt, failed to reflect their full experiences.

* * *

Relinquishing mothers who are still happy with their adoptions are often enlisted to discuss their experiences publicly. These opportunities might include speaking to prospective adoptive families on conference panels alongside their child's adoptive parents, or in small peer support groups for women considering adoption, or in online forums for women who have recently relinquished.

Megan's adoption agency even hired her soon after her adoption:

> I was hired as a birth parent counselor by the adoption agency, with zero experience except I had gone through it myself! I did it for about eight or nine months and then quit. First of all, it just brought up all my feelings. But also, the way that birth moms

were talked about in that office . . . it was unbelievable. Ridiculous. And the other women who worked there, they knew I was a birth mom, and they still said stuff like that around me. They would be like, "What do you mean, she changed her mind? I have parents who are waiting for her baby!" And I'm like, "That's *her baby*. Unless she signs something that says she's relinquishing her rights, that is *her child*, not anyone else's." It was a very bad experience. I actually got called into my supervisor's office because there was this one birth mom who said that after she talked to me that she was reconsidering. My supervisor said, "What did you say to her?" I'm like, "I didn't say anything negative. I just said, 'This is your choice.'" But they looked at birth parents as just people who were supplying babies.

Most of these mothers share their stories while they are still in their adoption honeymoons. As they become more critical of adoption, they either step back from that work (and often come to regret it) or are pushed out of that work because the agency does not want to provide a platform for more critical perspectives. Alicia had been fairly active in talking about her adoption when we first spoke, but a decade later she acknowledged that the agency had stopped inviting her to share her story and that it would be "pretty awkward" if they asked her to again:

I wouldn't say that I'm critical of adoption. I just say I am balanced. I don't know that agencies even see how adoption looks ten, fifteen years out. They don't follow up that long. I spoke to a prospective adoptive parents' group once. They had an adoptive parent, a birth mother, and an adoptee, and I think I gave them a lot to think about. We'll just put it that way, because I wasn't like, "Oh, adoption's wonderful!" I was like, "It sucks. It's hard. It was the right choice for our situation, but it is not good." You know, I definitely laid it out there, so I haven't been called again. And I'm kind of glad about that.

There is a mutually reinforcing dynamic here. The joyful stories are amplified, and the rest fade into the background.

Not every relinquishing mother is definitively traumatized. Human beings are resilient even when faced with severe traumas of violence and loss, and many mothers were able to cope well, find support, have grace for their past selves, take solace in the open adoptions they have with their growing children, and find joy and purpose in their lives. None of this resiliency means that their relinquishments were not traumatic; it merely speaks to the ability of people to find other sources of strength and hope. (The ways this strength is manipulated into cultural narratives designed to make relinquishing mothers feel *positive* about their adoption traumas will be explored in the following chapter.)

This pull between trauma and resiliency plays out in how women assess their regret around their adoptions. Many mothers easily and frequently expressed *dissatisfaction* with their adoption. Dissatisfaction suggested that if something had been different about the adoption—for example, if they had had more contact or a better relationship with the adoptive parents—they might feel more positive. However, *regret* was a more complicated sentiment, and one that carried the weight of wishing that the adoption had never happened at all.

When I asked mothers if they regretted their adoptions, many of them said they did, unequivocally. This pattern is consistent with a survey of birth mothers that found that nearly half of them regretted their decision. However, even among mothers who wouldn't precisely say they regretted their adoption, it was rarely because they were clearly happy with their relinquishment or believed it had been the best possible outcome.

For these mothers, a lack of regret was rooted in their capacity to forgive themselves and acknowledge that they did the best they could at the time. As outlined in Chapter 2, most of these women were simply trying to figure out a possible solution under circumstances of severe constraint. For example, Morgan described looking back on her decision:

> My mantra about it is that I did the best I could with the very limited resources I had. I try not to beat myself up for not standing up to my parents, who I'd never had to stand up to before. I try not to get too mad at myself for not doing that, especially at such a difficult time in my life. But generally—I don't know— I'm at peace with it, I guess. It just is what it is and it sucks, but I honestly don't attach too much sadness to it anymore.

Morgan's resignation reflects a recurring theme: How can I regret something where I had so little agency? Jessica described a similar feeling: "I don't regret the adoption, because it was traumatic but necessary. I can't regret it, because it's not like I had another choice. I can be angry that I didn't have another choice, but I don't regret what I did knowing that. He's taken care of, and I know that."

In asking these mothers about regret, I was effectively asking them to imagine an entirely different life for themselves and their children. If they undid the adoption, would they be married to their current partner? Would they have the other children they've had since the adoption? Would their relinquished child be the person they are now, the person they love just as they are? Vanessa explored the challenge of this question:

> It depends how you understand regret. I definitely don't feel like it was the best decision. I don't think it was necessarily the wrong decision. Obviously, I feel like if I had parented, that would have been a good choice. It's hard for me to sit here and see how my life is now: I have another beautiful daughter who I really love, and a husband. I think about how my life might be different if I had parented her, and I feel guilty because it's like I'm choosing the life with her over the life I have now, with my daughter. I do regret

that I didn't truly consider parenting, that I didn't try to make that work. I definitely have regrets in many ways, but at the same time I know that she's happy right now, and I just hope that she doesn't have issues growing up that stem from her being adopted.

Relinquishing mothers regretted a lot, including buying into the idea that adoption would be an easy solution. However, engaging with the counterfactual of what their lives would be like if they had *not* relinquished was not often a step they could take. Critically, a lack of regret does not mean a lack of trauma, nor does it mean that they felt the adoption was necessarily the right decision for them.

In addition to studying how women make decisions when denied abortion care (as discussed in Chapter 2), the Turnaway Study also looked at the longer-term outcomes for women who accessed the abortions they wanted compared to those who were denied access. My colleagues found that women who relinquish infants experienced the highest incidence of regret and the most negative feelings about their pregnancies, compared to both women who received the abortions they wanted and women who chose to parent after being denied abortion care. In fact, of the three groups, the relinquishing mothers had the hardest time emotionally, and they were far more likely than those who parented to wish that they still could have had their abortion. Yet over a longer period of time, there was little relationship between adverse mental and emotional health outcomes and the outcome of the pregnancy. This body of research reveals the complicated dynamics of regret, trauma, and mental health: mothers could experience the relinquishment as traumatic, yet still not regret it; they could regret it while finding mental and emotional well-being later.

This complexity is important because many of the mothers I interviewed turned to adoption because they believed they would be *less* likely to regret that outcome than if they were to have an abortion. The presumption of abortion regret is a common one, yet research shows that 95 percent of women who receive an abortion believe it was the right decision for them. It's clear that—despite anti-abortion messaging that has centered on abortion regret—a far higher proportion of women regret their adoptions than their abortions.

None of the relinquishing mothers that I interviewed between 2010 and 2020 felt *better* about their adoptions as time went on. However, there were two who did not feel worse. Their feelings were fairly stably positive at both interviews. I share Megan's story here, not because it's typical—it's not—but because it illustrates the type of rare adoption that seems to have been satisfying for her over time.

*   *   *

In the spring of 2000, Megan was just three weeks shy of graduating from high school when she found out she was pregnant. An eighteen-year-old white woman, Megan was very close with her mother—who herself had been a younger, single mom—and told her about the pregnancy right away. "You can't be a mom now. You're too young," her mom told her. Neither one of them really considered abortion; Megan just wasn't interested. She felt connected to her pregnancy and wanted to continue it.

But Megan felt very conflicted about parenting. Her ex-boyfriend was already dating someone else and was heading to college out of state in the fall. Raising her child would mean she'd need to live in her mother's basement and have her baby in day care all day, and then Megan would have to choose between spending time with her child and doing the evening college classes she'd been hoping and planning for. She worked in a day care and knew it would be a struggle to make ends meet—but ultimately it wasn't really about money for Megan.

I knew my finances would change, eventually. But I just thought about what my daughter's life would look like. Living in a basement. Day care during the day. Me in classes in the evening, or feeling just a little resentful that I wasn't. A father who didn't want to be involved. And working at the day care, I saw how the kids were never mistreated at all in their homes, but their mothers were young and tired, and I knew the kids weren't getting the love and attention that I wanted my child to have. Those kids just kind of went along for the ride, I guess; I didn't want that for my kid. I didn't want her to be just an accessory, where I was trying to go to school and work and still wanted to see my friends and I might end up resenting her, leaving her with a different babysitter all the time. I never wanted my daughter to feel like I resented her or that I wasn't giving my all to her. I just did not think as a single parent in the situation I was in, I could provide her with the level of emotional support and the kind of home that she needed. We would've had shelter. We would've had food. I would've figured those out. But I wanted more for her.

Megan was extremely clear that the decision to relinquish was her own. She has a support system of friends who would have helped her if she chose to parent, and while her mom was leaning toward the adoption, Megan didn't feel pressured by her. She did match fairly early with her daughter's adoptive parents and admits that she didn't want to let them down, but she also felt that they truly wanted what was best for her.

Megan had initially been drawn to Donna and Rich's profile because of how family oriented they were, their absolute commitment to the adoption even if the baby had a disability or health issue, and their commitment to an open adoption. "We were very open at the beginning," she said. "And that set the tone for the rest of our relationship."

However, Megan realized quickly that the adoption agency was, in a word, useless. They weren't especially proactive about helping her figure out an openness agreement, and they didn't seem invested in helping Megan, Donna, and Rich get off to a strong start. Instead, the three of them took it upon themselves to get to know each other: going out to dinner, visiting each other's homes, starting a friendship. Megan was still actively considering parenting, but she was clear with Donna and Rich: if I choose adoption, I'm choosing you. Megan would send them ultrasound pictures, but they never asked for them, and they let Megan lead the way.

The night after Megan signed her termination of parental rights, she was riven with anxiety and couldn't sleep.

I was just so worried. I didn't know how everything was going, so I called to check, and Donna was like, "Why don't you come over? You'll probably feel better when you see her in her new home." I was like, "I can do that?" She's like, "Sure. It's up to us. The three of us figure out how this works. Come on over." I went over there. It really helped, because I got to see her. She was home, and she was okay. I saw her in her little bassinet, so I knew exactly how she was doing. From there, I didn't see her too much at the beginning; it was about a month before I saw her again. I basically told Donna and Rich, "I don't want an issue, but I do think you need to bond as a family," because I didn't want to seem too pushy. Rich was just like, "It's fine. You're our family now. Anytime you want to come over, just give us a call." I kind of stayed away a bit, because it was hard on me to see her. Those were like the weird years, like I was having a lot of trouble with the adoption. It was emotional, obviously. I mean a major loss, your little girl. By the time Chloe was three, though, it turned around. I started to see her more and more. I got married soon thereafter, and she was my flower girl.

Chloe would grow up just about twenty minutes away from Megan, whom she called "Auntie Meg." And Megan was part of the family. Not only did she show up for Chloe's ballet recitals, but she tagged along for Chloe's brother's baseball games. She joined family beach vacations. She watched Fourth of July fireworks and dyed Easter eggs. She came along to the mall for back-to-school shopping or got a text if they were in a park nearby.

There was little about how Megan's adoption happened that set her on a better path. It didn't need to work out that way, and for most of the women I interviewed, it didn't. But whatever kismet conspired to bring Megan, Donna, and Rich together would ultimately let them build a foundation that would serve them well.

A decade later, Megan felt they were only closer. Donna would babysit Megan's nieces and nephews after school. Rich would lend Megan his large SUV to pick up items at the hardware store. "It's really just extended family at this point. The biggest thing is that it is just like any other relationship. It grows, it changes, and ours just happened to work out like this. It's not forced. I'm closer with them than I am with my own sister. We just clicked. But you can't plan on that. You can't plan on luck." Megan recognizes that her comparatively good fortune is independent of the system:

This has actually exceeded my expectations. I didn't think we would be this close, and actually I am very happy with it. I expected it to be more like, "Every three months we'll meet up, and you can see her and see how she is doing." But I think it turned into more of a relationship, and I am very pleased. I don't think I would have such positive feelings about the adoption in general if they had either backed out or limited the amount of contact that we thought we were going to have. It's actually just a mutual respect that we have for each other. They have always been incredibly respectful. Donna doesn't look at me like the vessel that produced her child. And she knows that Chloe needs me in her life. Once, when Chloe was about ten, she asked if she could call me Mom. And I said, "Well, that's something you should talk to your mom about," because I knew Donna would be like, "Yeah, call her Mom if you want." But I also told her that Donna was doing the work of taking care of her every day, and that made her fully Chloe's mom, too.

Chloe's mothers were able to validate each other and recognize that Chloe needed them both. And Donna was able to recognize that her family was predicated on Megan's relinquishment: when they held a party to celebrate the finalization of the adoption, she was conflicted on inviting Megan. She both wanted her there, as part of their family, but didn't want Megan to feel as if they were celebrating her loss. Few relinquishing mothers felt that their child's adoptive parents considered their emotional experiences in this way.

The value of openness for Megan, though, was not just for her own reassurance and well-being; it was of great benefit for Chloe. Megan was clear that she would never have relinquished Chloe if closed adoption had been the only option because she could not imagine her child not having any connection to her biological family. Yet, Megan recognized that adoption wasn't always easy for Chloe, that she struggled with loss. "I think as she's getting older, she's just being more authentic with me and not feeling like she has to impress me. But it's really taken her becoming an adult to get to that place." But her ability to answer Chloe's questions was, she felt, essential to her daughter's ability to feel secure enough to be vulnerable in those ways:

> She's asked me questions and that's been a great thing as she got a little bit older, she's been able to ask me questions about anything. I think that that really helped her, always having that availability with me. Once when she was probably, like, fifteen, she asked me, "What would you have done if you couldn't find parents that you liked?" And I was like, "Well, you would've come home with me." She's like, "Oh, okay." I told her: "The whole point of this was to find a family that I felt could give you the opportunities that

I couldn't, and if I couldn't find that, then you and I would've figured it out." I think that that really made a difference to her, because I could tell that that had been weighing on her mind, that I wasn't just casting her out into the world.

But Megan was still not overly sunny about the practice of domestic infant adoption overall. "I think I got very lucky that I had a good experience." When I asked if there were any systematic changes she wanted to see, she had a lengthy list: there should be less pre-birth matching with families (as early matching creates too much pressure); there should be less money involved; termination of parental rights should not be allowed within a week of birth, and there should be a thirty-day revocation period; openness agreements should be legally enforceable; adoption should be understood as a fully last resort. "If adoptive parents don't like it," she said firmly, "then they don't adopt."

And Megan was also not without conflicted feelings about adoption, even as she loved Chloe and her adoptive family and felt they represented a success story. She and her husband had decided never to have children, because she didn't want Chloe to see that she'd chosen to relinquish her and then raise her half siblings. She struggled with Chloe's adamant anti-abortion beliefs:

She goes, "Well, I wouldn't be here if you had an abortion." I'm like, "What we have is not very common. Our families got along incredibly well. That's not always the case. And you have to remember I was in a position where I was supported to get through a pregnancy. Like I had somewhere to live and health insurance." I'm glad I didn't have an abortion, knowing her, but I also never wanted an abortion. I wanted to bring her into the world. Not every woman is me, and not every woman has what I had.

Megan still described the relinquishment as a trauma, but she was able to find some peace in knowing that she did the best she could. "I don't know how things would have been different, but given the circumstances, I think I made the best choice that I could have at the time."

Paige

"It felt very much like: this is what you do because this is what a good Catholic does, and never mind the trauma that you're incurring."

Paige is a white woman who grew up in the Midwest. She relinquished her daughter, Abby, in 2006, during her first year of college. When we spoke ten years later, Paige had finished medical school and was working as a physician. She had not had any more children.

2010

I was in my first year of college, and I found out I was pregnant the day after Christmas. But I honestly wasn't sure what had happened. I knew who the birth father was, but I think I just kind of checked out. I hadn't been drinking. There wasn't any alcohol or drugs involved that I knew of. I told my parents that I didn't know what had happened. I was a virgin at the time that whatever happened happened. I was very confused as to how I could be pregnant, and then it really took a while to sink in.

After I told my parents that I was pregnant, we went to the hospital right away, so luckily I had prenatal care from the very beginning. The nurse said, "Well, what are your plans for this pregnancy?" I had never thought about being pregnant, ever. You know, crisis pregnancies only happen to other people. Right away I said, "Well, it's my baby. I'm going to keep it." I knew that for me, abortion wasn't an option. Abortion just wasn't part of my beliefs at that point. I consider myself pro-life, but I have to say that being pregnant and going through this whole thing have made me understand both sides better. And I think I was just still in so much shock that I hadn't even thought that maybe there was another option.

The next day, my mom talked to me about somebody that she knew whose daughter had also gotten pregnant and had placed in an open adoption. When she told me how the birth parents and birth grand-parents got to go and visit the little girl and all of that, it just seemed right. If open adoption hadn't been an option, I would definitely be raising her. But I was so removed from the situation at that point. I was only five or six weeks pregnant. Right away, adoption felt like a solution that I didn't have to think about too much. It just gave me something to focus on. Looking back, I can see that I wasn't thinking really clearly. I wasn't thinking about parenting at all. I just needed something that made sense. I needed some order, and I needed some control. For some reason, adoption felt like it did that. Even once I was in the hospital giving birth to her, everyone kind of stopped and was like, "Maybe we didn't look into parenting enough." But at that point early on, I was just determined to move ahead quickly.

My ob-gyn actually gave me a profile for an adoptive family. The ethics of this are still a little fuzzy? They put it in my chart. I looked at it and it was amazing. They resembled my family in a lot of ways, and it really was too much for me. It was the perfect match. I folded it up, got home, and threw it under my bed because it was just too much. After that, I visited with the adoption agency probably three, maybe four times, and after each time I would go home and pull out that profile from underneath my bed and I'd look at it and it would feel right. I had heard the baby's heartbeat and was starting to grow more and more attached to the baby, but I pushed that aside.

I reached out to the family in the profile. Every step in the adoption process made it more real. In my memory, we had just emailed back and forth continuously. But when I go back and look in my email, I would go two and a half, three, four weeks between emails. I think I misremembered because I felt like things were moving so fast, because that was all I had.

After I gave birth, we sent the adoption parents a picture of her right away, but other than that it was just us in the hospital—me and my family, and my daughter. The first day, it was just pure joy and everyone was so happy. Abby, other than her checkups, never left my room, so we did have a lot of bonding time. The morning of that second day is when it kind of struck me that this isn't how it's always going to be. That second day, they came up to the hospital just for a little bit, probably not more than an hour, maybe two. But even when they came, her mom said right away: "Are you sure that you want us to come up? Are you getting enough time with her?" Things like that. She was very, very sensitive. I could not have asked for a better hospital experience. I really, really couldn't have. She gave me my time, and I'm really grateful for that. That was one of those things that really helped. But that second day, I'm not sure that anyone in my family really knew which way this was going to go. After her parents visited for the first time, that's when we all kind of stopped and said, "How are we going to do this? Maybe we rushed into this too quickly."

I was having some second thoughts. My whole family offered to help. My parents would have supported me either way, and so they were willing to make it work. We definitely wavered. It's interesting looking back on it. I have since gotten my notes from my adoption worker, and she has in there that she didn't think I was going to be able to place. She had actually called the family and told them not to come because she didn't think I was going to be able to go through with it.

I don't know. It's interesting because I felt like I was pretty confident in my decision. I knew that I could do it. I was a nanny at the time. I knew that I could take care of children. I love children. I wanted children. But I also knew that at this point in my life I couldn't give that baby everything that she deserved. I just kept looking at her, and she was so perfect, in my completely biased opinion. I knew I wasn't what she needed, and I remember sitting and just crying and apologizing to her for not being good enough for her, not being everything she needed. And that made me feel awful, but at the same time, it also reassured me that this is what I needed to do. In order to give her everything that she deserves, I needed to give her this family.

Now her mom and I probably email every week, maybe every other week. Usually nothing big, other than just "Hey, how's it going? How's your week been?" Things like that. I am welcome to go and see her whenever I want. My medical school is actually only a little over an hour away from her. So that worked out well. So I see her probably at least once a month, if not more. I am pleased with the amount of contact. I've gotten to do a lot of things that I never thought I would be able to do with her. I was her godmother at her baptism. Once her family went away to a wedding when she was just one, and I got to babysit her for the whole week. Those are things that I never thought I'd be able to do, and ways that I've been able to be a part of my daughter's life that I never thought were possible, while still going to med school and working on everything that I had planned on working on before I got pregnant and placed.

I believe they do think of me as part of the family, and they have told me that. They told me that from the very beginning. That they weren't just adopting this baby, we were just going to be like extended family to them. They've welcomed my whole family in, with open arms. When you go into Abby's room, she has a big frame that I gave her with a picture of my whole family and her in the hospital, and it says, "Loved from the start." I feel like they will surround her with things that remind her who I am, and that she has always been loved and that there are already special people in her life.

I also coordinate a mentoring program online for birth mothers. I do outreach with the adoption agency that my daughter's family went through. I've gotten to speak at adoptive parent training. I've gone into high schools to talk to students about adoption, to tell my story. It's about putting a face on adoption rather than just, you know, *Juno*. Things like that. I think it's great. I've gone into high schools that are specifically for students who are pregnant. I think it's great that they are presenting adoption as another option to these high school kids. I wish it would have been presented when I was in high school.

I don't regret this adoption. I don't. It has been difficult. It felt like I was never going to smile again. It felt like I had gone through hell and back. But it's worth it for her. Seeing her happy and loved, and getting hugs from her. She has the life that I wish I could have given her. It took a while for me to accept that it was the right decision for myself. If it had been solely about me, I don't know if I could have made that decision. But I have always known that it was the right decision for her. And really, once you become a mom, that's all that matters.

The life she has is the kind of life that I hope to be able to give my children in the future. I cannot wait to have kids. I am very excited for that. I cannot wait to parent. I'm scared about how it's going to be going through having more kids. I'm a little bit excited about being able to be excited about being pregnant. I have really very mixed emotions about that. I'm terrified of never being able to get pregnant again. I've told many people they're going to have to lock me up in a room, a nice padded one, if I'm not able to get pregnant again. I'm sad when I think about going through another pregnancy only because I'm hoping that my next one will be in a committed relationship. And, while it will be great to have that support that I didn't have, to have somebody bringing me saltines, because God knows we're going to have to stock up for another nine months of that. But it might be hard to find a partner who is up to the task. It's going to take a special kind of guy to understand what I've been through, and especially the level of involvement I have with Abby. I'm definitely not going to choose a guy who's uncomfortable with adoption and all that comes with that over my daughter.

*   *   *

2020

I definitely have seen Abby less as she's gotten older, but the adoption is still pretty open. She is very busy in athletics and stuff. It's nice because now she has her own phone, so we can text back and forth, at least every other week. I usually send her some sort of text, just like, "Hey, how's your week going?" She's not super into texting, so I get a lot of one-word answers. But it's still something. My relationship with her parents has dropped off quite a bit, so it's nice that she has more control. If she and I are making plans to meet in person, I do always include her mom, but I don't really have a lot of direct contact with her parents anymore. I think it was just a natural thing, as I started communicating more with her and she is growing up. I don't really think that her parents consider me part of their family. Her mom maybe did for the first year, maybe. Her dad's pretty distant. I see other adoptions where birth mothers are remembered or thanked on birthdays, or invited to family things. That's never been our relationship at all.

I hope my relationship with her can get stronger. I hope that we can talk a little bit more. This year the night before her birthday I'd just been texting her, because I want her to understand more of her birth story. I texted her and I was like, "Thirteen years ago, I was just going to the hospital with you." And she texted back, "Do you happen to remember what time I was born?" I love that she's asking more of those questions. In the next ten years, I want her to be able to ask those questions and put together more of her story. I would love just more openness and more comfort, because I think I've done a lot of work around all of it and I feel super comfortable talking to her about those things and having those conversations. But I have to remember she's just thirteen and not quite there yet.

I don't feel like her parents have adequately addressed what it means to be adopted for her. She still does not know the circumstance of her conception, and that's a place where her parents and I do not agree. She also has this very anxious attachment. She's going to need a lot of therapy, too, and if I got to make the parenting choices, she'd already be in therapy because it's heartbreaking to see. When we have visits and it gets close to the time for me to leave, she just clings to me and says: "I love you, I love you. I miss you. I love you. I love you. I love you." It's heartbreaking, and that's going to be her path.

That time I babysat her for a week . . . oh, gosh. It was so much. It was so real and it was scary at times. When we talked about it before, did we talk about that was the first time she crawled out of her crib? Crawled out of her crib, fell on the floor. I felt like a failure. I remember just sitting on the floor, reading books with her, and I cherish those moments so much, just getting to be there without like anybody really watching over us. It was the only time since being in the hospital with her that it was just us. That was really sweet, and I really appreciate those times. "Appreciate" isn't even strong enough. I really cherish those times. But then there was this other side that really made me feel the "not good enough" part. Like: she is crawling out of her crib, and oh my god, she fell on the floor. I was mortified and like spent the rest of the week sleeping on the floor next to her crib. I wanted to make sure it didn't happen again. I was devastated at that point. I was, like, I should never be allowed to be alone with children, I guess.

I do still want to have more children. I don't know if I will. I might consider adopting. Maybe. Gosh, that would be so hard. I would consider it. But I almost feel like I would end up being biased and, like, pushing the mother to parent. I think it could work out if it was a situation where I could support her and help her figure out all her options. There's so much I would do for her just in terms of the whole process. I'd want to make sure that she was in a space where that was there and she felt empowered. I absolutely didn't feel empowered at all and spent the first twenty-four hours with her just apologizing to her for not being enough. That doesn't leave easily. So yeah, just trying as much as possible to empower her to make decisions that feel right and having it be completely unbiased, which is why I think a therapist, a competent therapist needs to be involved. I would consider adopting, but it's certainly not the route that I would want to go.

As far as my outreach around adoption, that has really stopped. I just kind of took a step back from a lot of it, including the online groups. I did it for a few more years, and then it got to be too much and I had to step back. I'm still in contact with a couple of other birth moms, mostly through Facebook. And I don't speak at schools anymore. I realized after a while, like, it actually really wasn't healthy for me to be doing, because I would get done and then I would want to drink. I realized there was a lot more work that I needed to do individually on that before I really engaged again in any of those things. I really haven't struggled with drinking, so it was an uncommon thing for me to like want to go home and have a drink. I think I almost felt kind of like this, like, caricature of this ideal birth mom. I was overcompensating so much with school, and I got really tired of hearing, "Oh, look at everything that you've been through with the rape, and then you chose life, and aren't you fabulous for doing that? And now you're going to be a doctor and you're helping children!" I can feel the activation and anxiety even when I'm talking about it now. But talking at those schools—it didn't feel genuine. It didn't feel like what my experience actually was. It felt kind of like we were just putting a nice little bow on it, and I think the incongru-ency was just too much. I felt like I was just being a rule follower still, and trying to do everything just right. I was like, "This is bullshit. I can't do it anymore."

I also just have this strong response to thinking about going to a Catholic school, and thinking about abstinence-only education. I re-member the morning after the rape, I didn't know that we had had sex because I just disassociated. But I knew something bad had happened, and I called my sister and asked her about Plan B, which I'd loosely heard of and didn't know anything about. But I said, "Oh, I didn't have sex with anybody." And she's like, "Well then, you don't need it." That's definitely something I've thought about a lot more, just in terms of how my life trajectory would have been a lot different. Obviously, I love Abby. But had I known then what I know now, that would have been . . . well, I just wish that could've been a conversation. The emer-gency contraception, and maybe abortion. I don't know.

During my pregnancy, I think I got to a place where I was just so tunnel-visioned around adoption. I needed one option, and then I needed to plan that option perfectly and do that perfectly. I really wonder if it was a trauma response, that hyperfocus, the need to mobilize, the fight-or-flight energy. And my identity had really been formed around being a good Catholic girl, and it was so clear I would choose adoption and do this, because that's what you do and you do this "selfless"—ugh, I can feel my gut tighten when people say that, or even just my saying it right now, because I don't know that I really felt like it was a choice. It felt very much like, this is what you do be-cause this is what a good Catholic does, and never mind the trauma that you're incurring. I think I needed to be able to control something, and that just seemed like that was the way I was going to keep social connections. There wasn't any pressure to do the adoption explicitly. But growing up in that environment, you know what "the right thing" is, what the proper thing is.

I think the most traumatic part of Abby coming into the world was leaving the hospital and leaving with her family. It sounds silly to say, but if all I had to deal with was the rape, that would've looked very different. But it's true. It was far more traumatic to place her for adoption. The pregnancy almost felt like an inescapable attack, like it was something that was happening to my body I couldn't get away from, and just had to endure. That's not what pregnancy's supposed to be. If it hadn't been the result of an assault, if it was with a partner who I cared about, I would've parented. Does it feel right to say that? I think so. The drive with which I pursued adoption, I don't think that would've been there if it weren't for the rape. My eighteen-year-old brain could have been in a very different place without that trauma. Obviously getting pregnant at that age wouldn't be ideal. But I feel like I wouldn't have been so frantic. When I think about how it actually was, I just see it as such a trauma response. I think I would've parented had I been with somebody that I cared about.

I don't consider myself pro-life anymore. That's interesting, that I said I still did think that when we first spoke. Because in my mind, as soon as I went through the pregnancy, I had switched, so that's really interesting that I said that in 2010. I was in such an insulated place. I also definitely don't identify as Catholic anymore, and so I just think I was so limited in what I'd been exposed to. I'm definitely pro-choice, and I wish there would have been a little bit more discussion around that. I think about Abby right now, and if she were to have something like that happen to her, I would absolutely want her to have all of the options, not just one. I hate how adoption becomes political. I feel like, in some ways, it's politicized just like abortion is. I don't want anyone to use my story as a reason why women shouldn't have the right to choose. It makes my skin crawl and puts me in this position of just wanting to scream. It just makes me vomit when people are like, "God bless you for choosing life." There are so many assumptions made, and it's so manipulative. I run in enough conservative circles that I do hear that a lot. It's kind of abusive to use people's experiences like mine as a way to push your own agenda, because you're making so many assumptions and you don't know. And the Republicans sure aren't going to be the ones paying my therapy bill, right?

5

Mothers, Martyrs, Myths

In 2009, seventeen-year-old Catelynn and her boyfriend, Tyler, were facing an unplanned pregnancy. In addition to navigating their own lives in "chaotic" households—an "unpredictable" mother for Catelynn, an intermittently incarcerated father for Tyler—they were trying to decide what life they wanted for their daughter, and they began to look at adoption. However, Catelynn and Tyler were making this decision with MTV cameras in tow. The cameras are still rolling. Catelynn and Tyler have had their adoption story told publicly, first on *16 and Pregnant* and then *Teen Mom*, for over fourteen years.

The reasons Catelynn and Tyler turned to adoption will not be surprising: the instability of their own homes was not what they wanted for their child. In one charged scene, Tyler's dad, Butch, yells at Tyler for considering adoption while Catelynn's mom, April, rolls cigarettes at the kitchen table.* Tyler shouts back that adoption will give their baby "a stable household," one that he never had. Angrily, he tells his dad that the upbringing he had is "not good enough for my kid. My kid deserves way better. Way better than *this*."

---

* April and Butch are actually married, making Catelynn and Tyler stepsiblings. However, as both teenagers are quick to point out, they were a couple before their parents were. During the first season of *16 and Pregnant*, Catelynn lives with April and Butch, and Tyler lives with his mother.

When Catelynn and Tyler first meet with a representative from Bethany Christian Services, she states: "You're in the driver's seat of your adoption plan. This is going to look and feel the way you guys want it to." Catelynn and Tyler are clear they want an open adoption, and they choose a picture-perfect family for their daughter: Teresa intends to be a stay-at-home mother and Brandon works in finance. ("Look at that house!" Catelynn exclaims as they page through the family profile binder. "It's a nice house," Tyler answers.) Catelynn describes the sense of turbulence in her own life when they meet Brandon and Teresa:

> I don't really have a really good stable household. My mom, she's had problems. I had to go live with my grandparents for seven months because I couldn't live where I was living. [She begins to cry.] I just want her to have better than what I had. And I know that I can't do that. I'm just doing the thing that I think's the best. I know that you guys can provide for her a lot better than I can.

After Carly is born, Catelynn does not want to look at the baby. Tyler holds Catelynn and whispers to her: "We can do this, honey. We can do this, I know it, okay? We can do this. This is all for her. All for her. She's going to have such a good life, honey. And she's gonna be so happy." Teresa gives Catelynn a bracelet that says "Always in My Heart" and shows her a matching one on her own wrist. "We're just going to be linked for life, and we can't thank you enough," she effuses.

After Carly leaves with her new parents, Tyler and Catelynn cry together.

"She's gone now," Catelynn says.

"But she's off to a better life," Tyler replies. He hugs Catelynn and pauses a moment: "I kept her blanket."

"Did you?" Catelynn asks quietly. "Good."

*   *   *

Several months later, Catelynn and Tyler appeared on the "Life After Labor" end-of-season special hosted by psychologist Dr. Drew Pinsky. "Such a courageous decision, both of you," Dr. Drew gushed. "Do you understand how extraordinary it was, that you guys were able to do that? . . . How, at seventeen, do you have the courage and the strength to stand up to your own family?" He goes on: "You take my breath away. Your strength and your courage . . . I feel so passionately that people like you need to be honored."

*   *   *

I watched *16 and Pregnant* in the summer of 2009 like it was my job, because it was. At the time I was interning with the Massachusetts Alliance on Teen Pregnancy, an organization that worked to increase support for pregnant and parenting young people across the commonwealth. Part of my job was to counter the cultural narratives about young parents that are not rooted in the best social scientific evidence and to galvanize these parents to care for their children and achieve success for themselves and their families. The contrast between the regressive stories I saw on MTV and the activism of the young parents with whom I was working during the day was sharp. These young women—lobbying at the statehouse for better policies to support young families, fighting for their right to finish high school, striving toward self-sufficiency, becoming good role models for their children—were supposed to be the immature ones? They lacked courage? They were selfish for wanting to raise their families? If Catelynn and Tyler were selfless, brave, strong, extraordinary by virtue of their relinquishment, what did that make those women who kept their children?

If the pain of relinquishment and the struggle of openness are the burdens that many birth mothers carry throughout their lives, then the persistent widespread misrepresentations of their stories make those burdens all the heavier. Over and over again, I heard from women who felt that birth mothers were alternately demonized and exalted in our popular culture, with their experiences diminished or misrepresented to serve broader aims or preconceived notions.

Sometimes this misrepresentation happened in small ways, with clear intent: the adoption agency who assembles a panel of happy relinquishing mothers to speak to prospective adoptive parents, only to push those same women aside when they become more critical; the anti-abortion movement that elevates birth mothers to make a case that adoption is a good and preferable choice. But these representations aren't relegated only to conservative or adoption-centric spaces; they are popular, mainstream, and deeply rooted in our culture.

I completed my first round of interviews in 2010, in the midst of a proliferation of modern adoption stories that were entering the cultural zeitgeist via some of the most popular or prestigious shows on television, Academy Award–winning films like *Juno* (2007) and *The Blind Side* (2009); and reality shows including *16 and Pregnant* (2009) and *Teen Mom* (2009), as well as more niche shows like *The Baby Wait* (2012) and *I'm Having Their Baby* (2012).

In most scripted adoption narratives, the relinquishing mothers are wholly absent, as on *Sex and the City* (2004) or *Modern Family* (2009), or on *Grey's Anatomy* (2010), when primary protagonists Meredith Grey and Derek Shepherd adopt their first child. Notably, all of these are international transracial adoptions in which the relinquishing mothers remain both narratively and physically remote from the stories of their children. They are never shown and never acknowledged. But many other adoption stories *do* include birth mothers in some way. When I asked relinquishing mothers about the portrayals that resonated with them—for better or worse—they listed depictions of birth mothers that careened from sainthood to stupidity, ineptitude to danger, indifference to obsession.

One frequently recalled story line was the final episode of *Friends* (2004), in which central characters Monica and Chandler complete their long journey to parenthood by happily adopting twins. Erica, the twins' birth mother, is introduced in a clumsy comedic mishap in which Monica and Chandler lie to her about their identities for an entire episode—yet after the mistruths are revealed, Chandler delivers a speech describing Monica as "a mother without a baby" and Erica chooses them despite their deception. Too naive and slutty to know who the father of her baby is without a sex ed lesson from Monica, too oblivious to recognize that she's in labor until Monica tells her she is, and too dim-witted to understand that she's having twins until mid-delivery, Erica has no backstory beyond her sexual history. Chandler is anxious when he learns that Erica is having twins, but Monica assertively shouts: "I don't care if it's two babies. I don't care if it's three babies. I don't care if the entire cast of *Eight Is Enough* comes out of there. We are taking them home because they are our children!" Mere moments later, Erica says goodbye to Monica and Chandler (with no moment of goodbye for the children she has just birthed) as she is wheeled out of the delivery room and never seen again. The adoption placement is the show's pinnacle, the end of the journey for these characters.

* * *

The trope of the birth mother who easily, happily walks away would become prominent just a few years later, with the wry comedy *Juno* (2007). Juno MacGuff, the film's eponymous heroine, is a scrappy high schooler who becomes pregnant, to the chagrin of all around her. She finds prospective adoptive parents in a classified ad and tells them she wants a closed adoption, no questions asked. At the end of the film, she hands off her son to adoptive mother Vanessa and says "I think, really, he was always hers," before bicycling to her boyfriend's house. While *Juno* received critical acclaim and an Oscar nomination for Best Picture, it was almost universally hated by the women I interviewed. "How much do I hate *Juno*? Let me count the ways," Erin quipped, while Vanessa was emphatically serious: "I watched *Juno* once, I hated it, and I will never be able to watch it again." Haley reflected:

> I feel like the media just always portrays birth mothers as people who are really incapable or whatever, but then they are saved by adoption. I think of *Juno,* and how she just has this baby and then like hops back on her bike and goes and sings a song with her boyfriend. That's not how it is at all—even the good stories. I didn't just hop back on the bike. I locked myself in my room for a month and a half and wouldn't eat anything. It's still devastating. It's not the easy way out, by any means, and I wish more people knew that.

Phoenix had additional logistical concerns for Juno: "Okay, this is such a small thing, but in the very last scene she's riding a fucking bike after having a baby? *Who is riding a bike right after giving birth?*"

While *Juno* remains an especially salient example, the mothers I interviewed have a long and detailed memory for stories about relinquishment in popular culture, and were especially attuned to stories that acknowledged the complexity of their adoption in any way. As Shelby described to me:

> I remember on an episode of *ER*—gosh, it aired before I was even pregnant, and then I latched onto that memory during my pregnancy—there was a doctor who was Chinese who got pregnant, and the baby's father was Black. And she asked her mother, "Can you love a baby who's part Black?" And her mother wouldn't answer, so she gave the baby up for adoption. And after he was born, she was crying and said that she was choosing her bigoted family over her son. But she did it anyway.

The character in question is Dr. Jing-Mei Chen, a Chinese American emergency room resident, and the *ER* episode was nearly twenty years old when Shelby described it to me in 2020. It seemed to resonate not just because of the issues of race it made explicit (especially for Shelby, a white woman who relinquished a Black biracial daughter), but because it portrayed a birth mother who was professionally accomplished and well-regarded. This reasoning is why several mothers mentioned a 2006 episode of *Grey's Anatomy* in which Dr. Izzie Stevens, a surgical resident, is revealed to have given birth and relinquished a daughter, Hannah, when she was fifteen years old. Hannah is brought to the hospital by her tearful adoptive parents because she needs a bone marrow transplant, and they hope Izzie will be a match. While Hannah refuses to meet Izzie, Izzie is able to look at her daughter through a hospital room window, at a tearful distance. "I didn't really like how Izzie didn't know them at all, and obviously had no relationship to her daughter," Erin told me. "But at least Izzie wasn't a drug addict; she was beautiful and a surgeon. It was wrong about adoption, but at least it wasn't a bad stereotype."

*   *   *

The bad stereotypes include the "scary birth mothers"—the impoverished, addicted, and often incarcerated Black and Latina mothers from *The Blind Side*, *Orange Is the New Black*, *Parenthood*, and *This Is Us*. "It feeds these ideas that we're people to be feared, that we're dangerous or scary. That we don't love our children," said Alicia. "It gives the idea that openness is risky because we are a threat to our children, that open adoption is or would be a scary thing." These portrayals also present adoptive parents as white saviors:

> The one thing that I can't stand is the whole white savior thing, like in *The Blind Side*. Like, "Oh, well, they adopted this poor Black child from the other side of the tracks." I will not watch

those movies. I have a visceral reaction to them. Just . . . no. The movie could be good, I guess, but I just don't like that idea of portraying adoptive parents as saving children.

Yet while many mothers resented the white savior trope, many of them accepted the premise of the "scary/dangerous birth mother" trope as they worked to distance their own stories from mothers who relinquished while they were addicted or incarcerated. In distancing themselves, they failed to recognize that they were often making judgments of worthiness, connection, capability, or capacity to love similar to those that had been used against them. These were nearly always white women, who felt the need to share how they were "not like other birth mothers," and reveals how the racialization of private adoption continues to create challenges in how adoption is understood and could be changed.

The "scary birth mother" trope feeds into another recurring plot: the birth mother as a "baby stealer," intent on regaining custody of her child. On *Desperate Housewives* (2006), Gabrielle, the would-be adoptive mother, is distraught when the baby's mother reclaims her. Gabrielle cries, "This is our baby! No! . . . You can't take her away! It . . . it's too late! We've already fallen in love with her!" On *Glee* (2011), mean girl cheerleader Quinn is set on revoking her daughter's adoption: "I have to get her back . . . We're gonna get full custody." (Given that Quinn's adoption has been finalized for many months, this scenario would be a legal impossibility. The outlandish plot device prompted activists to start an online petition demanding that the show's creators produce a public service announcement to "separate fact from fiction about adoption.") These portrayals misrepresent adoption as something other than the full and permanent transfer of parental rights, while *also* typically centering the deservedness of the adoptive family. On *Downton Abbey* (2014), when Edith *does* seem to undo her daughter's adoption and reclaim custody of her child, the decentering of the adoptive family challenged some viewers. After the episodes aired, one adoptive parent wrote: "No matter how happy I'd like to see [Edith], I also don't want to see the little girl's adopted parents in pain . . . [The adoptive mother's] love for her daughter has weight, too, and the show owes it to her character to honor it." This viewer's desire for story lines that privilege adoptive parents' desires is easily met by the majority of pop cultural offerings on the subject. I found that in portrayals of adoption decisions, sympathy for prospective adoptive parents abounds, with their love and their expectations of parenthood viewed as valid and worthy.

This sentiment holds true even when a relinquishment has not occurred but is merely being considered. Another plotline on *Grey's Anatomy* (2010) included young mother Sloan Riley, who had planned to relinquish her son but had second thoughts after he was born and her own father offered to help her raise him. Her father's colleague, Dr. Arizona Robbins, is a pediatrician who becomes infuriated by Sloan's reluctance to call the baby's prospective adoptive parents after the birth. As Arizona vents to a fellow physician:

> That poor baby's parents, just sitting there. . . . The mature, capable, financially secure, emotionally stable, loving parents, who were deemed fit by Sloan and the state of Washington, are sitting there by the telephone, staring at the sky-blue nursery walls that they just painted. Those are the parents. . . . She made the one sound parenting decision she needs to make. She found a lovely couple to raise her baby. And she did that months ago when she wasn't flooded with postpartum hormones or overwhelmed by heartfelt pleas from her dad.

By the end of the episode, the adoptive parents have arrived at the hospital and joyfully welcomed the baby. In contrast, on a 2012 episode of *Parenthood*, Zoe decides to raise her son after giving birth, and the story's focus is on potential adoptive mother Julia's

grief—her heartache, her confusion, her family's slow dismantling of the nursery. Similarly, on *A Million Little Things* (2020)
Eve devastates prospective parents Regina and Rome, who have
supported her throughout a complicated pregnancy, when she
decides to raise her son. "I'm so sorry," Eve tearfully tells them.
"You two have been nothing but kind. But that's just it—with
everything you've done, and all the support I've gotten from the
shelter, I realized for the first time I can do this. I can raise this
baby on my own." Regina and Rome are crushed: "He was *mine*,"
Rome says angrily, before he and Regina return home to sadly
pull sonogram images off their refrigerator.

My critique is not to minimize the grief of the (fictional)
hopeful parents in these scenarios, but to suggest that the cor-
responding grief of the (also fictional) relinquishing mothers is
rarely shown with such sympathy. One exception—which was
remembered by multiple participants for its rarity—was on a
2014 episode of *NCIS*, where an adoption fell through when the
mother chose to parent. The disappointed prospective father
said: "She saw the baby, and I guess she felt the same way we
felt when we first saw [the baby]. Can't fault her for that, right?"
Alicia remembered this brief moment very clearly:

> On *NCIS*, the would-be dad comes back empty-handed because
> the mom decided to keep the child. But instead of demonizing
> her, he actually said, "I can't blame her because she probably,
> looking at the baby, she probably felt the same way I did." Sorry
> to cry now as I'm remembering, but it gets me a little bit be-
> cause it's the one time I've seen in pop culture where it doesn't
> demonize the girl for keeping her kid. It doesn't say: Hey, that
> was a terrible decision. It really rips my heart out. It doesn't say
> the adoptive parents are more important than she is. It actually
> like validated her, that it was her kid, and that was like the one
> time I've seen in pop culture that did that. I've seen a lot of sto-
> ries both about glorifying adoptive parents but also like being

pretty harsh on birth mothers—sorry, it's not birth mothers, but women who decide to parent after considering adoption.

Phoenix sums it up: "Whenever you see stories about birth mothers, it's all about how they're causing trouble for adoptive parents or potential adoptive parents, it's not really about how they came to adoption." In our popular culture, either birth mothers happily move on after their adoptions (as in *Juno*) or their longing for their child renders them threatening, disruptive, pathological—an inappropriate parent.

Herein lies the cultural contradiction of how we portray adoption. We view certain parents as fundamentally incapable of and inadequate to the task of raising their children, but relinquishment demonstrates their worthiness. They are better parents *because they do not parent their child*; the permanent separation rendered by adoption redeems them of their deviations and deficiencies. Birth mothers are perfect mothers—the embodiment of love and self-sacrifice—until they express any desire to raise or know their child.

More recent shows have explored adoption with more nuance, most often by centering on adult adopted people. On yet another *Grey's Anatomy* episode (2019), surgeon Jo Wilson searches for the birth mother who relinquished her at a fire station safe haven site when she was five days old. She finds Vicki, who begrudgingly meets her at a diner, but she's furious at Vicki's apparent financial security and happy home and at her trite comments that she wanted Jo to have "a better life." Jo lashes out: "I didn't have a better life. I wasn't better off. No one found me adoring parents who were dying for a newborn of their own." (Given that Jo was an apparently healthy white newborn, this aspect of her backstory seems improbable.) Their conversation is angry, confrontational, and hurtful until Vicki gradually discloses her story of sexual assault, a hidden pregnancy, and a flood of love for baby Jo that couldn't quite overwhelm the memory of her rapist.

In response, Jo talks about her own abusive marriage and her decision to have an abortion. This response is an unexpected political retort, a suggestion that—given Jo's painful childhood and her mother's trauma from the pregnancy and birth—safe haven relinquishment is not an alternative to abortion. Jo asserts that her abortion has been an easier path to tread than adoption was for either her or Vicki.

This Is Us also explored much of this complexity. The show is premised on multiple series-long examinations of adoption, in which transracial adoptee Randall Pearson—who grew up as a Black son in a white family—struggles to come to terms with his identity and role in the family, while navigating a reunion with his birth father, William. Randall believes that his mother, Laurel, died soon after his birth. In an episode entitled "Birth Mother" (2021), Randall discovers Laurel's real backstory, which includes a distinguished and privileged upbringing in the South, a rebellious and carefree love of the outdoors, a decision to run away from her controlling family, and a path toward heroin addiction. After giving birth to Randall, Laurel overdoses and wakes up to nurses whispering that the baby is "better off" wherever he may be. She is incarcerated for several years, and, feeling unworthy of a relationship with her lost son, she returns to her childhood haven at her aunt's home. The story shows Laurel missing her child, grieving, and grappling with her loss and guilt. Laurel's friend tells Randall: "She said there wasn't a single night that went by when she didn't dream about you." It also goes on to show her finding peace, love, and reconciliation, while never forgetting her son.

In this story arc, *This Is Us* goes beyond the scary, addicted, incarcerated birth mother trope to add nuance and compassion, and to remove the fear and threat at the heart of the trope. Even though the episode aired after my interviews were completed, Shelby emailed me: "I will always remember that episode," she wrote. "I started watching *This Is Us* because I wanted to see a Black adoptee story, but I was knocked over by their decision to show a birth mom as a real person and let her be sad and guilty and then give her forgiveness. I cried the whole time watching it. I wish my daughter could see it."* She continued: "I guess people are discovering that birth mom stories are worth telling. That we're like, interesting people with complicated lives, and that it's worth looking at us beyond our ability to give children to other people."

Several mothers mentioned *The Handmaid's Tale*, an adaptation of Margaret Atwood's dystopian novel in which fertile women called handmaids are forced to bear children for infertile couples that uphold the totalitarian government of the Republic of Gilead.† "Honestly," said Vanessa, "*The Handmaid's Tale* feels like the truest depiction of birth motherhood. It shows the loss that these women feel, from having babies that are pretty much ripped from their arms, and they know the whole time someone else is going to raise their children, and they're going to raise them in a way that continues the beliefs that are used to hurt the handmaids. I think the show does a pretty good job of showing the anguish and the loss, and how much of a connection they feel to their babies." Amy described reading the novel as "painful"; she delayed watching the show as long as possible because it felt too close to her experience. "It really does feel similar. It feels like you're there to serve someone else's needs, and the children are just pawns who get moved around." That several relinquishing

---

* A few episodes later, Randall's sister Kate and her husband, Toby, are adopting a newborn daughter, Hailey. They plan on an open adoption, but Hailey's mother, Ellie, says she can't handle contact, that it would be too painful. Kate is upset by Ellie's withdrawal, and talks about the pain Randall experienced not knowing his birth family growing up. Here, the threat of open adoption is neutralized, and the value of having an engaged birth mother is articulated—not just for her sake, but for the sake of the child ("The Ride," *This Is Us*, February 23, 2021).

† As other scholars have noted, Atwood's original novel draws on the legacy of the narratives of enslaved Black women in the United States, including Harriet Jacobs's *Incidents in the Life of a Slave Girl* (discussed in Chapter 1). Native American author Tiffany Midge has also noted the parallels between *The Handmaid's Tale* and the real history of child-taking from Indigenous mothers.

mothers identified with this story, set in a patriarchal theonomic state ruled by regressive antifeminist ideologies, is perhaps the most telling example of where they feel the power in adoption is currently rooted.

I take the time to explore these pop cultural narratives about relinquishing mothers because they shape our sense of deservedness, our assessment of necessary support, and ultimately the political narratives that dictate our social policies around family and adoption. Critical adoption scholar Kimberly McKee makes this connection clear: "Such depictions of birth mothers as deficient or defective prevent these women—these allegedly 'bad' mothers—from entering our imagination as potential equals to the 'good' adoptive mother. Claudia Corrigan D'Arcy [a birth mother and activist] asks, 'Why is it so hard to see a birth mother as a real, live person? Both of the views—the sinner or saint, the Madonna or whore, the selfless or the abandoner—are just so limiting and not real. Instead, they are parts cast in this play we call adoption.' . . . It is nothing more than a parroting of the carefully honed adoption-marketing message."

The stories we tell about adoption are part of both cultivated and incidental efforts to promote adoption as a social good (as discussed in Chapter 1). These stories reflect the messaging found in aggressive online adoption advertising for those facing unplanned or crisis pregnancies (as discussed in Chapter 2), and the ways in which this contradiction is sold—to vulnerable pregnant women, to those seeking to build families, and to society at large.

* * *

In 2000, the conservative Family Research Council (FRC) released a report detailing the reasons that pregnant women visiting crisis pregnant centers refused to (or were reluctant to) consider adoption. According to the report, the women expressed very negative ideas about relinquishment, equating it with abandonment and deception and considering it an unbearable sacrifice.

Their primary recommendation? "Everyone's perception of adoption must be changed." But despite the FRC's analysis, data show that Americans already have consistently positive opinions of adoption. (The Dave Thomas Foundation has found in repeated surveys that over half of adults have "very or extremely favorable" assessments of adoption, with only 2 percent having "not at all favorable" opinions.) But this generally favorable opinion has little bearing on individual decisions. What the FRC *actually* wanted to shift was how the general public and pregnant people think of relinquishment. The FRC details exactly how this should happen:

> Adoption must be repositioned so that it is no longer perceived as an unbearable loss and shameful action for a mother or an irreparable injury to the child. The language of adoption itself must change. Adoption is a choice made by a courageous and loving mother to provide a better life for her child than the life she has known. It is a heroic act of selflessness that serves to redeem her character and lay the groundwork for her own better future. The result for the baby is a home with a family that is strong and secure. Adoption creates a family, and the individual to whom chief gratitude is due is the woman who gave that baby life in abundance. Images promoting adoption typically focus on the children and the adoptive couples. Birthmothers are rarely portrayed. That must change. Pregnancy resource centers need to present them in terms that evoke admiration, honor, and respect.

A 2007 follow-up report from the Family Research Council and the National Council for Adoption was unironically entitled "Birthmother, Good Mother: Her Story of Heroic Redemption" and found that the recommendations of the earlier report *did* resonate with vulnerable expectant women. The specific communications strategies outlined included: "deliver[ing] the messages through birthmothers that sometimes choosing adoption is what it means to be a good mother," "includ[ing] birthmothers in messaging by having them speak directly to pregnant women considering adoption," and "show[ing] women who have gone on in their lives to become successful, both professionally and personally." The report recommended using media and public relations efforts to help women understand these messages in advance of unplanned pregnancies, including adoption discussion in sex education classes, educating healthcare workers, and "hav[ing] events for birthmothers to keep them in touch with other birthmothers." For those with financial or political interests in promoting adoption, these recommendations became marching orders.

Of course, adoption agencies have a deep investment in this work and often devote resources to promoting precisely these messages in exactly these ways. Some of this outreach is via direct advertising to encourage expectant parents to consider adoption. Sociologist Elizabeth Raleigh found that one agency spent upwards of 20 percent of its full budget not on care for expectant parents or long-term support for adopted people, but on marketing. "This figure brings into stark relief the paradox of private adoption: it is a profession devoted to child welfare but sustained by advertising for children and customers," Raleigh writes. Importantly, selling the idea of adoption is necessary for adoption agencies to sustain themselves as businesses—and marketing themselves as serving the best needs of children and families *is* part of that. The demand for babies is so much higher than the number of infants available that agencies have every interest in promoting adoption as a social good. "At the end of the day, we are a business," says Abigail, a domestic adoption provider interviewed by Raleigh. Similarly, in her study of an adoption agency, anthropologist Kathryn Mariner found that "cash flow was tied directly to the flow of babies . . . Mission and money, it turns out, were never mutually exclusive."

Adoption agencies are not the only organizations promoting the "birth mother as good mother." For example, there are many groups that work to provide adoption-positive trainings to healthcare professionals who work with pregnant people, such as the National Council for Adoption's Infant Adoption Awareness Training Program (as discussed in Chapter 2). There are also key organizations that work with state governments and local school boards to incorporate pro-adoption messaging into sex education curricula across the country. In Utah (where the state requires that each student receives a presentation on adoption once in middle school and again in high school), organizations provide presentations that "discuss and evaluate the adoption option as a positive alternative," while in Tennessee and Alabama, public school curricula that "examine the benefits of choosing adoption for a pregnant teen" are offered from an organization that also provides religious education.

Other organizations underwrite larger-scale public education campaigns. Both federal and state governments invest in advertising to promote adoption from foster care—and while these ads do not draw on the "birth mother as good mother" mythology in the ways other campaigns do, they still increase the ubiquity and salience of pro-adoption messaging. More specifically, Save the Storks, an anti-abortion organization that dispatches vans equipped with ultrasound machines across the country to serve as crisis pregnancy centers on wheels, ran a "Life's About Choice" campaign to "shine a light on the beauty of choosing adoption." LDS Family Services, an organization established by the Church of Jesus Christ of Latter-day Saints, ran a public service announcement campaign with over 35 million television views and 169 million radio exposures to "promote adoption as a positive option" and to "recognize the birth parent who selflessly and courageously chooses adoption" among both Mormon and non-LDS audiences. These organizations—and indeed, most Americans—will not see anything nefarious in promoting adoption. Who could see anything wrong in a pro-adoption message? I would suggest, however, that that merely begs the question and illustrates how deeply the idea of adoption as a social good has become in our culture.

One of the most determined and intentional adoption-promoting forces in this cultural conversation is BraveLove, a nonprofit organization (that is not affiliated with an adoption agency) that seems manifested directly from the pages of the Family Research Council and National Council for Adoption's "Birthmother, Good Mother" report recommendations. Founded in 2012, BraveLove works to "change the perception of adoption through . . . communication that conveys the heroism and bravery a birth mother displays when she places her child with a loving family through adoption." On their website, BraveLove asserts that they are "not an adoption agency . . . not a pregnancy resource center or church ministry." However, a separate interview with founder Ellen Porter, herself an adoptive mother, describes how she was inspired to start BraveLove after meeting with the president of Gladney Center for Adoption (one of the largest adoption agencies in Texas), who later served on BraveLove's founding board, and the president of Thrive Women's Clinic (an anti-abortion crisis pregnancy center). A recent tax filing from BraveLove further outlined their relationship: "More women in unplanned pregnancies know that adoption is an option because nearly 1,000 pregnancy centers nationwide have access to BraveLove's adoption resources . . . BraveLove's network of partner agencies spans nearly all 50 states." The majority of these partner agencies are church-affiliated (mostly evangelical or Catholic). BraveLove's message is a simple one: relinquishment is a "selfless, difficult, and loving act" that is "complex, messy, and beautiful." Their strategy is similarly straightforward: to "inundate" our culture with "brave adoption stories" by working to "create, curate, and distribute multichannel media content."*

BraveLove's work consists primarily of content distribution: sharing videos and quotes from birth mothers, as well as organizing local "birth mom dinners" across the country. For Christina (whose story you will hear next) and a few other mothers that I interviewed, these story-sharing opportunities and community conversations were very valuable: they were a way to feel connection and pride in their adoption, and most important, they were a way to feel less alone. For women who relinquished primarily because of lack of support, the relationships formed in a pro-adoption space validated them. For those who relinquished because they felt shamed or embarrassed by their pregnancy or single motherhood, the BraveLove narrative affirmed them as worthy and caring. For those who relinquished because they felt they lacked the power to shape their life circumstances, BraveLove was a space created to "empower" them and to enable them to see themselves as courageous in their surrender. Outside of overtly anti-abortion spaces, relinquishing mothers have few of these opportunities for redemption and validation.

Crucially, BraveLove's publicly facing stories make space for pain, sadness, and loneliness—otherwise, relinquishing mothers would likely not feel any connection to their messaging at all. One Instagram post included a quote from Katie, who identified as both an adoptee and a birth mom: "I love how BraveLove puts a spotlight on how bravery, pain, and joy can exist in one story, but still is undeniably beautiful. . . . What a bittersweet love

---

* BraveLove has also entered the knowledge-generation space, recruiting the birth mothers with whom it is connected to participate in research interviews and focus groups in partnership with academic researchers and the National Council for Adoption. I did not recruit via BraveLove, but several of the mothers I interviewed were or had been connected with the organization—and many of those who were not and have never been still had opinions on the group and others like it.

story." Another, from Laura, reads: "While I have felt *heartache*, I have also felt *peace*." Yet another: "Adoption isn't easy, it's not all rainbows and butterflies, but I know I made the right decision for my baby. I put his needs before my own and chose the best I could for both of my children." In each story and dozens of others like them, the acknowledgment of hardship is made before the adoption decision is reaffirmed as ultimately beautiful, peaceful, correct. When reading these BraveLove posts, remember Taylor, who had also shared her story with them during her adoption honeymoon:

> It's really hard for me to look at those posts, or interact with birth moms who are still in that, like, "unicorns and rainbows" mindset about adoption. I was there. There is still evidence out there of me feeling very positive about adoption. There are some articles, blog posts. I wrote a BraveLove post! I was feeling great about adoption. Now I've gotten as much of it taken down as I can.

Now Taylor cringes to remember her glowing words. She asked if BraveLove would share more of her current, more critical thoughts about relinquishment and adoption, and did not receive a reply.

Other mothers are similarly critical. They are as offended by BraveLove's portrayals of birth mothers as they are by dismissive racist stereotypes that portray birth mothers as "crack whores" who are "unloving."* Melissa shared that she "hate[s] presenting birth moms as selfless angels. That's just not realistic. When we're

---

* Again, this language is fraught, and their engagement with these racist tropes was somewhat convoluted. Did they object to the "crack whore" stereotype because it's inherently racist, offensive, and inaccurate, or simply because it didn't apply to them and they didn't want to be understood as in that same category? Unfortunately, it seems more likely the latter—yet another indication of the ways that the racist structures of adoption and the whiteness of many relinquishing mothers prevents them from seeing the connections between their adoptions and other systems of family regulation and separation.

pregnant, we're not sitting here going, 'How could we change a family's life and give them the gift of a child?'" She laughs and continues: "Being pregnant like that, it's a very painful, disorganized place to be, and you're just trying to figure something, anything out. To present us as angels and selfless people, it's a bunch of bullshit." Moreover, for many it felt disingenuous: "The more people praise birth moms, the more I know they hate us," Shelby said. "They think we're worthless, that our children need to be saved from us. And they use flattery to cover it up." She sees the praise as mere marketing and messaging, not genuine admiration. "If they took the money they spent telling me how empowered I am for giving up my kid, just a small part of that money, and gave it to me when I was pregnant, I would actually have *been* empowered to raise her."

Despite its ties to anti-abortion pregnancy centers, Brave-Love purports to be apart from that political debate. Its website reads, "Is BraveLove a pro-life organization? BraveLove is pro-adoption. Whether pro-life or pro-choice, we support a woman choosing to place her baby with a loving family through adoption." This effort to situate pro-adoption rhetoric within an apolitical space is essential to then *re*introducing those ideas as nonpartisan and universally acceptable when they reappear in political contexts.

One such reappearance was during President Donald Trump's 2018 State of the Union address, to which he invited New Mexican police officer and new adoptive father Ryan Holets. "Last year, Ryan was on duty when he saw a pregnant, homeless woman preparing to inject heroin," Trump shared. "When Ryan told her she was going to harm her unborn child, she began to weep. She told him she did not know where to turn, but badly wanted a safe home for her baby. In that moment, Ryan said he felt God speak to him: 'You will do it—because you can.' He took out a picture of his wife and their four kids. Then he went home to tell his wife, Rebecca. In an instant, she agreed to adopt. The

Holets named their new daughter Hope. Ryan and Rebecca: you embody the goodness of our Nation. Thank you, and congratulations." The entire assembled chamber rose to its feet in applause. Phoenix, watching at home, felt differently:

> I remember Trump's State of the Union address, where he shouted out a cop who adopted the baby from the mother who was addicted. Almost all the coverage was praising this cop as a hero. And I'm like, "Are you fucking kidding me?" Yes, she's unhoused and she's struggling with addiction, but this guy who has the power to arrest her comes along and says, "I'll take your kid off your hands." That is such an abuse of power. I was furious. But that story isn't actually that far off from a lot of birth mother experiences. There is a power differential.

This small family unit assembled through adoption—Ryan in his dress blues, Rebecca in her pearl earrings, and baby Hope sleeping peacefully through the din in a pink swaddling blanket—somehow came to represent the best of our country. No one needed to know if Hope's mother found housing, addiction treatment, medical care, or safety in order to proclaim this a happy ending, but Phoenix and other relinquishing mothers noticed it right away. "Ugh, whatever," Shelby grumbled to me, reflecting on the incident. "Cop takes baby, everyone claps, including the Democrats—it's the story of this country. Then six months later they're all upset when babies are taken from their mothers at the southern border. And they should be upset about that! But the hypocrisy is real. And stupid."

The focus on the solidity and sanctity of adoptive families is indeed nonpartisan and has always been. Yet there are some indications that perhaps those on the left are beginning to engage in closer scrutiny of the adoption system than they have previously. In his 2021 proclamation for National Adoption Month, President Biden acknowledged that it was necessary to "improve our efforts to keep families together, prevent the trauma of un-necessary child removal." A year later, his 2022 proclamation fo-cused on "celebrat[ing] families that create safe and supportive homes and families that are made whole through adoption," and failed to make such an acknowledgment—a deeply disappoint-ing omission given that it came the same month that the Su-preme Court was hearing oral arguments in *Haaland v. Brackeen* (the case that challenged the Indian Child Welfare Act), and mere months after the *Dobbs* decision, which relied heavily on promoting adoption as a solution to curtailing abortion access. However, the policies outlined by the Biden administration (in-cluding making the adoption tax credit fully refundable and fighting discrimination against gay, lesbian, and transgender adoptive parents) included extending the adoption tax credit to legal guardians, including grandparents and other relatives, who care for children within their own extended families. This proposal is small, tentative, and insufficient—but also perhaps a start toward considering whether the full separation of children from their families of origin is necessary if the country is willing to make a minimal investment to help them remain part of their families and communities.

It may seem a far leap from MTV to BraveLove to presiden-tial politics, but the ubiquity of the narrative across platforms and messengers makes it all the more essential to understand that these messages are *not* prevalent because they are true re-flections of what relinquishment and adoption look like today, but instead because the curators who shape them often have a tangible or ideological investment in portraying adoption posi-tively. Whether it's Dr. Drew encouraging a live studio audience to applaud Catelynn and Tyler for relinquishing their daughter, or President Donald Trump encouraging a joint session of the United States Congress to applaud an adoptive father for sav-ing a baby, the universal ovation is in the service of transferring babies from those with less social privilege to those with more.

* * *

The inherent contradictions of the "birth mother as good mother" message always eventually break through. On *Teen Mom* (MTV's sequel series to *16 and Pregnant*), the cracks appear as early as the first season. As the story of Catelynn and Tyler continues, we hear Catelynn's scripted voice-over sharing: "As painful as it was, we know adoption was the right choice for our daughter, Carly." Yet she is later shown sighing with irritation because she doesn't know Carly's last name or the city where she lives. "I think I've just been depressed lately because I feel like if Brandon and Teresa decided to, then they wouldn't have to tell us anything. It just scares me, because what if in the future they don't want us and they cut off all ties?"

This anxiety simmers through seasons to follow: from the second season, when they have their first in-person visit with Carly; into the third season, when Catelynn attends a birth mother retreat to seek support from other relinquishing mothers; and into the fourth season, when they meet Carly, Brandon, and Teresa in New York City, just after Carly's second birthday. After Carly leaves, Catelynn comments: "I'm a little bit heartbroken for some reason. I know that even though I was young, I still could have been a really good mom. She just seems fun."

In the middle of Manhattan, Tyler hugs Catelynn, in a scene reminiscent of them standing outside the hospital just after Carly was born. "Sometimes I wish I had her," he says.

"Me too."

"I try so hard not to cry and act like I'm happy. But sometimes I'm just not. I'm sick of holding it back," he tells her.

The fifth season of *Teen Mom* resumes three years later, and Catelynn and Tyler are thrilled to be expecting again. They excitedly drive to get their first ultrasound, the camera framing a "Pro-Life Generation" sticker on their car's rear window. Dawn, the counselor from Bethany Christian Services with whom they worked for Carly's adoption—the one who told them that they were "in the driver's seat" for their adoption—attends their baby's gender reveal party. (Offscreen, Dawn partners with the anti-abortion organization Students for Life to film videos promoting open adoption and retweets BraveLove articles.)

Tyler's and Catelynn's joy is marred when Teresa, the adoptive mother, becomes upset that Tyler has shared photos of Carly on his and Catelynn's Facebook fan page. (Catelynn had warned him they'd be mad, but he pointed out they'd recently made their own public appearances with Carly on behalf of Bethany Christian Services.) "This whole adoption thing was supposed to be a lot different, in my opinion. I pictured it being way different than it is now," he fumes, turning directly to the camera: "If anyone's pregnant watching this, pick . . . pick the right couple."

He turns back to his pregnant girlfriend: "Let's just pop this kid out so—"

"She won't replace [Carly]," Catelynn interrupts.

Tyler, exasperated, vents: "The thing is, we *don't* have the right to [post pictures]. We don't. We signed everything away. We don't have no rights at all." Later, he continues:

> I'm done putting myself in adoptive parents' shoes. I've done it for five years. It's all I've ever done. I want you to sit with me now. . . . For the past couple years, I've been doing this, where I've been preparing myself for the day they say, "That's it, we're done." And if it happens, I'm not going to have to deal with the hurt, saddened little girl. You are, not me.

The cameras roll on: Catelynn and Tyler get married (Carly is a flower girl; Teresa helps Catelynn put on her veil). Catelynn gets pregnant again and then again; they buy a house; Catelynn candidly struggles with anxiety and depression; they go two years without seeing Carly.

In the seventh season, the families visit again. Catelynn is happily overwhelmed to see Carly with her younger sisters, and bereft when she leaves: "To see your kids together, and then watch them go away. It almost doesn't feel right. I don't think anything ever changes . . . what you're feeling."

During a conversation with Dr. Drew in the season finale, Cate-lynn names adoption as one of her traumas and maintains that "25 percent of birth mothers experience PTSD [post-traumatic stress disorder]." Dr. Drew does not engage with this statistic.

Christina

"There is a side of the pro-life movement where I feel like the only focus is on the baby, and the women are getting forgotten. That's how I felt when I actually stepped into my role where I work right now. I was like, 'Well, what about the women?'"

In 2012, Christina (who is white) was thirty-three years old and in a long-term relationship. She was living in the Northeast when she found out she was pregnant but moved home to the South (where she had grown up) by the time her daughter was born.

I was happy with my boyfriend, and so when I found out I was pregnant, it was just more a story of a normal surprise pregnancy. But then my boyfriend told me that I needed to have an abortion and that our relationship was over. I scheduled an abortion appointment, but with, like, my faith, my upbringing, I never felt like abortion was the right decision for me. Having an abortion felt like giving up. I was struggling, living away from my family, finding out I was pregnant all of a sudden, dealing with this.

My boyfriend and his mother were really, really pushing for an abortion, really coercing me. They even offered me money at one point to have an abortion. I told him he was making me feel unsafe. I finally called my mom and told her, and she actually gave me what I would call the politically correct answer: "It's your body, it's your decision. Your dad and I will support you in whatever decision you make." But then she called me right back, to make sure that I knew I had options other than an abortion. I canceled my appointment, and soon I moved home and started looking at adoption.

Throughout the process, no one really talked to me about parenting or what that would look like. I mean, having it be almost nine years later, my heart says yes, I would have liked to have that conversation. But it's kind of hard to have that perspective because I'm coming from a place of knowing what I know now versus how I would've felt in that moment. But yeah, I would have appreciated thinking more about parenting. At the center where I work now, they would have been able to help me get pretty much everything I needed to start parenting, in exchange for attending parenting classes.

The people in our church community were so helpful. They helped me find a job, and they suggested a couple that was looking to adopt. I remember one member asking me, "Is there anything we can do for you, Christina?" And I said, "You know, I'd really love a support group." So she put one together. She had a couple of other women who were choosing adoption at the time.

When I picked the adoptive parents—well, every birth mom that I've ever met and talked to, when she chose her baby's family, she just knew. That's how it was with Jared and Kelly for me. I never doubted that they were supposed to be my daughter's parents. In our conversations together, I knew I wanted the adoption to be very inclusive. I wanted them to come to doctors' appointments and birthing classes. But we weren't talking about openness yet. I definitely wanted openness. I never wanted to be a mystery to my daughter, and I knew openness would help me, too.

Right after Audrey was born, Jared and Kelly got to meet her right away while I was still in the operating room. In the recovery area after my C-section, I remember seeing Kelly was holding Audrey, and tears were just streaming down her face. I was worried something was wrong, but they were just so overjoyed.

I was really super sick, so I was out of it, and I ended up needing a blood transfusion. But I did get to spend some time with her. I was really censoring myself, though, holding back because I knew she wasn't mine. The morning I was being discharged, I got up super early and I just sobbed in the shower. Sorry, I'm going to cry now remembering it, but . . . but I was so proud of myself because I had changed her diaper and fed her and dressed her on my own, because it was like I had proven to myself that I could do it.

We had actually planned a ceremony at the church in the hospital, and it was very sweet. I held Audrey through the whole service. It's videotaped. I've never watched the video and I don't really remember a whole lot about it, other than it was very sweet. Then of course she was able to go right home from the hospital, and then my friends, they took me home with them.

I remember the first couple of weeks were the hardest. I don't know what part of it was like the postpartum hormones and what part of it was true grief. There were times where I would just be crying, and usually it was my mom who would comfort me.

I got to see her a couple of times at church early on, and I was very intentional about going to church so I could see her. But then I felt like seeing her that way was really preventing my growth and healing, so I found my own church. Now I really just see her a few times a year. Her adoptive father doesn't really allow me to visit anymore. Around her birthday last year, I said to Kelly, "I would love to schedule a time to bring her birthday gifts." And Kelly said, "I'm sorry, but Jared won't allow any visits right now." And this was before COVID; it's not that. When I asked why, she said that I needed to give it some time. There's something strange going on, and I don't understand it. Right now when there's silence and there's no reason behind it, at least that I can understand. It feels like they're hiding something, and that's very unsettling to me.

I want Audrey to know that I'm always here for her. I always want her to feel comfortable asking me any question, even if it's a hard question about why my relationship with her dad didn't work out or why I chose adoption. I would love for her to be able to hear the answer from me, because I know she has started asking those questions. I've never been a stranger to her. She's always known who I am. Last time I saw her, she just peppered me with her seven-year-old chatter and her questions, and it was very sweet. I don't even know what story she's being told now, which is slightly heartbreaking, you know? I don't even know what stories she's being told about me.

Support from the agency was so limited, and it felt very transactional. After the adoption, the agency was like, "Okay, we're done with you. Thanks, bye. We got what we wanted." And that's just very sad to me. So I've gotten pretty involved in birth mother communities. I've been to a few retreats, and I'm involved with BraveLove and their events. And I've hosted a few dinners here. My involvement goes in waves. For example, I remember probably the first year I was just super, like, gung-ho and, like, all pro-adoption and wanted to shout it from the rooftops. In year two, I kind of withdrew and was just going through another angry phase. I was just mad. I still feel anger sometimes because I still have a dream to be married and have a family, and things don't look like how I imagined. I was sad, a lot, that Jared and Kelly got to be happy and I didn't. But the support groups are helpful to an extent. Probably the most helpful was the actual in-person support group we had here locally, until then the other girls moved away.

*   *   *

But I really like BraveLove, I've always appreciated their mission to paint birth mothers in a positive light. I think I love most that the focus is on birth parents and the reminder that birth parents, especially birth mothers, are an important part of adoption. And then also, I love that they are out there promoting adoption as a choice, if a woman does find herself unexpectedly pregnant. It's just a place to feel comfortable and validated. It makes me proud to be a birth mom.

That's why I got a job at the pregnancy center where I work now. I wouldn't be working there otherwise. We offer free pregnancy tests. We also counsel on all three options, although I will tell you that adoption gets shut down pretty fast—they just aren't interested, really. Usually most women who come in are either going to parent or they want to have an abortion. We also offer free ultrasounds to confirm pregnancy, but then we also have a baby parenting program and then a diaper parenting program. We serve women from twenty-four weeks pregnant up through the baby's first year with material items. Pretty much everything you can think of for a baby!

I'm pro-life. I don't know. I think that term gets a bad reputation. I think there's a misconception that we pressure women not to have abortions, but we just want women to be educated about all of their options. We can't legally refer for an abortion,* but there isn't any

---

* This interview was completed in 2020, when abortion (and referring for abortion) was

shame or condemnation if a woman does choose to have an abortion. In fact, we help with post-abortive healing, if that's necessary. I'm pro-life in the sense that I feel like the woman gets forgotten about. There is a side of the pro-life movement where I feel like the only focus is on the baby and the women are getting forgotten. That's how I felt when I actually stepped into my role where I work right now. I was like, "Well, what about the women?" You know, to be supportive of their choice, especially after they've made it. We really want her to not have an abortion. We want to be supportive of her caring for the baby, too, if she chooses to parent.

The way that my social worker always explained it to me is that usually women who are most capable of parenting are the ones who make an adoption plan, which I know is true for me. I very much could have parented, but I made an adoption plan because I wanted what was best for her. But then mothers who are, like, addicted to drugs or in jail, they won't consider adoption at all. I honestly can't read into people's minds, but I know there's a stigma out there of, like, how could you give your baby away, or, you know, of being a bad mother because of that choice. And I know not everybody thinks that way, but I still think it's out there.

I've always said that I never doubted my decision, and I guess I trust that that was the path for both of us. But sitting where I am right now with the silence, especially from her adoptive father, and just not understanding his reasoning or logic, that has been really hard. There's no doubt that I could have parented her, though, so it's hard to feel confident in my choice. That's been really hard to navigate—I feel like I don't have say in anything because I surrendered my rights. I don't really wish what I have now on any other birth mom. There'll always be women who choose adoption, but I want it to be better for the women to come.

---

legal in all fifty states. What Christina likely means is that it was against the policy of the center to refer for abortion, as it is for most crisis pregnancy centers.

Kate

*"I've never met anyone—they might exist in this world,
but I've never met any, and I know a lot of birth
mothers—who, if they had the power to change the other
things about their lives, like having more support, more
cash, more something . . . I don't know anybody who
would, all things considered, choose to place their kid for
adoption."*

**In late 2000, Kate (who is white) was nineteen and in her second
year of college when she and her boyfriend, Pete, found out she was
pregnant. Her small, prestigious New England school did not have
much in the way of support for pregnancy and parenting students,
and the assumption seemed to be that she would get an abortion.
But having grown up in the anti-abortion movement in the Midwest,
Kate did not want an abortion. She dropped out of college.**

2010

I went back to Ohio at the end of the semester and was living with my
parents. That didn't work out because my mom was totally flipping out
that I was pregnant. She actually suggested that I go out of state and
disappear. I felt that I wasn't a different person because I was pregnant, and I didn't have to hide or be ashamed of myself. But it wasn't
working out living with my parents, so I moved in with my grandma
and worked three different jobs.

You have to understand that my family is Catholic, and super pro-
life. Growing up, my family members always worked in the parish
church, and my parish was a major hub of the Ohio pro-life movement. It's weird to think about now, because my experience with adoption has totally changed the way I think about abortion politics, but at
that moment I was very solidly pro-life. Abortion was not an option for
me—and I don't think it was an option for Pete, either.

I wasn't even thinking about adoption at first, because I felt like a mother as soon as I found out I was pregnant. I felt like I had this serious obligation to him, and no holds barred, I was going to make sure he was okay. I wanted to parent him. I was really concerned about finances, though, and I had never lived on my own. Pete had dropped out of school when I did. He lived in a shitty one-room apartment, a studio in an attic. My family was not even interested in meeting him. They thought he was the devil. There was all this tension regarding our relationship, the pregnancy, and neither of us knew how to live on our own. Could we even figure out how to survive as individuals, in addition to how best to care for our son?

But probably, in all honesty, I think I just needed more confidence in myself. And I think that could've been achieved by just having a different attitude about me being a single person being pregnant, especially in my family. My pregnancy was a major drama crisis in my family. From the get-go, there was something already deficient in me by virtue of the fact that I had gotten pregnant. I was already "flawed" in terms of my ability to not only provide financial stability, but also in my ability to provide moral or familial stability—even though I had this super intense, very directed commitment to him, which apparently didn't count for anything. But I think, in retrospect, that those feelings should have counted. They didn't, though.

I don't have super crisp, clear memories of that entire time. I thought I looked into adoption early in my pregnancy, but then when I went back and looked at my calendar, I had only really started investigating adoption in the last two and a half months of my pregnancy. I worked really hard to figure out the whole adoption process, the laws and everything. I made an interview questionnaire and went and interviewed a bunch of attorneys and adoption agencies. I was really put off by a lot of the attorneys because they were basically like, "Who are you to be interviewing me for the job?" But I wouldn't back down. I had always had a pretty clear vision of what I thought my obligations were to my son. I felt really bonded to him as soon as I knew I was pregnant. One of those obligations was that I had to be present in his life, at least psychologically, so that he would never feel that he was not wanted. If he had any questions, I wanted to be freely available to answer those for him. And I wanted, essentially, him to experience all the love that was available to him. I had this really specific idea of what I thought my job was. I wanted to get it right. I had this idea that I could have an A+ adoption: that even though I knew adoption was hard, I could be intentional and make it happen in a way that would be good for him.

We eventually worked with an agency, but we found one family we were really drawn to. When you've not been a parent—like I wasn't—I felt like my model for who parents should be was just a family that looked like my parents—even though I wouldn't have necessarily parented the way my parents raised me. I basically looked for a replica of my own situation: I wanted a Catholic family, a big family, a boisterous family, an educated family. And the agency found me a family exactly like that.

After Kate had chosen adoptive parents, the rest of the adoption process went very quickly. It culminated with an entrustment ceremony at Kate's family's Catholic church, during which she handed her newborn son, Francis, over to his new family. She signed her termination of parental rights in the sacristy of the church. Just a few weeks later, she went back to school, where her coping mechanisms (as she described them) were "kicking ass" at school, earning straight As, and immersing herself in anti-abortion work.

I started getting really involved in pro-life activism, because I had fulfilled this pro-life expectation of what you're supposed to do as a single person. My approach was: "I need to be really public because I did this adoption, and my adoption is going to work out just as I planned. Things are going to be great." That was my outlook for that first year. I'm talking about adoption in my daily living, and I'm also doing adoptive-parent training sessions where I'm the featured birth mother, talking about how hopeful and proud I am, and whatever.

But everyone around me at college was really pro-choice, and I was really out of sync in my beliefs. But there was one super conservative professor I intentionally sought out. He is actually one of the legal scholars credited with developing the Born Alive Infant Protection Act of 2002. He knew about my pregnancy, and he treated me like a demigod. I was *it*. He would make little sidebar references to me, in the middle of class, without acknowledging they were about me. He'd say, "Somebody in this classroom has done the most heroic thing ever." He actually eventually wrote me a reference to law school, and in his reference he said how, in choosing adoption, I had implicitly understood that I wasn't good enough to be a mother and that I shouldn't have been having sex and all of that stuff—in my law school reference. The whole thing was disgusting and crazy. But at the time, I really liked him, because I felt alone and he was there putting me up on a pedestal.

I'm in the middle of this adoption honeymoon, and around Francis's first birthday, I'm excited to have a meeting with his adoptive parents. Pete and I asked them if we could have an adults-only conversation: just to kind of talk about where we've been, how we feel about it, where we want to go, which I think is totally a legit conversation to have on the one-year anniversary. But they didn't understand what there was to talk about.

I had these grand plans about what I thought our adoption was going to be, and I thought I had articulated those ideas in a really clear, plain way. Even though I was only nineteen years old, I was serious about the commitment that I wanted to make to this whole thing. In those early conversations, pre-placement, we spelled out the kind of contact that we would want, the frequency of contact that we would want. We talked about those things. But there was a lot we didn't talk about, and we needed to. I didn't know to—or know how to—press through those awkward moments, to get to those deeper ideas of what adoption means to them on a philosophical level. We just talked details, schedules. And we matched on those surface-level things. But now that we've been living in this adoption for ten years, I've come to find out that our philosophies about how we feel about adoption were very different.

For example, I imagined openness as that we were all connected.

I loved *them* because they were the parents of my son. I wasn't expecting to be a part of their everyday family life or anything like that, but I thought of them as being a part of my larger kinship circle and my larger family. I don't feel like they feel that way. I feel like they participate in the open adoption as a favor to me, because they said they would or because maybe I needed it for my grieving processes. I don't know if they think of open adoption as necessary for the benefit of Francis.

It was clear, after that one-year conversation, that they didn't really think of me as part of their family at all. So after that particular conversation, I had this second, consolidated loss.

After I went back to school, I lost it. I fell into the deepest depression. I dropped out of school again, but this time because I flunked out. I was totally in my own head for about four years after that, trying to figure out how I, who had put so much thought and effort into negotiating this system of adoption, had ended up here. I had fought so hard for a good adoption, and I couldn't even pull it off. And I had a big realization that there were other larger, systemic things at work that really couldn't necessarily be overcome by a birth mother by sheer tenacity and will.

I know without a doubt that my nineteen-year-old self did everything she could to give her son the best chance. I weighed my options, and I chose adoption. But in retrospect, now that I know more, I see how my choice was framed by a lot of things that I didn't understand at that moment in time. I signed the papers, and I chose. I don't know. I never want to rob anyone, including myself, of agency in choosing those things. But here's the thing: I've never met anyone—they might exist in this world, but I've never met any, and I know a lot of birth mothers—who, if they had the power to change the other things about their lives, like having more support, more cash, more *something* . . . I don't know anybody who would, all things considered, choose to place their kid for adoption. It has a lot to do with external factors that are not within their control. If I had a choice to change those external factors, I would've changed those up and parented.

Thinking about how, even before I did the adoption, I had ideas about the *right* kind of family or the *right* kind of mother, and those same ideas were now working against *me* simply because I was a single person and young. I was an educated Christian middle-class white girl, which usually constitutes some serious privilege in this world. What was it about my experience that didn't constitute privilege anymore? And the only thing I can think of is that I was not married. In my context, in a conservative Catholic family, that was just like a freakin' no-go. Nothing else mattered. I feel like a lot of the people who consider adoption are essentially people like myself, who come from a particular demographic or perhaps have a particular ideological investment in pro-life stuff. The issues that birth mothers face are issues that everyone faces: relationships with their family, financial issues, racism, classism, sexism. All the things that make a woman consider adoption; everyone faces those things. It's not like I am a *particular* kind of woman who's *particularly* poorly suited to parent a child. I was just somebody who in that moment was really impacted by a lot of these ideas, and I folded, essentially.

I would never, ever suggest that someone do an adoption. Everything about how I was brought up says that abortion is wrong. But in choosing this, I would never, ever wish this experience on anyone. And I would never strategically use adoption as a way to mitigate or negotiate the abortion issue, and I think that people who suggest that girls do adoptions instead of abortion just don't know how difficult and challenging adoption can be.

I mean, the adoption is definitely the worst thing that's ever happened to me, definitely. That is mitigated by the fact that my son is the best thing that's ever happened to me. It's kind of like a weird dynamic where he is literally the best thing that's ever happened to me, just because he's totally fantastic and I'm so lucky to be the person that brought him into the world, and I'm so fortunate to know him, even though I know him on this really weird and limited basis. But he is literally the best thing in my life. And so, in losing that relationship with him, it's clearly the biggest loss I could experience. The adoption has monopolized everything about my mind and my life to the point where I'm going to be doing this forever, because I think it's important. It's literally reoriented everything about my life.

* * *

2020

I spoke with Kate again in 2020, ten years after our first interview. She was married and parenting three younger children. Despite being heavily involved in work around adoption for many years after our first conversation, she was not as active in that community at the moment, for a variety of reasons. She mentioned that she didn't speak very much about her own adoption anymore. Her visits with Francis had tapered off over time, and at the time of our interview, she hadn't seen him in person for about three years. "That was not my decision," she clarified.

I don't absolve nineteen-year-old Kate, but at the same time, I don't fault her, because I do know that in all the things that I did back then, I was trying my best to be a responsible person—however "responsibility" was framed for me at the time. I know that I tried really hard, but there's also times when I look back and think, like, "Wow. You got duped by yourself, by your own blind commitment to certain kinds of principles that you hadn't fully investigated or questioned." That's not an indictment of nineteen-year-old Kate. She did her best.

Even though my beliefs at the time were deeply about Catholicism, it wasn't strictly religion—it was very linked to a far-right conservative political ideology. From middle school on, I listened to Rush Limbaugh every single day. I taped off the radio while I was at school, so I could go back and listen to Rush Limbaugh when I got home. It truly is *that* brand of thinking. It's not just this religious redemption thing that adoption becomes in that framework. It's also very linked to ideas about punishment: punishment for slipping out of line in any direction, and punishment especially for being a woman who slips. I don't believe that I "slipped." I don't believe that framework anymore, but I think I did at the time.

It's not just a religious framework of responsibility. It's that you have the responsibility to act in ways that live out your political values. I don't have really strong memories of that time in my life, but I know that I loved my kid and I know that I didn't want to lose my kid. So I know that there was nothing in me that said: "Yeah, I want to do an adoption, because it's what I really want to do." Instead, it was: "I have to do this because it's what it means to live out a pro-life ethic." It meant that I needed to save the baby from suffering any of the punitive consequences—social or spiritual—that I had brought upon us by my alleged personal failings. Which would essentially have been having sex outside of marriage as a young adult.

What I'm describing here is actually not so far away from what motivates me now to do justice-focused work. I honestly attribute my interest in social justice to my very partisan, Republican Catholic grandma, who literally dragged me all over the place to pray in front of abortion clinics, going to all sorts of Republican political rallies. That engendered in me this idea that things were wrong out there in the world and that it was my responsibility to do something about it.

My awareness of the political nature of my former belief system has changed, and I think that parenting has also changed me, of course. When I was pregnant with my second child, their due date was around the same time as Francis's. So the entire time I was pregnant, the seasons were the same. All these things around me paralleled what I saw when I was pregnant with Francis. That was hard. But the biggest challenge was a lot of anxiety about control and self-determination. I was constantly in conflict with my healthcare providers because I didn't trust anyone to care for me in the ways that I wanted to be cared for, because in my first pregnancy I wasn't presented with any choices. I was just told by my doctor—who was assigned to me by my mother and who also went to my church—how my birth was going to be. It felt like choice and agency were the most important things for my second pregnancy. It wasn't just about the birth. It was about my relationships with my family and how much access they had to me and my child. I would not let anybody visit me at the hospital. Nobody was allowed to come visit me, because this was my time and my space. When I went home from the hospital, nobody was allowed to come visit me because I didn't want anybody touching my kid. I just wanted the entire experience to be for me. That made it hard, obviously, because when you have a newborn it actually helps to have people around.

There was something incredibly important, striking, tragic, melancholy, beautiful—I don't even know how to describe it—about especially the early months that my second child was here. That pregnancy was already on the same timeline, but remarkably—and I think cosmically—they ended up being born on the exact same day. The same birthday, thirteen years apart. Literally with every day I have with my second child, I see the things that I have missed. It almost feels like in real time because, at this moment, Francis would've been doing this when my second child was doing this, because of the birthday alignment. That's just kind of how it feels psychologically to me. There was just this enormous appreciation, I think, of being in my second child's life, and of seeing all the things that I had missed. I knew that I was missing out on parenting, you know, but I didn't really know what that was until my second child arrived.

There was that kind of understanding of the depth of what I had lost. I got a richer picture of what that was. But parenting also made me think about new forms of trauma or tragedy. I knew that there were relationships now between my kids that had been lost. Those losses were just abstract possibilities before, but now they were real. If anything, whatever hope that I have carried with me as I navigate open adoption for now two decades, I felt like I've also been carrying the hope of my kids, too, the hope of my parented kids that this relationship with Francis would turn into something closer to what I had originally intended, or at least it would be easier to explain to my parented kids why it's not that way. I don't know.

But the fact that I now parent other children hasn't changed what I want out of the relationship with Francis. And being a parent to little kids, I honestly don't even think it would change the logistics. Should Francis express any interest in me and in developing our relationship, that is a top priority. I've always known that that would be a priority, from the beginning. I'm prepared to spend whatever money I need to, drive anywhere I have to, to make sure I can be there if Francis calls. I would do that. I still feel the same way, whether that would mean dragging my kids to another state for a visit, or having conversations with my parented kids that are hard for me emotionally. I'd do it. But all of this is theoretical anyway because it hasn't happened.

My fourth pregnancy was different—it was unplanned. That was the first time I ever considered abortion. My third child was only nine months old when I found out I was pregnant. My partner and I were already feeling so overwhelmed and completely, totally broke. That was the first time in my life that I've ever had a real discussion about that particular option. I seriously considered it, to the point that I told my sibling I was thinking about it, and they were completely fine and supportive. But I also think the same old shit, the same old pro-life shit slips in after the fact, when I look at my youngest child and I think, *Oh, if I had had an abortion, this person would not be here with me right now.* I consider that to be an intrusion in how I want to be thinking and living my life. Maybe I'm being too hard on myself.

Honestly, my feelings about being a mother help me hold contradictory ideas in place. I've never had an abortion, but every time I read stories about people who face tons of obstacles to making decisions about their pregnancies, I see them now as people making decisions out of mercy and compassion and love for their own selves, their unborn baby, and their families. When I see people trying to navigate their reproductive lives, I see only lots of love and good judgment under often the most crushing of circumstances. I used to just uncritically consider them to be soulless. I really felt that way back then. I'm actually so ashamed of the fact that it took my own experience with feeling disempowered to start to see how other people were experiencing those same dynamics in other circumstances. That's straight-up shameful. That's certainly a white lady thing, to wait until it impacts you to actually start to think critically, but that is definitely what happened.

It's honestly hard for me to talk about this still. I believe that the reproductive and sexual control of women's bodies is a key feature of not just sexist oppression but lots of different forms of oppression. I really, truly believe that self-determination is beyond important for resisting and dismantling the hierarchical systems of value that produce oppression and stratification. I believe categorically, for any reason, people should be able to make decisions about their bodies, and I don't think that people have abortions without real, intentional consideration of what they need for themselves. People know their own lives and they know what they need. I say that and I believe it and I also believe, because I feel like it's been ingrained into my head, and I haven't been able to figure out a way out of it, that abortion ends a human life. I also believe that. I grapple with this, and maybe this is why I don't want to talk about it. I also believe that we can have abortions if we think it's right for us. My old belief system could never accommodate ambiguity or a contradiction; my current belief system can accommodate those things, and those things sit side by side.

For me, as someone who's in an adoption that I would describe as profoundly unsatisfactory and very disempowering, I appreciate and have an interest in adoption processes and adoption professionals that are going to work hard to facilitate the necessary high-stakes conversations between prospective families—not just the birth parents, but the adoptive families—to try to see about structuring forms of communication that meet everybody's expectations and can evolve. I want that to happen. But there is something that seems incomplete when you're thinking about where adoption fits into a reproductive justice framework. *What is your role in creating the conditions that would make your work obsolete?* I want to ask these agencies. *What is your investment in the placement in the first place?* That's a political tension, and I don't know if so-called feminist adoption agencies are unpacking it, if they're wrestling with it right now, if that means that they shift their portfolio from adoption to something else. I don't know what that means for them. And I don't know if they're having those conversations, but it feels like anybody should be, if they care about reproductive justice.

6

To Parent the Children We Have

As Kate's story illustrates, the anti-abortion movement may celebrate birth mothers, but its understanding of adoption does not resonate with relinquishing mothers for very long. Most of the mothers I interviewed identified as pro-choice, even if they were uncomfortable with abortion—and for many of them, the adoption had prompted them to see the necessity of abortion for others, if not themselves. Yet even if they held strong opinions about how adoption should change (which many of them did), few of them felt they had an alternate movement or space to engage in advocacy that would support families and honor their own experiences. For some, this lack of engagement was rooted in feelings of inadequacy and trauma post-relinquishment or in the work of daily survival taking up their time and energy. Others worried such engagement would jeopardize their relationship with their child (or, if the child was under eighteen years old, with their child's adoptive parents), or—very often—didn't know where to look beyond the anti-abortion movement.

Traditional white-women-led reproductive rights and feminist movements have never held a critical analysis of adoption, nor have they made space for birth parents. Indeed, like Norma McCorvey, many relinquishing mothers—particularly those from the baby scoop era—have always felt alienated from "choice"-centric feminist spaces that prioritized the professionalized voices of doctors and lawyers over the voices of impacted people. Mary Anne Cohen, a relinquishing mother, was one of the founders of Concerned United Birthparents (CUB), the earliest birth parent advocacy organization. CUB was established in 1976 "to promote the general mental health and welfare of birthparents located through the United States," and much of their early work is chronicled in historian Rickie Solinger's book *Beggars and Choosers: How the Politics of Choice Shapes Adoption, Abortion, and Welfare in the United States*. Solinger's work is some of the earliest to make very explicit the connections between adoption and reproductive justice, but as Mary Anne Cohen reflected decades later: "I felt [the book] was skewed toward a feminist and pro-abortion slant that was not really there for many of us early activists, who initially just wanted to find and reconnect with our kids, and tell the world what had happened to us. We did not all think of ourselves as feminists." Yet even mothers who were more likely to identify as feminists felt let down by the movement. At one gathering of the American Adoption Congress in 2014, adoption advocate Leslie Pate Mackinnon spoke on a panel entitled "Without Option, It's Not a Choice," and referred to feminism as "that movement that let us down before," for failing to consider the constraints under which so many relinquishing mothers (particularly of the baby scoop era generation) lost their children.

Many such "pro-choice" organizations have—not unlike adoption agencies—always believed there were people worthy and unworthy of parenthood and been comfortable with having the choices of others constrained. As researcher and writer Liz Latty argues:

> Mainstream feminism—feminism by and for middle and upper-middle-class white women—has historically gotten behind adoption. Feminists have supported the rights of single people and same-gendered families to adopt, the rights of adoptive

families in contested adoptions, and policies intended to get children into adoptive homes faster. What's missing from mainstream feminism is any explicit support for families of origin: the parents who have to lose their children, the families that must be dismantled in order for adoptive families to be built.

Of course, the shortcomings of mainstream feminism are felt well beyond the specific group of people impacted by adoption.

In the early summer of 1994, a group of Black women gathered in Chicago. They were responding to an immediate concern about the Clinton administration's healthcare proposal, in which reproductive healthcare had been deprioritized in the face of firm Republican opposition. However, they also felt compelled to address a greater series of omissions from the white-women-led reproductive rights movement that focused on choice, while neglecting to consider the ways racist power structures, poverty, policing, and other unjust systems constrained the choices available to women of color, transgender and nonbinary people, and other marginalized groups. From this meeting, the critical framework of reproductive justice emerged. Loretta Ross, one of the Black founding mothers of the reproductive justice movement,* describes how reproductive justice goes beyond the debates about pregnancy choice to include work that "fight[s] equally for 1) the right to have a child; 2) the right not to have a child; and 3) the right to parent the children we have" as well as "the necessary enabling conditions to realize these rights." Three years later, SisterSong Women of Color Reproductive Justice Collective would be founded to help build a national reproductive justice movement.

As a critical framework, the claims of reproductive justice

* Loretta Ross herself was pressured to relinquish her son when she gave birth at age fifteen in 1969, after a pregnancy that was the result of incestuous rape. Her decision to parent cost her a scholarship to Radcliffe College (Loretta J. Ross Papers, Smith College).

to assert for the right "to parent the children we have" seem to make it an intuitive space for an analysis of relinquishment. Yet that claim was rooted in a history of the Black and Indigenous people, whose parenthood was most often policed and denied, and whose families were so often separated by the state. While mothers in private adoptions often feel resonance with reproductive justice as a *theory*, forging connections with reproductive justice as a living *movement* has proven harder. For so long, relinquishing mothers were mostly white middle-class women, who did not often draw connections between their losses and the injustices of separation faced by families of color. Without such connections, meaningful movement building is impossible.

Instead, the work of building these connections has largely fallen to adopted people—often transracial and transnational adoptees of color. In *Outsiders Within: Writing on Transracial Adoption*, editors Jane Jeong Trenka, Julia Chinyere Oparah, and Sun Yung Shin write powerfully:

> Our definition of feminism includes a commitment to reproductive justice for all. At the heart of our adoptions are the reproductive choices of our mothers—choices that were most often made in the context of limited option. For us, reproductive rights can never be reduced to the right to a safe and legalized abortion or freedom from dangerous contraceptives or forced sterilization. Instead, we must work to create and sustain a world in which low-income women of color do not have to send away their children so that the family that remains can survive. Our feminism demands that we critique a global system that bequeaths power to some mothers but not to others. It calls on us to reconsider the myth that we have been told about our birthmothers and to challenge ourselves to move past our own pain to see the limited survival choices given our mothers and communities that led to our adoptions.

Their reclamation and redefinition of feminism offers an essential paradigm for considering adoption within reproductive justice, and the crisis provoked by the *Dobbs* decision has reinvigorated efforts to make such connections more overt and prevalent within that movement.

"The idea of adoption as a reproductive justice issue struck me as intuitive," Tiffany HyeonBrooks, an internationally adopted person and reproductive justice advocate, told me, "but I couldn't find much out there at first." There was scholarship around reproductive justice theory, but there were few established reproductive justice movement spaces that centered adoption. In August 2022, a mere two months after the *Dobbs* decision, HyeonBrooks gave a talk entitled "An Adopted Person's Lived Experience and Expertise at the Intersection of Reproductive Justice, Adoption, and Survivorship" at the annual conference of SisterSong. Importantly, HyeonBrooks had already attended SisterSong's conferences in the past—she did not show up for the first time asking them to consider adoption, but drew on her deep knowledge of and commitment to the reproductive justice movement in making these connections. She began to work to create space for adopted people to feel welcome and see themselves in the reproductive justice movement. Though she was nervous about what the reception might be, the audience welcomed her perspective. HyeonBrooks shared:

> It's not that repro justice left us out, or that the movement is gatekeeping conversations about adoption, but I also didn't see proactive involvement. I want to help build more explicit and open conversations about adoption in these spaces—I want to create an adoptee caucus at SisterSong, or build adoptee-centered spaces at Collective Power [another key reproductive justice organization]. . . . With *Roe* falling and so many adoptive parents on the Supreme Court talking openly about adoption, it

makes these connections to adoption accessible for the broader movement for the first time.

HyeonBrooks wasn't the only one who felt this omission. T. Sheri Amore Dickerson, an adopted person, was deeply involved in the movements for social and reproductive justice as a founder of Black Lives Matter Oklahoma and a board member of the Women's March. Dickerson attended HyeonBrooks's talk and felt an immediate connection:

> I have realized how much of my lived experience as an adoptee colors my reproductive justice lens, but it wasn't until the session with HyeonBrooks at the SisterSong conference that I felt seen as an adoptee in the RJ space. . . . Being Black, Indigenous, and queer from Oklahoma, these are identities I bring with me to all movement spaces. But I rarely get the chance to talk about my experience as an adoptee and never have had the opportunity to do so with other adoptees.

For both Dickerson and HyeonBrooks, the centering of adoptees is important to doing the work of reproductive justice well, and the task is more urgent than ever. HyeonBrooks later wrote:

> Right-wing movements have taken hold of adoption narratives. Because of that, and because there's a fear that talking about adoption will detract from efforts to advance and sustain abortion rights, reproductive justice movements have been reluctant to talk about adoption. This does a disservice to our movements because adoption touches on so many reproductive justice issues and adoptees can be a powerful force for building the movement and acting as political allies. Many of us are looking for a movement home in this way.

HyeonBrooks was very eager to continue to build connections between adoption and the reproductive justice movement, and was certainly open to the idea of co-creating these conversations with relinquishing parents. Yet she acknowledges that, thus far, the work has been almost entirely adoptee-led. There are relatively few relinquishing mothers from private adoptions who engage openly and deeply with the reproductive justice movement.

* * *

Kate Livingston* and I first met in 2010, over lunch between sessions of the Alliance for the Study of Adoption and Culture conference, held that year at the Massachusetts Institute of Technology. We ended up at a nearby pizza place, eating slices so large and greasy that we both needed multiple napkins to make it through the meal with any semblance of dignity (and still my notebook from that day remains smudged with orange spots). That day I heard Kate's adoption story—which you have just read—for the first time.

Kate's life and my own ran in parallel in many ways before intersecting that April afternoon: we were about the same age; we grew up in neighboring states; we attended neighboring undergraduate schools in bucolic western Massachusetts. Kate was a fellow doctoral student at the time and would soon finish her women's, gender, and sexuality studies dissertation on the role of anti-abortion politics in adopted people's access to original birth certificates in her home state of Ohio. We came to the same space by different paths: I was seeking to understand the political through the collection of personal stories; Kate was seeking to understand her personal experience through a political and gendered analysis. As she reflected:

---

* Dr. Kate Livingston is the only research participant in this project identified by her actual name, with her permission. Other writers, scholars, and advocates who contributed as nonparticipants are also named.

> If you would've had this conversation with me five years ago, before I had a feminist framework for understanding what happened, I never would've thought that I could even get close to being happy again. And I feel like having this particular framework to think about adoption is getting me closer to that.

Kate brought a specific scholarly expertise to her understanding of adoption, but the political intersections and the core, justice-based themes that she articulated were shared by many of the mothers I interviewed.

Around the time of our first conversation, Kate founded (and went on to serve as the director of) the Ohio Birthparent Group. In creating this space for "peer support, advocacy, and community education," she was able to merge her personal experience and her academic and political perspectives into a supportive community for birth parents that created space for considering reproductive justice. In her essay "Adoption as a Reproductive Justice Issue" critical adoption scholar Kimberly McKee cites the Ohio Birthparent Group as a "key emerging organization" in "advocat[ing] for the rights of birth parents." McKee goes on to offer a vision of what a true consideration of adoption from a reproductive justice paradigm might mean: "Incorporating adoption into discussions of reproductive justice recognizes how some women's motherhood is encouraged while other women face barriers" and "using a reproductive justice lens to understand adoption puts birth mothers' lack of rights in conversation with theory and praxis that moves to the center women's rights to parent with dignity, if they elect parenthood." It is necessary to consider the context in which relinquishment occurs to understand what reproductive justice means, what adoption means, and how we can newly understand connection and family.*

---

* In her early scholarship, Kate writes about "the birthmother dilemma" in which birth mothers "find they must simultaneously undermine and embrace normative constructions of family" in order to be acknowledged. She asks: "Do we articulate ourselves

For Kate, traditional pro-choice/"pro-life" dichotomies fail to consider the conditions under which adoptions occur, including her own relinquishment. "Now that I'm out of the anti-abortion space, I'm struggling with the bigger challenge of considering what adoption means as part of reproductive justice," she told me in 2020. "It has always been incredibly frustrating to me as a birth parent and as somebody who's invested in reproductive justice, to see 'feminist' considerations of adoption that are grossly oversimplified. I know people in abortion-centric orgs who think that by merely offering adoption as an option, that they're doing feminist work. I know of adoption-focused orgs that say they're doing feminist work by being willing to make abortion referrals. On both accounts there's a failure to think through the full scope of what it means to account for adoption in reproductive justice work."

In December 2021, Kate and I participated in a joint interview, along with adoptee memoirist Angela Tucker and reporter Kathryn Joyce, to respond to Justice Amy Coney Barrett's questions in the *Dobbs v. Jackson Women's Health Organization* oral arguments. In those arguments, Justice Coney Barrett relied on the idea that relinquishment of infants offered a meaningful and appropriate alternative to abortion access for Americans. Kate's own experiences and her political framing of them in the context of reproductive justice allowed her to respond forcefully: "What's happening at the Supreme Court right now is that a bunch of people who don't live my life, who don't live Angela's

---

as 'natural,' biological mothers at the risk of shoring up the heteronormative family forms that exclude us? Do we stress the constructed nature of kinship and give up our most salient claim to legal and social recognition in the current socio-political climate? Either choice produces our exclusion and fails to account for the complexity of our subjective experiences, our relationships, and our place in the large social fabric of family life." Here, Kate goes beyond the limitations of choice-based politics in understanding the process that drives relinquishment, but identifies the limits of traditional feminist discourses in understanding birth motherhood—as it is lived over a lifetime—at all (Kate Livingston, "The Birthmother Dilemma: Resisting Feminist Exclusions in the Study of Adoption," in *Adoption and Mothering*, Demeter Press, 2012).

life, are using us as a tool to further their own agenda. They're co-opting our lives and our stories."

*   *   *

Kate's story brings many answers to that key question: Where do relinquishing mothers go next? For many mothers, it can be hard to find supportive spaces—which is often what they need first—that make room for them to move toward a bigger understanding, let alone offering opportunities for organizing.

When Angie Swanson-Kyriaco was pregnant in 1998, she had few places to turn. Her controlling boyfriend assured her he'd get the money for an abortion, but he continually came up short, until she was past the point in pregnancy when she could obtain one. Even as the Planned Parenthood clinic turned her away, she remembers being treated with kindness, compassion, and a freedom from judgment that she hadn't encountered in many other places—not throughout her fraught Catholic upbringing, and certainly not in the context of her abusive relationship. Looking back, Swanson-Kyriaco sees how much of her life was shaped by misogyny, and how entrenched her feelings of shame and self-hatred were during her early adulthood. She was vulnerable, overwhelmed, and in real crisis when the adoption attorney (whom she shared with the adoptive family) promised her an open adoption, without a real explanation of what that might mean.

After she relinquished her daughter, Swanson-Kyriaco struggled to get back on track. Within a year after she had given birth, her car was repossessed and she became homeless; soon after her daughter's first birthday her boyfriend left town and she never heard from him again. Swanson-Kyriaco struggled with deep depression and suicidal thoughts, feelings exacerbated by her lack of contact with her daughter (even though she'd been assured of an open adoption), as the adoptive parents never allowed more than the very minimal information they felt obligated to provide.

Years of waiting tables and slowly rebuilding her life went by. "My self-esteem was so low and so damaged, I never quite knew what I wanted to do," she told me. "But I knew I wanted more." She had never forgotten the care she'd received at Planned Parenthood, and soon began volunteering and stuffing envelopes at her local affiliate. Eventually, Swanson-Kyriaco moved from volunteer to employee, and she would go on to serve as the call center manager, the clinical services coordinator, and finally the director of executive and board affairs at her regional Planned Parenthood affiliate, all while finishing graduate school. At the same time, she became more deeply involved in Democratic politics, and her political awareness grew as she began to engage in state and local campaigns. Yet still, through this accumulated professional experience and political engagement, she remained mostly secretive about her experience as a birth mother.

"I think many birth parents feel timid, or don't know where to start," Swanson-Kyriaco said. "It took me a long time to gain confidence in how I was thinking and feeling. So often birth parents are told 'be quiet' or 'you're too sensitive.' They are also still struggling with the shame of relinquishment and, many times, just trying to navigate their own survival and well-being—they aren't necessarily in a position to spend time or emotional energy on advocacy."

Yet that time did eventually come, when in late 2021 Swanson-Kyriaco became the executive director of MPower Alliance, an organization "dedicated to significantly improving the lives of birthmothers through supportive services, community-building, and advocacy." MPower Alliance is one of just a few support organizations not affiliated with an adoption agency that specifically works with more recent birth parents. (On Your Feet Foundation and the Ohio Birthparent Group would be others.) The core of MPower's work has always been support: weekend retreats for mothers, counseling grants, peer support, educational or vocational grants, online support groups, and emergency resources. Over the years, they've helped over a thousand relinquishing parents, with everything from no-fee therapy to school tuition to moving expenses, to smaller costs like day care registration fees, car repairs, medical bills, even menstrual products.

MPower Alliance was founded by an adoption attorney and has long been led and funded by donors who are adoptive parents. It has been an uphill effort for Swanson-Kyriaco to begin bringing a more critical and political framework of adoption to her work. She wants to lead an organization that is able to bring more transparency to adoption, to acknowledge the injustices and inequities, to engage with the argument that adoption is not a replacement for abortion, and to forge connections with other reproductive justice organizations. For Swanson-Kyriaco, this paradigm is part of how MPower will care for the parents who seek services: "We welcome everybody where they are, and don't expect them to adhere to narratives that they have given a 'gift' or that they're damaged, helpless, or that they're heroes." This approach is a new one for MPower Alliance, whose leaders have previously leaned firmly toward an apolitical neutrality. It is also potentially an important step in helping a new generation of relinquishing parents contextualize their individual losses within a broader social discourse.*

*   *   *

An organization like MPower Alliance, which provides tangible support while allowing mothers to feel critical about adoption, is essential in an environment where most post-adoption support is agency-provided. Independent, nonagency spaces allow relinquishing mothers to begin to consider their own power as advocates—for themselves and their children.

Historically, birth mother activism has always been rooted in adoptee activism, as relinquishing parents support the organizing of their collective children. These efforts have included, for exam-

---

* In the spring of 2023, Swanson-Kyriaco parted ways with MPower Alliance. While the decision was difficult for her, she shared with me that "this change will allow me to continue my activism and advocacy that is in alignment with my values and focused on reproductive justice and reducing the number of unnecessary adoptions."

ple, fighting for open access to original birth records for adopted people, or lobbying for citizenship for all transnational adoptees.* Yet while most of the mothers with whom I spoke supported such measures, they also felt uniquely prepared to bring to light the deeply unethical practices that they had experienced.

Many of the relinquishing mothers I interviewed had a very clear sense that they wanted adoption to be different, but not always how or to what degree. Their suggested reforms are unsurprising: they wanted real options counseling that included information about abortion and—more important to them—concurrent parenting planning, so that they felt they had access to all their options throughout their pregnancy and after giving birth. They wanted greater clarity around their legal rights both before and after relinquishment, and a better understanding of the limits of openness agreements and what their relationship with their child might be like (both legally and practically) after signing their termination of parental rights. They wanted longer revocation periods during which they could change their mind and regain their rights, and access to crisis care that would help them care for their newborn while they considered what was possible. They wanted agencies to provide real lifelong support for their mental health and well-being, and for negotiating ongoing relationships with their child and their child's adoptive family. Nearly universally, they wanted money to play less of a role in the practice of adoption—whether in an agency's pursuit of profit or nonprofit sustainability, or in the reasons behind their own relinquishment, or in the cost to would-be adoptive families.

Some of the articulated desired practices seemed at first mutually exclusive. For example, mothers rejected pre-birth matching

---

* The Child Citizenship Act of 2000 ensures automatic citizenship to transnationally adopted people who were fully adopted and under eighteen years old when the law went into effect. However, adopted people who were born before 1983 did not have automatic citizenship, and some have been deported to their countries of origin. The Adoptee Citizenship Act would rectify this omission, but as of this writing, it has not yet passed Congress.

between expectant parents and prospective adoptive parents as unethical; they described the sense of obligation they felt to deliver a child for the hopeful parents (and, in several cases, excited would-be older siblings). Yet they also wanted a deep focus and prioritization on openness that, in their vision, required a more extended relationship and understanding of one another. In these dual desires, expanded models of community care—particularly kinship networks, which are central to an understanding of parenthood in more communal cultures—offer a possible paradigm. The seeming tension around pre-birth matching is actually a conflict only if we see adoption as the permanent removal of a child from those networks.

Many of their stories tell of agencies or adoption professionals who walk the murky line between the merely unethical and the outright illegal, revealing the ways in which current laws are insufficient in even minimally protecting the interests of expectant and relinquishing parents. For example, as discussed in Chapter 3, it's clear several agencies were manipulating information to avoid the implications of the Indian Child Welfare Act, which is a federal crime. I also heard stories of mothers being asked to sign papers consenting to the adoption before the baby was born.

"I don't think that's legal," I told one.

"Oh, no," she said, sighing, "it's not. But they told me to leave the date line blank and that they'd file the papers after he arrived. They said it would be less overwhelming to sign it before. So that's what I did."

Other mothers had to sign contracts saying they would pay the would-be parents' legal fees if they decided to parent, a cost which would be unimaginable to most mothers who are considering relinquishing precisely because they have no financial resources in the first place. Some unscrupulous attorneys would aggressively encourage expectant parents to accept help paying for groceries and rent throughout their pregnancy, and then, after the baby was born, present an itemized list of expenses for which they would be responsible if they did not relinquish. Several were told by the adoptive families' lawyers that they'd be prosecuted for "adoption fraud" if they did not relinquish, or that the attorney would call child protective services to remove the newborn if they expressed a desire to parent after giving birth. (After chronicling a particularly egregious story of attorney misconduct, the mother told me: "Well, and then after all that, I heard he was awarded the [congressional] Angels in Adoption award. It's almost like they tried to give it to the worst possible person in the universe.")

One mother who helped support other women who faced coercion during their adoptions recounted:

> So in this state, the law is that you can terminate your parental rights at twenty-four hours, and then attorneys will tell moms that they have thirty days to revoke their consent. And that seems reasonable—you have about a month to change your mind. But they trick you, because if you want to revoke, you have to have a "best interest" hearing. And: the adoption attorneys are friends with all the judges. The adoptive parents have your baby. You've terminated your rights. You haven't had your baby. They hire an aggressive attorney who is friends with the judge, and you can't afford any attorney, and you lose. And hearings get postponed all the time—months and months later. The next thing you know it's been fifteen months, and maybe the judge will just say, "Sure, you'd be a good parent. But it's been fifteen months and this is the only parents the baby has ever known. I'm not taking the baby away." Case closed.

The imbalance in legal power is yet another reflection of the disparity in socioeconomic power between relinquishing and adoptive families; the adoptive families are more likely to have better—or at least some—lawyers. In many states, relinquishing parents *share a lawyer* with the adoptive parents during the adoption finalization, but the lawyer is paid by the adoptive parents, creating unbalanced representation.

When one relinquishing mother tried to speak up publicly about the injustices she encountered, her agency sent her a cease-and-desist letter. Another mother was forced to delete her blog criticizing her agency, when they said they would advise her son's adoptive parents to cut off contact if she did not. In a 2020 lawsuit, Bethany Christian Services sued Valerie Garcia, a relinquishing mother, alleging "she [had] defamed them with more than 1,000 'false and disparaging' social media posts. . . . Garcia has called Bethany's adoption services a 'scam' and accused Bethany of 'fraud,' as well as 'illegal adoptions and predatory behavior.'" (In 2021, a judge found that Garcia's claims of "reproductive exploitation and coercion" and accusations that BCS "traumatized" her were "materially false" and "not of a public concern." Garcia was ordered to remove her social media postings and barred from publishing any further defamatory statements about BCS.) Based on my findings, these examples—the cease-and-desist letters, the threats of cutting off contact, the defamation lawsuit, all in response to mothers who were publicly critical of their adoptions and agencies—might serve to silence other mothers.

Far from being exceptional, these egregious examples are ubiquitous. However, even in an adoption that does not involve coercion, legal manipulation, or deceit, there is still often a level of indifference toward the expectant parent's well-being—a routine omission of care that reveals, markedly, whom the system is designed to serve.

Susan Dusza Guerra Leksander, an adopted person, birth mother, and adoption provider, has written about the pursuit of ethical adoption, and what it includes: a recognition that racist and patriarchal structures have "historically dehumanized people seen as unworthy of parenting"; an acknowledgment of the "gains and losses" inherent in adoption; a genuine counseling process that provides access to all options, including family preservation; an exploration of whether kinship placement is possible. If the expectant parent still wishes to move ahead with adoption, Leksander talks about preparing them for an adoption:

> This means educating them about their rights, reassuring them they can change their mind at any point without guilt, avoiding the pressure of "matching" them with potential adoptive families early in their pregnancy, searching for potential families beyond our pool if needed who meet the expectant parents' desires for their children, discussing the benefits of open adoption and the availability and limits of contact agreements, explaining what their placed child will need from them as they grow, and offering post-placement counseling.

Leksander is also quite clear: "We are not in the business of 'finding babies' for people." Importantly, Pact, the agency for which she works, does not rely on adoption to financially sustain itself as an organization. They also provide educational programming, family camps, support groups, and mental health programming, services that (along with philanthropic donations) ensure Pact's sustainability.

This differentiation in funding streams is a meaningful one, even for a nonprofit organization. In her ethnographic study of a nonprofit adoption agency, anthropologist Kathryn Mariner described the situation thus: "From my vantage point, it seemed as though expectant mothers were frustratingly slipping through [the social workers'] grasp[s], despite [their] numerous efforts to retain them. This is not to say that [they] did not believe wholeheartedly that expectant mothers had a legal right to parent, and they did their best to support mothers in making that decision, but their existence as brokers—and adoptive parents themselves—depended on relinquishment." Thus, while other small adoption agencies must either more aggressively pursue pregnant people and work to ensure relinquishments occur in order to cover their operational costs, Pact will remain open whether or not it facilitates adoptions, making it an anomaly within the adoption industry. This practice gives the organization an opportunity to prioritize its values of choice, autonomy, and lifelong support in striving toward ethical adoption. Such thinking is also as much about improving what adoption can look like for those already living it.

* * *

Beyond adoption reform, the advocacy to which most of my participants felt deeply drawn was the work of family preservation, or individual and societal efforts to create the conditions that allow people to parent the children they have.

Since losing one of her own children to adoption, Renee Gelin has been tireless in her work for family preservation. In 2011, Gelin founded Saving Our Sisters (SOS) as a small grassroots collective of birth mothers who wanted to help other women who hoped to parent but who were feeling pressured into adoption. Today, SOS is a nonprofit organization with a network of volunteers—mostly relinquishing mothers and adopted people—that spans the country.

The needs of the women who reach out to SOS are clear: "Money, obviously, but more and more it's also affordable housing. The wait lists for affordable housing are years long, and they don't have years to wait. They're pregnant and they need housing now. I also need housing that they can sustain, because I don't want to get them just through the birth. I need to get her in a place with rent she can afford, so that she's not homeless with a six-month-old." Gelin also helps women get enrolled on WIC and other public benefits, and file for child support. For women who feel resistant to accepting public support, she reminds them: "This is what your child needs you to do right now. You're doing this to keep your family strong." Gelin estimates that a few years ago, most of the women she worked with just needed about $500 to keep their children. But now, with the dearth of housing, it's up to about $2,500, to help them afford rent for a few months until they can return to work after birth.

Despite this increase, SOS remains scrappy and practical when it comes to helping mothers, relying on word of mouth on social media to find mothers in need of support, and on "Buy Nothing" Facebook groups to help them find the baby supplies they need. But much of what Gelin believes they offer is just a community of support. "Being a parent isn't always easy," Gelin says candidly. "This work is about not damning them for having a moment of weakness."

Katie Burns, a fellow mother of adoption loss, does volunteer intake for SOS. When she began, women would call in, asking for housing or parenting resources in a specific state or locality, and Burns would dig into the research for them. She pulled together resources for housing, child care, and transportation, and began compiling them all on her website, the Family Preservation Project. This work feels satisfying to Burns, a self-described "doer" with long personal roots in activism—with the anti-abortion movement: "I was raised in the church and the pro-life movement. That was all I knew growing up. As young as I can remember, we went to the March for Life every January. It was a very pro-life household. So it was very confusing when I was pregnant at eighteen, and I was told I couldn't come home with a baby. They told me I had to place the baby for adoption."

After a disillusioning adoption, Burns remained active in anti-abortion work for a time, including joining the board of a crisis pregnancy center. But for her, preventing abortions is now increasingly about supporting families.

I looked at the reasons women were getting abortions, and they were the same reasons that women were having adoptions.

Usually money. The responses to this information didn't make sense to me. I was on the board at a crisis pregnancy center, because I wanted to help families. But the national pro-life movement wasn't doing anything about it. I am still uncomfortable with abortion, but I don't want to own anybody's choice. I want people to have options, and we need better parenting options. I became disillusioned with the pro-life movement because no one is involved in supporting parents—it's just about pushing adoption. . . . I just want to help people parent if that's what they want.

Gelin does not share Burns's discomfort with abortion. For her, it's very clear: "I've had an abortion and done an adoption. Abortion doesn't register on the scale. Adoption has devastated me."

When we spoke about a month after the *Dobbs* decision, Gelin was anxious about the potential increase in vulnerable mothers: "It's a very scary thought. We rely on the resources to help these parents be the kind of parent they want to be. With women being forced to carry pregnancies to term, you're creating more parents who need more resources. We do not have a system to support these families. We do not have the social structure. It's a huge concern. I was so anxious the other night that I couldn't sleep. What are we going to do? How are we going to find more housing?" Her long-term dream is an apartment complex with every stage of transitional housing, a commune of mothers who are all parenting without partners and can help each other. "It's about being a village."

Burns is right, after all, that some of the reasons women have abortions are not so different from many of the reasons women relinquish infants for adoption. (For both groups, the most common reasons are financial, along with not feeling like they were prepared to parent, or not wanting to share a child with their current partner.) Yet from a movement-level perspective, few elected officials that proclaim themselves "pro-life" seem to understand the ways that supporting parents might avert abortions.

When it comes to public policy, the states with abortion bans are the least likely to have a social safety net that supports mothers and families: they are unlikely to have paid family leave or expanded Medicaid, and they have higher rates of children living in poverty and both infant and maternal mortality. The same state governments that want to ban abortion don't seem inclined to want to make parenting any easier, either. As Katie Burns, the relinquishing mother who was active in the anti-abortion movement, describes: "The pro-life movement knows this, but they don't vote in a way that matches. They don't vote in a way that supports families. We are not a family-friendly country. There's political talk about how important family is, but if you need help keeping your family together, you're a bum or a leech on the system. But I don't see it that way. I see families in need that just hit a lot of dead ends."

The desire to parent that I found at the heart of many relinquishing mothers' stories is a narrative lost in the rhetorical contrast of abortion and adoption. More often than not, adoption is not about "saving babies" from abortion. Instead, adoption is about transferring infants from mothers that have become convinced—by virtue of their poverty, their youth, or their single status, or all three—that they are poorly prepared to parent. While adoption has been framed as the political common ground in the abortion debate, supporting people in parenting probably ought to have been the goal that both sides of the aisle rallied around.

Indeed, many of the types of reforms that work in the service of family preservation are widely about making parenting easier for *all* American families, and thus are often intuitive and popular. Most of the mothers I interviewed wanted to parent but could not afford it. How would they pay for stable housing, sufficient food, safe child care? The United States makes parenting uniquely untenable; parents in other developed countries do not grapple with these challenges in the same way. Of countries in the Organisation for Economic Co-operation and Development (OECD), the United States ranks among the *lowest* in spending on family benefits, child care, and early childhood education, and yet is above average on gross childcare fees as a percentage of average earnings.* (In contrast, countries that rank near the top of the OECD rankings—Iceland, Sweden, Norway, France, New Zealand—have among the lowest domestic relinquishment rates in the world.) The United States is also by far the worst on parental leave: while other OECD countries average just under fifty-two weeks (an entire year!) of guaranteed *paid* leave, the U.S. is the only country that does not guarantee any leave at all. In short: in the United States, parenting is more expensive, and you have less help. Independent of considerations about adoption, this toll makes parenting downright untenable for many. Many Americans are having fewer children than they want, or no children at all, simply because the cost is too high.

Yet even relatively modest investments in families can keep them together. Sociologist Sarah Cowan examined the impact of the Alaska Permanent Fund dividends, through which all Alaskans receive an annual cash payment. She found that household cash disbursements of $3,000 per year increased short-term fertility rates, especially among socioeconomically disadvantaged groups. When you give people the resources to make parenting just a bit easier, a bit more affordable, they have and raise the children that they want. Research has found that a 5 percent increase in food assistance reduced states' foster care caseloads by up to 14 percent, and that raising the minimum wage by just one

---

* None of this suggests that countries with stronger social safety nets don't have their share of challenges with adoption. Low numbers of domestic relinquishments often translate to high rates of transnational adoption; for many years, Scandinavian countries with very low domestic adoption (particularly Denmark and Sweden) had very high rates of children adopted from South Korea and Chile, for example. The work of Korean Swedish adoptee and critical adoption scholar Tobias Hübinette explores the dynamics of transracial and transnational adoption in these countries in particular depth.

dollar reduced child maltreatment reports by 10 percent. And there are bigger solutions to further address these inequities, if we are willing to deploy them: rental and mortgage assistance, public housing, family shelters; Head Start and early childhood education; expanded child tax credits. This list of policy priorities were all part of President Joe Biden's 2021 American Rescue Plan—and during the time they were in effect, they halved child poverty. This legislation is some of the most radical family preservation policy ever passed in the United States.*

We could decide to devote these resources to keeping families together. We've done it before in false starts and small steps, but we have the evidence to know it works. Yet we still allow our public spending to flow to anti-abortion crisis pregnancy centers, biased options counseling, and tax credits and subsidies for adoptive families. Indeed, the Adoption Tax Credit for adoptive families is as high as $16,000 per adoption (and increasing every year), and much of this credit can be claimed *even if the adoption is not completed.* In recent years, policymakers have made the Adoption Tax Credit refundable, pushing the budget line item to over $1 billion each year. Additionally, private philanthropic dollars pour into nonprofit adoption agencies, crisis pregnancy centers, and adoption marketing. A fraction of this combined public and private outpouring of money could render much of the adoption system moot.

An understanding of family preservation is essential to a reproductive justice framework for adoption. Yet this goal still cannot serve those who do not wish to continue their pregnancies and have no desire to parent. A reconsideration of adoption does not suggest that every pregnant person is ready or willing to be

---

* It is in this understanding of family preservation that the overlaps between private adoption systems and family policing systems are readily apparent, because efforts to limit the scale of either will limit the scale of both. It's important to note that there is far more organizing around family preservation and family policing abolition than there is around the private adoption system (see, for example, the Movement for Family Power, UpEND Movement, JMACforFamilies, and other organizing by impacted people).

a parent with just some more support; instead, it is premised on the necessity of abortion access—abortion that is not just legally available but affordable, local, supported, destigmatized. Some of the relinquishing mothers who did not fully consider abortion and wished they had said they were prevented from doing so because they believed misinformation about abortion: they thought abortion might jeopardize their future fertility, or that they might be traumatized or regretful about having an abortion. None of these beliefs are supported by our best evidence about abortion, but they still keep people—including many mothers who will go on to relinquish—from fully considering all of their choices. Indeed, a better understanding of adoption and the ways it fails to serve the women who relinquish should only strengthen the arguments for meaningful abortion access. Adopted people who have a commitment to reproductive justice understand this deeply, and often confront it when asked by flippant anti-abortion advocates, "Would you have rather been aborted?" any time they are critical of adoption. Stephanie Drenka, an internationally adopted person, offers this response: "The point is not whether I'm 'grateful' my birth mother didn't abort me; it is that she deserved to make her own choice." Reproductive justice allows us to sincerely value both family preservation and reproductive autonomy.

*   *   *

There are many organizers, most of them adopted people, who resist the very idea that ethical adoption practice is possible. They are adoption abolitionists.

Adoption abolition is rooted in many traditions including Black queer feminist socialism and Black Marxist thought, and is evolving in theoretical partnership with fellow abolitionist movements: prison and police abolition, border abolition, and of course, family policing abolition, as well as the broader dismantling of racial capitalism.

For many, the instinctive understanding of adoption abolition suggests either compulsory parenthood or the maintenance of children in unsafe or unloving homes, or both. But an adoption abolition framework isn't about banning adoption in the same way that the anti-abortion movement is about banning abortion. Amanda Transue-Woolston, a social worker and activist, describes this distinction:

> "Anti-adoption" is . . . a strawman used to suggest that any person who acknowledges problems or struggles in adoption must therefore not want children to have homes. . . . Literally no one argues for kids to not have homes. . . . People are more concerned about folks not ever saying anything bad about adoption than they are about adoption actually not being bad.

Abolition is about creating the conditions under which adoption, as it is practiced today, becomes obsolete. Specifically, it is about creating conditions under which families are not separated as a result of systemic oppression, coercion, and carceral systems, and in which children are not commodified and displaced for the benefit of others' family-making desires and a lucrative industry.

As abolitionist geographer Ruth Wilson Gilmore describes, "Abolition is about presence, not absence. It's about building life-affirming institutions." Adoption abolition, then, is rooted in the ideals of reproductive autonomy, family preservation, and community care, but it is also about creation and building something new. As writer, researcher, and abolitionist Liz Latty argues: "No one is saying there aren't people who can't or don't want to parent. Nor is anyone saying that harm does not happen to children in their families of origin. We're actually recognizing these experiences very deeply. We want to support existing and build new systems of care and kinship that do not continue and reinforce the harms caused by these industries and institutions."

Nearly all of the work building a movement for abolition is

done by adopted and formerly fostered people, who have come to it in different ways. (This leadership is in contrast to child welfare and family policing abolition organizing, which is often led by impacted parents.) Transnational adoptee Nicole Eigbrett reflects on her growing connection to that framework:

> I still have a lot to learn, but right now my journey has led me to be in the adoption abolitionist community. I recognize myself as part of a global community of people who have been displaced, stolen, and colonized. I want to work toward a world where adoption is no longer necessary. . . . Adoption has been incredibly normalized in this country, so rarely do you find people who aren't adoptees interrogating the historical context of transnational and transracial adoption, or the imperialism, colonialism, and state violence that makes adoption possible. As a transnational adoptee, I cannot unlink adoption from the U.S.'s global white supremacist imperialist project; from the foreign policy and the wars that lead to destabilization in other countries; from the profit-making adoption industry that followed. Everyone just wants a happy story, which often means that in order for the little brown child to be embraced by their new white family, their family and story of origin had to be erased. It assumes that the birth parents did not deserve or were not allowed to raise their child, and wouldn't receive rehabilitation or the resources they needed to be a thriving family. This is all a form of white supremacy.

Eigbrett is drawing connections not just to the abolitionist idea of "organized abandonment," but to a global movement of adopted and fostered people. In his essay "The New Abolition: Ending Adoption in Our Time," writer and scholar Daniel Drennan El-Awar reflects on global activist efforts: Korean adopted people fighting to shut down adoption in their country of origin; investigations into and repatriations of stolen children from Guatemala, Argentina, Spain; the reclamation of children in countries that were, for long periods of time, source countries for international adoption. He suggests: "I sense that we are reaching a crucial turning point both for adoptees and their families, as well as for source countries and their communities, in which the very institution of adoption is challenged and critiqued not in terms of its reform, but openly and honestly in terms of its abolition. . . . The time has thus come to structurally, culturally, economically, legally, and politically dismantle adoption."

This dismantlement includes a new orientation to how most Americans have come to understand the process of caring for children and families. Adoption abolitionist Joon Ae Haworth-Kaufka describes a series of abolition tactics: the decommodification of children and the categorization of for-profit adoption as human trafficking; the implementation of anti-racist and adoptee-led regulation of the adoption process; the preservation of the identities of adopted people (including access to original birth certificates and records); the banning of transracial adoption except under extreme circumstances; the broadening of understanding of adoption within contexts of colonialism and white supremacy; and, essentially, the centering of the voices of adopted people. These practices, along with the destigmatization of infertility, access to true reproductive healthcare (including sex education, birth control, and abortion), the prioritization of family preservation efforts (including housing, guaranteed basic income, compassionate addiction treatment, and anti-poverty measures), and the promotion of guardianship arrangements over full permanent adoption, all move us closer to a world without adoption as it is currently practiced.

For Benjamin Lundberg Torres Sánchez, an adoption abolitionist, the question of abolition is a simple one: "Can young people receive the care they need without being made a legal stranger to their families? We have the power to imagine the support structures that transform the material conditions that make adoption seem inevitable, and have to continue to raise our collective expectations of what is possible through organizing and popular education." They argue that many approaches to adoption reform (in contrast to abolition) are rooted in what makes adoption "feel better" and about what concessions power brokers can make—but not about a deeper rethinking of what people and families need. For Lundberg Torres Sánchez, this conception is not about reimagining but remembering: "What we're asking for is that everyone takes great care of each other. We don't primarily need to reimagine this as much as we'd need to dismantle everything that suppresses Indigenous, Black, Queer, and Crip ways of being, making, doing kinship. This is where a historical, dialectical materialist analysis rather than an idealist analysis is so critical. The practices for care have existed prior to this moment."

*   *   *

If we were to make contraceptive and abortion access real in this country, and if we were to make parenting truly tenable for those who want it—ambitions that, admittedly, seem very far away on this arc toward justice in our post-*Dobbs* nation—adoption would be exceedingly rare. And what of those in more dire circumstances? Parents who are homeless or incarcerated when their children are born? Or have an addiction to drugs and are unable to care for themselves, let alone a newborn? Or are facing a mental health crisis that compromises their ability to parent safely? Or are trapped in an abusive relationship with a partner that could be dangerous to their child? I have shared stories of women in all of these circumstances throughout this book. What would happen to them if we actually built the systems that could support and serve them? These challenges are why reproductive justice is the necessary movement in which to reconsider adoption, as it not only "demands that the state . . . not unduly interfere with women's reproductive decision-making, but it also insists that the state had an obligation to help create the conditions for women to exercise their decisions without co-ercion and with social supports." It envisions a world with paths to justice other than incarceration, with paths to healthcare that are affordable and meaningful, with paths to safety that include not just a child, but their parents, too. And for those who are still not able to parent, it offers something other than the policing, separation, and shame of the current family regulation system, and something other than the full permanent transfer of parent-ing rights and gaslighting of the current private adoption sys-tem—it embraces supported crisis care, kinship arrangements, and temporary guardianships that leave open opportunities for reconciliation and reconnection with families and communities of origin.

When I began this project nearly fifteen years ago, I had very little sense of how these mothers' stories might unfold, no political agenda with regard to adoption, and no credible sus-picion that *Roe v. Wade* would be overturned before this book was finished. The world I have worked to document is already changing as I finish writing, and there is, as ever, more work and research to be done. For example, I interviewed only two relinquishing fathers, and their stories are not included here; they remain an important variable in understanding the context and practice of domestic adoption. There is also an open ques-tion of what adoption will look like in this post-*Dobbs* world in which access to abortion is curtailed and denied, as we face the prospect of relinquishments meaningfully increasing for the first time in several generations. Many of these questions will not be mine to answer, and I look forward to more scholarship (and more knowledge generation rooted outside of traditional academic spaces) led by adopted people and relinquishing par-ents that explores the costs and consequences of adoption in this country, and more advocacy led by impacted people that makes overt the connections between private adoption and the family regulation system as well as the historic and ongoing legacies of family policing and separation. This book is just one part of expanding understandings of adoption developing not just in traditional academic spaces, but in the organizing made possible when impacted people are able to find each other in an increasingly interconnected world. In this necessary work, I hope the experiences of parents who have relinquished infants for adoption—along with adopted people—will be centered.

This book may be uncomfortable reading for those who have never considered the practice of adoption deeply, and especially those whose families have been happily formed by adoption. But neither the solidity, safety, and love of many adoptive families nor the stories of those happy adoptions negate that adoption is a practice rooted in inequity. If we understand adoption as a practice intended to meet the needs of children and not the dreams of would-be parents, then the desires of those who wish to become parents through adoption are not truly relevant to whether adoption, as it is currently practiced, should continue to exist. Relinquishing parents do not owe anyone their child.

Ultimately, adoption is an inherently conservative institution, one that represents a refusal to both support and care for American families at the most basic level, and one that precludes the conditions that make reproductive freedom possible. It is conservative in that it upholds regressive narratives about what types of people are worthy parents (who are, *most often,* white heteronormative nuclear families with financial stability)—but it is also conservative in that it offers a private solution to public challenges and shortfalls. Rather than supporting vulnerable families with a real and robust social safety net, it instead facilitates the transfer of infants and children. If we lived in a more equitable world, a world shaped by reproductive justice, adoption would fade into obsolescence and be viewed as a social and systemic failure. Having heard the stories of these relinquishing mothers, we can and must do better for them and their children.

Appendix A

Study Methodology

This research draws on the lived experiences of American women who relinquished infants for domestic adoption between 2000 and 2020, with data collection via in-depth qualitative interviews.

2010 Cohort. In early 2010, as part of my doctoral dissertation, I conducted open-ended interviews with forty mothers whose adoptions occurred between 1962 and 2009. These women were initially recruited through in-person and online support groups and message boards, with additional snowball sampling (interpersonal referrals from other participants). Of these women that I interviewed in 2010, seventeen of them had relinquished between 2000 and 2010. In late 2020, I reached out to all of them to ask if they would be willing to be interviewed again. After contacting them via email, all seventeen women agreed to speak with me again. The focus of this book is on adoptions that occurred since 2000, but all of the interviews conducted in 2010—including those with women whose adoptions occurred earlier—have informed my analysis.

2020 Cohort. At the same time that I recontacted and reinterviewed the subsample of 2010 participants, I recruited an additional cohort of sixty mothers who had relinquished *since* 2010. As in 2010, these participants were recruited via online groups for birth parents. These groups were purposively chosen to include a range of geographies and approaches to support. Some were professionally facilitated groups associated with adoption agencies or churches; some were local chapters of larger groups; many were small local groups that seemed to be unaffiliated with other organizations. Some were volunteer-led; others were professionally facilitated.

For both cohorts, the request for participants spread beyond these groups. Ultimately, participants reported finding out about the study from eight different online groups (four birth mother support groups that were unaffiliated with any organization, two that were affiliated directly with the organizations I contacted, two that were affiliated with adoption agencies), several group email listservs, several adoption agency listservs, and numerous personal contacts (either previous participants who shared with other birth parents they knew, or others in the adoption community who saw the call for participants and forwarded it to their personal network without responding themselves). It is clear that the call for participants spread organically through these groups, as many of these are open only to those who identify as birth mothers or who have placed infants through a specific agency. Many mothers in the 2010 cohort reported that they were no longer active in online groups, either because the agency-sponsored message boards had been closed or because they no longer felt the community was relevant to their lives. Additionally, because these groups represented a range of ideologies around adoption—with several promoting and embracing adoption, and others being more critical—the use of these groups as sites of recruitment should not suggest that these women are particularly more in need of support than other relinquishing mothers.

Interviews. Initial interviews for the 2010 cohort were done in person, when possible, or over the phone. All 2020 interviews were completed via phone, due to the COVID pandemic. Interviews generally last 90 to 120 minutes (follow-up interviews were shorter).

Participants. My sample included seventy-seven people who

relinquished infants for domestic private adoption between 2000 and 2020, including seventeen that I interviewed in both 2010 and 2020. Four participants relinquished infants from multiple pregnancies. The majority of participants were white (n=55); seven identified as Latina, five as Black, two as Asian American, and eight as bi/multiracial (including several with Indigenous/Native backgrounds, but only one an enrolled tribal member). Eighteen participants were adopted themselves (with experiences with private adoption, foster care, and stepparent adoption). One participant identified as nonbinary but did use the word "mother" to describe themself. At the time of their adoptions, participants ranged in age from sixteen to forty-three years old, and their adoptions occurred in twenty-seven different states.

I have changed or removed all names and identifying information for participants throughout the book, with the exception of one participant who chose to be identified so that I could include discussion of her public advocacy and scholarship. Advocates and scholars who have shared their thoughts, stories, and expertise in non-research-participant capacities are identified by name.

Participants were paid for their participation in this research in appreciation of their time and recognition of their contribution to this work and scholarship.

This research was approved by the Boston College Institutional Review Board (2010) and the University of California, San Francisco, Institutional Review Board (2020).

Appendix B

A Note on Adoption Language

Language around adoption creates chasms: people with similar experiences are divided between those who stand proudly with a given descriptor and those who consider that same word a slur.

For example, some of the women I have interviewed like the term "birth mother," feeling it is an accurate, neutral descriptor. Others prefer "first mother" or "natural mother," but aren't offended by "birth mother." Some consider "birth mother" an outright insult. There is similar contention around the word used to describe the act of terminating one's parental rights so that a child will be adopted by other people. Women who feel they were constrained, pressured, and coerced into their adoptions prefer the words "relinquishment" or "surrender" over "choice"; others prefer the word "placement" as reflective of their intentionality.

These debates about word choice are not new and are often a reflection of the gap between "positive adoption language" (PAL), as formalized in 1979 by adoption social worker Marietta Spencer, and "honest adoption language" (HAL), a counterpoint framework proposed in 2003 by the nonprofit organization Origins Canada. Most adoption agencies rely heavily on PAL, using words such as "placed for adoption" or "made an adoption plan" to focus on the legal legitimacy of adoption, convey adoption as the choice of the birth parent, and attempt to reduce stigma or prejudice associated with adoptive families.

* * *

In contrast, HAL was developed by adopted and birth/first parent advocates who feel PAL is inherently coercive and leads to erasure, and that HAL better reflects the experiences of many women who surrender children for adoption. This framework conveys that "birth parents" are legitimate (if not legal) parents, that adoption is rarely a freely made decision, and that the mother does not regularly have agency within the adoption process. Karen Wilson-Buterbaugh, the executive director of both the Baby Scoop Era Research Initiative and Origins International, wrote in her book *The Baby Scoop Era* that PAL has "proven to be a useful tool for the Adoption Industry and people who adopt to reframe adoption in such a way as to make it more socially palatable to the public. However, this more recent 'redefining' also renders invisible some inconvenient truths which should be held under greater social scrutiny, and dismisses the experiences of many who have been affected by this industry."

In 2010, the website of the National Council for Adoption endorsed PAL as choosing "emotionally 'correct' words over emotionally laden words. We speak and write in appropriate adoption language with the hopes of influencing others so that this language will someday be the norm." But norms change, even at the NCFA. By 2018, the NCFA website acknowledged that there was room for a wider range of "accurate" language around adoption: "Of course, 'accurate' language is subjective and always evolving, and you should choose words that are both accurate and feel right to you."

Over the years, many birth/first/relinquishing mothers have alternately embraced, accepted, or tolerated the name "birth mother," while others have rejected it completely. The advocacy group Concerned United Birthparents (CUB) was founded in 1976 to organize mothers who relinquished infants during the 1950s and '60s, and originally coined the term "birth mother." Yet many CUB members today are critical of this phrase (though the organization still uses this word in their name). Karen Wilson-Buterbaugh considers the term "birth mother" offensive and argues that it negates and denies the existence of an ongoing relationship between mother and child post-surrender, working to create "exiled" mothers. In contrast, BraveLove, the "pro-adoption movement" founded online in 2012 by an adoptive mother, fully celebrates the language of "birth mom." Many younger women that I have interviewed similarly feel comfortable with the term.

Given this history, it is impossible to respectfully use the same words to describe these groups, and I do not try to do so. Instead, I specifically asked all the participants their thoughts about the words used to describe them. If a person expressed a clear preference for a name that describes their relationship to adoption, I have followed that choice. Thus, you will see "birth mother," "natural mother," "first mother," and "relinquishing mother" used throughout the text. I have also chosen to write "birth mother" as two words, rather than one; I similarly use "adoptive mother" to describe women who have legal parental rights via adoption. I hope, with this context, that "birth" and "adoptive" are understood as descriptors indicating the relationship of a woman and an adopted person, and that these word choices do *not imply* that birth mothers' sole relationship to their child is limited to a biological one. I have similarly tried to mirror participants' own language choices with regard to "placement," "relinquishment," and "surrender." I avoid referring to pregnant women as "birth/first mothers," and use that phrase only to describe women whose parental rights have already been terminated.

* * *

I am also aware of language around the children placed for adoption, who, of course, do not remain children. The continual referring to people who are adopted as "adopted children" can be viewed as an ongoing infantilization of them. Unless I am speaking about a child, I try to use "adopted person" (or occasionally "adoptee" if I know the person to whom I am referring is comfortable with that word). If a parent-child relationship needs to be made clear, I use "adopted son/daughter/child" to describe an adopted person, but those terms are meant to convey familial relationships, and not youth.

The language used within state systems is an additional challenge. Wording such as "child protective" or "child welfare" services suggests that protection and welfare are indeed the primary purposes of such agencies. But my research (and to a far greater degree, the organizing and scholarship of many others) sees the harms and separations inherent in this work. Thus I chose to use "family regulation" or "family policing" systems, using "child protective services" or "child welfare agencies" only when specifically discussing named agencies, organizations, or legislation that uses this language.

Finally, my words throughout the text are often gendered (using "women" and "mother"). I do not mean to erase the experiences of nonbinary or transgender people who have given birth and relinquished their parental rights. However, I do want to acknowledge that my research has been primarily on women (with one nonbinary participant, who still used the word "mother" to describe themself), that most of the sources I cite specifically use gendered language and their research was limited to women, and that the systems that underlie adoption relinquishment are heavily rooted in ideas of gender and motherhood, specifically.

Acknowledgments

I must first express my deepest gratitude to the mothers who shared their stories with me; I hope I have been a worthy steward.

This book would not have been brought to the world without the insight of Elisabeth Dyssegaard at St. Martin's Press and Tanya McKinnon and her team at McKinnon Literary, all of whom immediately and intuitively understood the story I wanted to tell and the urgency with which I felt it needed to be shared. Renee Bracey Sherman not only made all these connections possible but has been an essential partner in my thinking on reproductive justice and one of my dearest friends. Dani McClain, with deep expertise and thoughtful editorial skill, helped ensure I was able to deliver this book with an alacrity that would not otherwise have been possible. Lisa Munro and Chris Vogel were essential to mitigating the disaster that was the first draft of my citations.

I am perpetually appreciative of my brilliant colleagues at Advancing New Standards in Reproductive Health (ANSIRH) at the University of California, San Francisco, including Molly Battistelli, Lori Freedman, Heather Gould, Diana Greene Foster, Daniel Grossman, Stephanie Herold, and Carole Joffe, and for the mentorship of Tracy Weitz. Thank you to Peggy Fledderjohn and her incredible team for transcribing all my many hours of interviews so diligently. My former colleagues from the Massachusetts Alliance on Teen Pregnancy—most particularly Patricia Quinn and Natasha Vianna—shaped my early thinking on this project more than they know.

I am very grateful to the Society of Family Planning, the David and Lucile Packard Foundation, and an anonymous funder for supporting my work on adoption for the last many years.

The production of knowledge is always a collective effort, and this book draws on over a decade of conversations, collaborations, and research. I am indebted to many other researchers and advocates who have shaped my understanding of adoption, relinquishment, and reproductive justice. My research draws on the prior work of many scholars and writers, most notably Laura Briggs, Ann Fessler, Laury Oaks, Dorothy Roberts, and Rickie Solinger, and the reporting of Kathryn Joyce and Rebecca Nagle; I encourage interested readers to engage with their work. I am very especially grateful for the thought partnership of Laura Callen, Jessica Harrison, Liz Latty, Benjamin Lundberg Torres Sánchez, Kate Livingston, and Angie Swanson-Kyriaco. This appreciation extends to the many mothers and adopted people who have provided reflections and expertise throughout the course of my studies of adoption: Janine Baer, Katie Burns, Sarah Burns, Claudia Corrigan D'Arcy, Tony Corsentino, Renee Gelin, Rebekah Henson, Rachel Herndon, Susan Ito, Gregory Luce, Susan Dusza Guerra Leksander, Leslie Pate Mackinnon, Kat Nielsen, Samantha Shields, Lisa Marie Simmons, Amanda Transue-Woolston, and Lina Vanegas. I have strived to elevate the work of adopted scholars and writers throughout this book; they include: Amanda Baden, Rebecca Carroll, Nicole Chung, Daniel Drennan ElAwar, Susan Devan Harness, Tobias Hübinette, Tiffany HyeonBrooks, Ann Fessler, JaeRan Kim, Betty Jean Lifton, Kathryn Mariner, Kimberly McKee, Michele Merritt, Elizabeth Raleigh, Angela Tucker, and others. My thinking has also benefitted immensely from reading memoirs by Candice Cahill, Melissa Guida-Richards, Jenny Heijun Wills, Harrison Mooney, and Lauren Sharkey. I am further grateful to many adopted voices that I know only on social media (Twitter, Instagram, and TikTok) whose work has been important to my thinking.

Thank you to Valentin Bolotnyy, Elizabeth Corman, Sarah Cowan, Parker Dockray, Poonam Dreyfus-Pai, Jaclyn Friedman, Alison Kiehl Friedman, Will Hemmings, Jenny 8. Lee, Jake Maguire, Jim McCollum, Sally McCollum, Malinda Seymore, and Carmel Shachar. As always, my endless gratitude for my friendships with Catherine Downs, Sarah Hudson, Stephanie Lee, Zoe Mercer-Golden, and Lauren Snyder; they variously provided support, feedback, food, and comic relief throughout the writing process. Many more thanks to Lindsay Lassman and Elena Lewis for helping make space in my life and calendar to finish this project.

To Sandra Resendez, every day, for helping me be the best researcher and mother I can be—this book could not have happened without her. To my parents for their love and support; to my sister, Meredith, for always being my first and best editor. To my husband, Andrew, for the partner he has always been. And to my children: it is because my love for you is both infinite and unremarkable that I have been able to understand these stories on the deepest level, and because of you that I can never stop working for a more just world.

Notes

Introduction

2 *In recent years, only about 19,000 women:* Gretchen Sisson, "Estimating the Annual Domestic Adoption Rate and Lifetime Incidence of Infant Relinquishment in the United States," *Contraception* 105 (2022): 14–18.

3 *Just a few years earlier:* Ann Fessler, *The Girls Who Went Away: The Hidden History of Women Who Surrendered Children for Adoption in the Decades Before* Roe v. Wade (New York: Penguin, 2006).

4 *The show's reality TV lens:* Jessica Grose, "Does MTV's *16 and Pregnant* Keep Girls from Getting Pregnant?" *Slate,* February 22, 2010, https://slate.com/human-interest/2010/02/can-the-mtv-reality-show-16-and-pregnant-keep-teens-from-conceiving.html.

5 *most people seeking abortions:* Guttmacher Institute, "Induced Abortion in the United States," September 2019, https://www.guttmacher.org/fact-sheet/induced-abortion-united-states.

5 *On an anniversary of* Roe v. Wade: Obama White House Archives, "Statement by the President on *Roe v. Wade* Anniversary" (Washington, DC, 2012).

5 *a decade later President Donald Trump:* Ed Lavandera, Jeremy Harlan, and Wayne Drash, "Trump Honors Police Officer Who Adopted Baby from Mom Addicted to Heroin," CNN Health, February 7, 2018, www.cnn.com/2018/01/30/health/police-officer-trump-state-of-the-union-opioid-crisis/index.html.

5 *The March for Life's 2014 theme:* March for Life, "Adoption: A Noble Decision," March for Life, 2014, https://marchforlife.org/adoption-a-noble-decision.

5 *the Supreme Court case allowing gay marriage:* Melissa Murray, "One Is the Loneliest Number: The Complicated Legacy of Obergefell v. Hodges," *Hastings Law Journal* 70, no. 5 (2018): 1263–72.

6 *The Congressional Coalition on Adoption:* Congressional Coalition on Adoption Institute, "CCA Members," CCA Institute, https://www.ccainstitute.org/congress-caucus/cca-members.

6 *To the extent that adoption has been understood:* Liz Latty, "Adoption Is a Feminist Issue, but Not for the Reasons You Think," The Establishment, April 19, 2017, https://theestablishment.co/adoption-is-a-feminist-issue-but-not-for-the-reasons-you-think-93ba3824bcbb/.

6 *Justice Amy Coney Barrett asked:* Supreme Court of the United States, oral argument, *Dobbs v. Jackson Women's Health Organization,* Washington, DC, December 1,

2021, https://www.supremecourt.gov/oral_arguments/argument_transcripts/2021
/19–1392_4425.pdf.

1. The Domestic Suppliers of Infants

13 *She was furious when she realized the* **Roe** *case:* Norma McCorvey with Andy
Meisler, *I Am Roe: My Life, Roe v. Wade, and Freedom of Choice* (New York: Harper-
Collins, 1994), 127–28.

14 *"Then she handed me the baby":* McCorvey with Meisler, *I Am Roe,* 131.

14 *"I spent years searching":* Norma McCorvey with Gary Thomas, *Won by Love:
Norma McCorvey, Jane Roe of Roe v. Wade, Speaks Out for the Unborn as She Shares
Her New Conviction for Life* (Nashville, TN: Thomas Nelson Publishers, 1997), 29.

14 *"My heart melted":* McCorvey with Thomas, *Won by Love,* 106.

15 *"I am a rough woman":* McCorvey with Meisler, *I Am Roe,* 3.

15 *her late-in-life confession:* AKA Jane Roe, directed by Nick Sweeney (FX,
May 22, 2020), https://www.hulu.com/series/aka-jane-roe.

16 *During the* **Dobbs** *oral arguments:* Supreme Court of the United States, oral
argument, *Dobbs v. Jackson Women's Health Organization,* Washington, DC, December 1, 2021, https://www.supremecourt.gov/oral_arguments/argument_transcripts
/2021/19–1392_4425.pdf.

17 *To understand contemporary adoption:* Some of the arguments in this section
draw on those I made previously in an article in *The Washington Post* ("Alito Touted
Adoption as a Silver Lining for Women Denied Abortions") on July 6, 2022.

17 *"Still holding me in her arms":* As cited in Walter Johnson, *Soul by Soul: Life
Inside the Antebellum Slave Market* (Cambridge, MA: Harvard University Press,
1999), 35.

17 *an estimated half of all slave trades:* Anita Sinha, "A Lineage of Family Separation," *Brooklyn Law Review* 87, no. 2 (2022).

17 *"When my master found that":* Harriet A. Jacobs, *Incidents in the Life of a
Slave Girl,* Project Gutenberg, 1861, https://www.gutenberg.org/cache/epub/11030
/pg11030-images.html.

17 *former slave owners argued:* Laura Briggs, *Taking Children: A History of American Terror* (Oakland: University of California Press, 2020).

18 *They could rarely hide well enough:* Brianna Theobald, *Reproduction on the
Reservation: Pregnancy, Childbirth, and Colonialism in the Long Twentieth Century*
(Chapel Hill: University of North Carolina Press, 2019).

18 *the children faced abuse and coercive assimilation:* Andrea Smith, *Conquest:
Sexual Violence and American Indian Genocide* (Durham, NC: Duke University
Press, 2015).

18 *In an infamous 1892 speech:* Richard Henry Pratt, "'Kill the Indian in him,
and save the man': R. H. Pratt on the Education of Native Americans," Carlisle
Indian School Digital Resource Center, Dickinson College, https://carlisleindian
.dickinson.edu/teach/kill-indian-him-and-save-man-r-h-pratt-education-native
-americans.

18 *One such child was Hazelle:* "Hazelle Boxberg," National Orphan Train Complex Museum and Research Center, https://orphantraindepot.org/wp-content/uploads
/2021/08/Hazelle-Boxberg.pdf.

18 *As Charles Loring Brace, founder of the New York Children's Aid Society:*
For more on the Orphan Trains, Charles Loring Brace, and the Children's Aid So-
ciety, see: Marilyn Irvin Holt, *The Orphan Trains: Placing Out in America* (Lincoln:
University of Nebraska Press, 1992); Viviana A. Rotman Zelizer, *Pricing the Priceless*

Child: The Changing Social Value of Children (Princeton, NJ: Princeton University Press, 1994).

19 **As sociologist Viviana Zelizer states:** Zelizer, *Pricing the Priceless Child,* 171.

19 **"The woods are full of people eager to adopt":** Both quotes from the Boston probate court judge and *The New York Times* are in Zelizer, *Pricing the Priceless Child,* 190.

20 **As gender studies and adoption scholar Laura Briggs chronicles:** The full quote, from Laura Briggs's *Somebody's Children: The Politics of Transracial and Transnational Adoption* (Durham, NC: Duke University Press, 2012), reads:

> "In fact, every generation in the twentieth century faced a 'baby famine.' In the 1920s, adoptable children were said to be so scarce that in 1929 the *Philadelphia Record* ran a front-page banner headline that read: 'Chronicle of a Search for a Homeless Waif in Philadelphia—Where There Aren't Any.' In the 1930s Paul Beisser, president of the Child Welfare League of America, [testified] . . . that on average there were twelve applicants for every adoptable child in the United States. In the 1950s, similarly, when the American Child Welfare League first began placing children with disabilities, the organization justified 'special needs' adoptions again because of the shortages in available (nondisabled) infants. In 1955, Estes Kefauver said, in opening the hearings on 'black market' adoption: 'There has been tremendous increase over the last 10 years in the demand for children for adoption. As a result, the demand has far exceeded the number of babies available.'" [6–7]

20 **Into this opportunity for profit stepped Georgia Tann:** The stories of Irene Green, Grace Gribble, and Mary Owens are all drawn from Barbara Bisantz Raymond's incisive history, *The Baby Thief: The Untold Story of Georgia Tann, The Baby Seller Who Corrupted Adoption* (New York: Carroll & Graf, 2007).

20 **Over the course of her career:** Briggs, *Somebody's Children.*

21 **After World War II, the United States:** Elaine Tyler May, *Homeward Bound: American Families in the Cold War Era* (New York: Basic Books, 1988).

21 **In contrast to baby farmers of the 1870s:** Zelizer, *Pricing the Priceless Child.*

21 **about 4 million American infants were relinquished:** Penelope L. Maza, "Adoption Trends: 1944–1975," Child Welfare Research Notes #9, U.S. Children's Bureau, August 1984, 1–4, Child Welfare League of America Papers, Box 65, Folder "Adoption—Research—Reprints of Articles," Social Welfare History Archives, University of Minnesota.

21 **a collision of social factors:** Sandra L. Hofferth, Joan R. Kahn, and Wendy Baldwin, "Premarital Sexual Activity Among U.S. Teenage Women over the Past Three Decades," *Family Planning Perspectives* 19, no. 2 (1987): 46–53; May, *Homeward Bound*; Rickie Solinger, *Wake Up Little Susie: Single Pregnancy and Race Before Roe v. Wade* (New York: Routledge, 1992).

22 **"One of the questions that come up":** Ann Fessler, *The Girls Who Went Away: The Hidden History of Women Who Surrendered Children for Adoption in the Decades Before Roe v. Wade* (New York: Penguin, 2006), 188.

22 **But they were framed as a path toward redemption:** Solinger, *Wake Up Little Susie.*

23 **while nearly 9 percent of all infants born:** Christine A. Bachrach, Kathy Shepherd Stolley, and Kathryn A. London, "Relinquishment of Premarital Births: Evidence from National Survey Data," *Family Planning Perspectives* 24, no. 1 (1992): 27–32, 48.

23 **there was also less of a market for Black babies:** Leslie J. Reagan, *When Abortion Was a Crime: Women, Medicine, and Law in the United States, 1867–1973* (Berkeley: University of California Press, 2022); Briggs, *Taking Children.*

23 ***Most white prospective parents:*** Ellen Herman, *Kinship by Design: A History of Adoption in the Modern United States* (Chicago: University of Chicago Press, 2008).

23 ***Those separations were more rooted in punishment:*** Briggs, *Somebody's Children.*

23 ***The 1950s and '60s also saw the systematic removal of Native children:*** Lauren van Schilfgaarde, "Native Reproductive Justice: Practices and Policies from Relinquishment to Family Preservation," Bill of Health, the Petrie-Flom Center Staff, Harvard Law School, May 12, 2022, https://blog.petrieflom.law.harvard.edu/2022/05/12/native-reproductive-justice-adoption-relinquishment-family-preservation/.

23 ***Anthropologist Susan Devan Harness:*** Susan Devan Harness, "Voices of Indian Adoption," Bill of Health, Petrie-Flom Center Staff, Harvard Law School, May 12, 2022, https://blog.petrieflom.law.harvard.edu/2022/05/12/voices-of-indian-adoption/.

24 ***"I am now in my homeland":*** Susan Devan Harness, *Bitterroot: A Salish Memoir of Transracial Adoption* (Lincoln: University of Nebraska Press, 2018), 290.

24 ***Adoption historian Ellen Herman chronicles:*** Herman, *Kinship by Design,* 287–88.

24 ***the National Association of Black Social Workers issued a statement:*** National Association of Black Social Workers, "Position Statement on Trans-Racial Adoptions," September 1972, https://cdn.ymaws.com/nabsw.site-ym.com/resource/collection/E1582D77-E4CD-4104-996A-D42D08F9CA7D/NABSW_Trans-Racial_Adoption_1972_Position_(b).pdf.

24 ***the Indian Child Welfare Act (ICWA) was enacted:*** Kathryn E. Fort, "The Indian Child Welfare Act: Preserving Families Is in Children's Best Interests," Bill of Health, Petrie-Flom Center Staff, Harvard Law School, May 12, 2022, https://blog.petrieflom.law.harvard.edu/2022/05/12/the-indian-child-welfare-act-preserving-families-is-in-childrens-best-interests/.

25 ***the domestic adoption rates were at an all-time low:*** Bachrach, Stolley, and London, "Relinquishment of Premarital Births"; Anjani Chandra, Joyce Abma, Penelope Maza, and Christine Bachrach, "Adoption, Adoption Seeking, and Relinquishment for Adoption in the United States," *Advance Data* No. 306 (May 11, 1999): 1–16.

25 ***These efforts were reinforced federally:*** Dorothy E. Roberts, *Torn Apart: How the Child Welfare System Destroys Black Families—and How Abolition Can Build a Safer World* (New York: Basic Books, 2022).

25 ***Legal scholar Dorothy Roberts tells the story of Valerie:*** Dorothy E. Roberts, *Shattered Bonds: The Color of Child Welfare* (New York: Basic Books, 2002).

26 ***international adoption into the U.S. doubled:*** "International Adoption Rate in U.S. Doubled in the 1990s," Population Reference Bureau, January 13, 2003, https://www.prb.org/resources/international-adoption-rate-in-u-s-doubled-in-the-1990s/.

26 ***Most of these adopted people:*** Laura Briggs, "Feminism and Transnational Adoption: Poverty, Precocity, and the Politics of Raising (Other People's?) Children," *Feminist Theory* 13, no. 1 (2012): 81–100.

26 ***as countries limited the exporting of their children for a variety of reasons:*** Sarah Neville and Karen Smith Rotabi, "Developments in U.S. Intercountry Adoption Policy Since Its Peak in 2004," *Adoption Quarterly* 23, no. 1 (2020): 63–83.

26 ***The culture around international adoption also shifted:*** Amanda Baden, "Intercountry Adoption: The Beginning of the End," Rudd Adoption Research Program,

University of Massachusetts, Amherst, 2019, https://www.umass.edu/ruddchair/sites/default/files/rudd.baden.pdf.

26 *in line with the recommendations of the United Nations Convention on the Rights of the Child:* Neville and Rotabi, "Developments in U.S. Intercountry Adoption Policy Since Its Peak in 2004."

26 *By 2020, there were only 1,622 children:* "Adoption Statistics," U.S. Department of State, Bureau of Consular Affairs, https://travel.state.gov/content/travel/en/Intercountry-Adoption/adopt_ref/adoption-statistics-esri.html.

26 *"negroes are themselves both perverse and comparatively indifferent":* As cited in Sinha, "A Lineage of Family Separation."

27 *Even the Freedmen's Bureau:* Briggs, *Taking Children.*

27 *The Orphan Trains were run:* Holt, *The Orphan Trains.*

27 *"There entered a God-given purpose in my heart":* Regina G. Kunzel, *Fallen Women, Problem Girls: Unmarried Mothers and the Professionalization of Social Work, 1890–1945* (New Haven: Yale University Press, 1993), 9.

28 *The echoes of Native boarding schools:* Amy Littlefield and Tina Vasquez, "Amid Chaos, Bethany Christian Services Raises Money Off Child Separations," Rewire News Group, July 6, 2018, https://rewirenewsgroup.com/article/2018/07/06/amid-chaos-bethany-christian-services-raises-money-off-child-separations/.

29 *the Trump administration used the legal precedents:* Maggie Blackhawk, "The Indian Law That Helps Build Walls," *The New York Times,* May 26, 2019, https://www.nytimes.com/2019/05/26/opinion/american-indian-law-trump.html.

29 *at times of crises it reemerges:* Kathryn Joyce, K. "Ukraine's Kids and Adoption: Will an Ugly History Repeat Itself?" *Salon,* March 22, 2022, https://www.salon.com/2022/03/22/ukraines-kids-latest-target-for-the-christian-adoption-industry/; Karla Zabludovsky, "Most Children in Haitian Orphanages Aren't Orphans—But US Missionaries Take Them Away from Their Families," *BuzzFeed,* February 7, 2022, https://www.buzzfeednews.com/article/karlazabludovsky/missionaries-orphanages-haiti; Alan Cooperman, "For Tsunami Orphans, a Christian Home," NBC News, January 12, 2005, https://www.nbcnews.com/id/wbna6819471.

29 *Even the definition of "orphan" endures:* "Orphan Process," U.S. Citizenship and Immigration Services, https://www.uscis.gov/adoption/immigration-through-adoption/orphan-process.

29 *Critical adoption scholar Kimberly McKee describes these:* Kimberly D. McKee, "White Supremacy, Christian Americanism, and Adoption," *Adoption and Culture* 9, no. 1 (2021): 84–111.

31 *I found that the number of adoptions represented approximately 0.5 percent of all births:* Gretchen Sisson, "Estimating the Annual Domestic Adoption Rate and Lifetime Incidence of Infant Relinquishment in the United States," *Contraception* 105 (2022): 14–18.

32 *For most of the 1990s, researchers found that:* Bachrach, Stolley, and London, "Relinquishment of Premarital Births"; Brenda W. Donnelly and Patricia Voydanoff, "Factors Associated with Releasing for Adoption Among Adolescent Mothers," *Family Relations* 40, no. 4 (1991): 404–10; Newlyn B. Moore and J. Kenneth Davidson Sr., "A Profile of Adoption Placers: Perceptions of Pregnant Teens During the Decision-Making Process," *Adoption Quarterly* 6, no. 2 (2002): 29–41; Pearila Brickner Namerow, Debra S. Kalmuss, and Linda F. Cushman, "The Determinants of Young Women's Pregnancy-Resolution Choices," *Journal of Research on Adolescence* 3, no. 2 (1993): 193–215; Linda F. Cushman, Debra Kalmuss, and Pearila B.

Namerow, "Placing an Infant for Adoption: The Experiences of Young Birthmothers," *Social Work* 38, no. 3 (1993): 264–72.

32 *does not seem to reflect relinquishing mothers today:* Gretchen Sisson, "Who Are the Women Who Relinquish Infants for Adoption? Domestic Adoption and Contemporary Birth Motherhood in the United States," *Perspectives on Sexual and Reproductive Health* 54, no. 2 (2022): 46–53, https://onlinelibrary.wiley.com/doi/abs /10.1363/psrh.12193.

33 *Compared to data for all American births:* "Quick Facts," U.S. Census Bureau, https://www.census.gov/quickfacts/fact/table/US/PST045221.

33 *the rate of Medicaid coverage for all women:* Joyce A. Martin et al., "Births: Final Data for 2018," *National Vital Statistics Reports* 68, no. 13: 1–47, https://stacks .cdc.gov/view/cdc/82909.

34 *In her work looking at the experiences of mothers in the baby scoop era:* Rickie Solinger, *Beggars and Choosers: How the Politics of Choice Shapes Adoption, Abortion, and Welfare in the United States* (New York: Hill and Wang, 2001), 67.

35 *In a 2014 report:* Ryan Anderson and Sarah Torre, "Adoption, Foster Care, and Conscience Protection," Heritage Foundation, January 15, 2014, https://www .heritage.org/marriage-and-family/report/adoption-foster-care-and-conscience -protection.

35 *Due to legal requirements:* Ryan Morgenegg, "LDS Family Services No Longer Operating as Adoption Agency," Church of Jesus Christ of Latter-day Saints, July 1, 2014, https://www.churchofjesuschrist.org/church/news/lds-family-services-no -longer-operating-as-adoption-agency; Kathryn Joyce, "Why Is the Mormon Church Getting Out of the Adoption Business?" *The Daily Beast,* June 23, 2014, https:// www.thedailybeast.com/why-is-the-mormon-church-getting-out-of-the-adoption -business; "Pausing New Infant Adoption Applications," Bethany Christian Services, June 27, 2022, https://bethany.org/help-a-child/adoption/us-infant-adoption.

35 *In her 2013 book* The Child Catchers: Kathryn Joyce, *The Child Catchers: Rescue, Trafficking, and the New Gospel of Adoption* (New York: PublicAffairs, 2013), xii.

36 *Moore argues that adoption is a way of living the gospel:* Russell Moore, *Adopted for Life: The Priority of Adoption for Christian Families and Churches* (Wheaton, IL: Crossway Books, 2009).

36 *In fact, they often have living parents:* E. J. Graff, "The Lie We Love," *Foreign Policy,* October 6, 2009, https://foreignpolicy.com/2009/10/06/the-lie-we-love/.

36 *Looking specifically at the crisis in Haiti:* This analysis of the Haiti crisis relies on Kathryn Joyce's *The Child Catchers,* a book I strongly recommend for a deep analysis of the Christian movements around adoption.

37 *The left-leaning think tank Center for American Progress:* "What Is Hillary Clinton's Greatest Accomplishment?" *Politico Magazine,* September 17, 2015, https:// www.politico.com/magazine/story/2015/09/carly-fiorina-debate-hillary-clintons -greatest-accomplishment-213157/.

37 *President Joe Biden noted the beginning of National Adoption Month:* The White House, "A Proclamation on National Adoption Month, 2021," Washington, DC, October 29, 2021, https://www.whitehouse.gov/briefing-room/presidential -actions/2021/10/29/a-proclamation-on-national-adoption-month-2021/.

37 *When Russia invaded Ukraine in early 2022:* Orion Donovan-Smith, "Lawmakers Call on State Department to Let Ukrainian Kids Awaiting Adoption Come to U.S. Immediately," *The Spokesman-Review,* March 24, 2022, https://www.spokesman .com/stories/2022/mar/24/lawmakers-call-on-state-department-to-let-ukrainia/.

38 *sociologist Joshua Gamson acknowledges:* Joshua Gamson, *Modern Families:*

Stories of Extraordinary Journeys to Kinship (New York: New York University Press, 2015), 16.

38 **As I wrote with fellow sociologist Jessica Harrison:** Gretchen Sisson and Jessica M. Harrison, "What We Get Wrong About Adoption," *The Nation*, December 7, 2021, https://www.thenation.com/article/society/adoption-politics/.

39 **adolescent motherhood is almost exclusively the domain:** Arline T. Geronimus, "Damned If You Do: Culture, Identity, Privilege, and Teenage Childbearing in the United States," *Social Science and Medicine* 57, no. 5 (2003): 881–93; Frank F. Furstenberg, *Destinies of the Disadvantaged: The Politics of Teenage Childbearing* (New York: Russell Sage Foundation, 2007).

39 **Social science research has found that:** Geronimus, "Damned If You Do: Culture, Identity, Privilege, and Teenage Childbearing in the United States"; Arline T. Geronimus and Sanders Korenman, "Maternal Youth or Family Background? On the Health Disadvantages of Infants with Teenage Mothers," *American Journal of Epidemiology* 137, no. 2 (1993), 213–25; James McCarthy and Janet Hardy, "Age at First Birth and Birth Outcomes," *Journal of Research on Adolescence* 3, no. 4 (1993): 373–92; Frank F. Furstenberg Jr., J. Brooks-Gunn, and S. P. Morgan, *Adolescent Mothers in Later Life* (New York: Cambridge University Press, 1987).

40 **One longitudinal analysis found:** Arline T. Geronimus, Sanders Korenman, S., and Marianne M. Hillemeier, "Does Young Maternal Age Adversely Affect Child Development? Evidence from Cousin Comparisons," *Population and Development Review* 20, no. 3 (1994): 585–609; Kristen Anderson Moore, Dona Ruane Morrison, and Angela Dungee Greene, "Effects on the Children Born to Adolescent Mothers," in Rebecca A. Maynard, ed., *Kids Having Kids: Economic Costs and Social Consequences of Teen Pregnancy* (Washington, DC: Urban Institute Press, 1997).

40 **After studying adolescent childbearing for over forty years:** Furstenberg, *Destinies of the Disadvantaged*, 3, 73.

40 **children raised by parents in high-conflict marriages:** Kelly Musick and Ann Meier, "Are Both Parents Always Better Than One? Parental Conflict and Young Adult Well-Being," *Social Science Research* 39, no. 5 (2010): 814–30.

40 **sociologist Christina Cross found that:** Christina J. Cross, "Racial/Ethnic Differences in the Association Between Family Structure and Children's Education," *Journal of Marriage and Family* 82, no. 2 (2019): 691–712.

41 **Another study found that the particularly ungenerous social supports:** David Brady, Ryan M. Finnigan, and Sabine Hübgen, "Rethinking the Risks of Poverty: A Framework for Analyzing Prevalences and Penalties," *American Journal of Sociology* 123, no. 3 (2017): 740–86.

41 **including 11.6 million children:** Emily R. Shrider, Melissa Kollar, Frances Chen, and Jessica Semega, *Income and Poverty in the United States: 2020*, U.S. Census Bureau, Department of Commerce, September 2021, https://www.census.gov/content/dam/Census/library/publications/2021/demo/p60-273.pdf.

41 **nearly one in six American children live in poverty:** Cassandra Robertson, Tara McGuinness, and Monée Fields-White, "Raising Young Kids in America Has Become Hell, and the Government Should Finally Acknowledge That," *The New Republic*, August 11, 2022, https://newrepublic.com/article/167369/young-children-parents-seniors-government-programs.

41 **Over 6.4 million children live in households:** "Food Security Status of U.S. Households with Children in 2021," U.S. Department of Agriculture, https://www.ers.usda.gov/topics/food-nutrition-assistance/food-security-in-the-u-s/key-statistics-graphics/#children.

41 **on any given night, 175,000 children:** The 2021 Annual Homeless Assessment Report (AHAR) to Congress, U.S. Department of Housing and Urban Development, Washington, DC, https://www.huduser.gov/portal/sites/default/files/pdf/2021-AHAR-Part-1.pdf.

43 **One of the largest adoption agencies in the country:** "Pausing New Infant Adoption Applications," Bethany Christian Services, https://bethany.org/help-a-child/adoption/us-infant-adoption.

43 **one director of a recently closed agency:** Kathryn A. Mariner, Contingent Kinship: The Flows and Futures of Adoption in the United States (Oakland: University of California Press, 2019), 179.

43 **The National Republican Senatorial Committee:** National Republican Senatorial Committee, "Initial Takeaways from Opinion Research on Abortion" memo, May 3, 2022.

43 **Texas congressman Dan Crenshaw tweeted:** Crenshaw, Dan [@DanCrenshawTX], "Less abortion, more adoption. Why is that controversial?" Twitter, May 2, 2022, 11:34 P.M., twitter.com/DanCrenshawTX/status/1521332386184769541.

2. Choosing Life

61 **That means that a full 91 percent of women denied abortions:** Gretchen Sisson, Lauren Ralph, Heather Gould, and Diana Greene Foster, "Adoption Decision Making Among Women Seeking Abortion," Women's Health Issues 27, no. 2 (2017): 136–44.

62 **myriad ways that abortion is excluded:** In her book No Real Choice: How Culture and Politics Matter for Reproductive Autonomy (New Brunswick: Rutgers University Press, 2022), sociologist Katrina Kimport describes this as "unchoosing" abortion—that is, the decision not to have an abortion as separate from the decision to have a baby, even if those choices are related and appear to be one and the same to an external observer. Instead, Kimport describes, a pregnant person might "unchoose" abortion for myriad reasons unrelated to a proactive desire to parent: they cannot afford an abortion; they lack the resources, knowledge, flexibility, or time to navigate their state's byzantine restrictions on abortion access; they are uncomfortable with the idea of abortion, either broadly or personally. Of the few women I interviewed who considered adoption their first choice, most were in this category.

62 **about half of all pregnancies conceived outside of marriage:** Christine A. Bachrach, Kathy Shepherd Stolley, and Kathryn A. London, "Relinquishment of Premarital Births: Evidence from National Survey Data," Family Planning Perspectives 24, no. 1 (1992): 27–32, 48.

62 **there were an estimated 175,000 adoptions:** Penelope L. Maza, "Adoption Trends: 1944–1975," Child Welfare Research Notes #9, U.S. Children's Bureau, August 1984, 1–4, Child Welfare League of America Papers, Box 65, Folder "Adoption—Research—Reprints of Articles," Social Welfare History Archives, University of Minnesota.

62 **there were an estimated 1.2 million abortions:** Carole E. Joffe, Doctors of Conscience: The Struggle to Provide Abortion Before and After Roe v. Wade (Boston: Beacon Press, 1995).

63 **400,000 births to unmarried women:** Stephanie J. Ventura and Christine Bachrach, "Nonmarital Childbearing in the United States, 1940–99," National Vital Statistics Reports 48, no. 16 (2000): 1–40.

63 **the relinquishment rate of infants born to unmarried American women:** Anjani Chandra, Joyce Abma, Penelope Maza, and Christine Bachrach, "Adoption, Adoption

Seeking, and Relinquishment for Adoption in the United States," in *Advance Data* 306 (1999): 1–16, https://stacks.cdc.gov/view/cdc/13614.

63 **it led to a decline in the adoption rate:** Marianne Bitler, and Madeline Zavodny, "Did Abortion Legalization Reduce the Number of Unwanted Children? Evidence from Adoptions," *Perspectives on Sexual and Reproductive Health* 34, no. 1 (2002): 25–33.

63 **women began to feel greater autonomy over all their choices:** Brent C. Miller and Diane D. Coyl, "Adolescent Pregnancy and Childbearing in Relation to Infant Adoption in the United States," *Adoption Quarterly* 4, no. 1 (2000): 3–25; William D. Mosher and Christine A. Bachrach, "Understanding U.S. Fertility: Continuity and Change in the National Survey of Family Growth, 1988–1995," *Family Planning Perspectives* 28, no. 1 (1996): 4–12; Rickie Solinger, *Wake Up Little Susie: Single Pregnancy and Race Before* Roe v. Wade (New York: Routledge, 1992).

63 **In a survey of over 5,000 abortion patients:** Diana Greene Foster, Heather Gould, Jessica Taylor, and Tracy A. Weitz, "Attitudes and Decision Making Among Women Seeking Abortions at One U.S. Clinic." *Perspectives on Sexual and Reproductive Health* 44, no. 2 (1996): 117–24.

63 **Another study of interviews with 70 women:** Paula Sachdev, *Sex, Abortion, and Unmarried Women* (Westport, CT: Greenwood Press, 1993).

63 **These feelings about adoption were equally held:** Leslie Cannold, *The Abortion Myth: Feminism, Morality, and the Hard Choices Women Make* (New South Wales, Australia: Allen & Unwin, 1998).

64 **"I don't want to give my child away to nobody":** Rachel K. Jones, Lori F. Frohwirth, and Ann M. Moore, "'I Would Want to Give My Child, Like, Everything in the World': How Issues of Motherhood Influence Women Who Have Abortions," *Journal of Family Issues* 29, no. 1 (2008): 79–99.

64 **Only 25 percent of those denied abortions:** Sisson, Ralph, Gould, and Foster, "Adoption Decision Making Among Women Seeking Abortion."

64 **One study of teen mothers:** David J. Kallen, Robert J. Griffore, Susan Popovich, and Virginia Powell, "Adolescent Mothers and Their Mothers View Adoption," *Family Relations* 39, no. 3 (1990): 311–16.

65 **the Opt Institute, a conservative adoption-promotion think tank:** George Barna, "Adoption and Its Competitors," Opt Institute, Cultural Research Center at Arizona Christian University, December 4, 2022, https://www.optinstitute.org/news/adoption-and-its-competitors.

65 **Kate McKinnon played Supreme Court Justice Amy Coney Barrett:** *Saturday Night Live*, NBC, May 7, 2022.

66 **less than 1 percent of women seeking abortions:** M. Antonia Biggs, Heather Gould, and Diana Greene Foster, "Understanding Why Women Seek Abortions in the US," *BMC Women's Health* 13, no. 9 (2013), article no. 29.

67 **posters that read "We Will Adopt Your Baby!":** Molly Olmstead, "The Real Story Behind the 'We Will Adopt Your Baby' Couple Is So Much Worse Than the Meme," *Slate,* June 30, 2022, https://slate.com/news-and-politics/2022/06/adopt-your-baby-meme-abortion-protest-roe.html.

67 **why so many first mothers in the baby scoop era faced compounding and enduring traumas:** Ann Fessler, *The Girls Who Went Away: The Hidden History of Women Who Surrendered Children for Adoption in the Decades Before* Roe v. Wade (New York: Penguin, 2006); Solinger, *Wake Up Little Susie.*

70 **sold a set of paid services:** "Kindred + Co Profile Books," https://kindredand.co/profile-books, accessed August 2022; "Google Adoption Ads." My Adoption

Advisor, https://myadoptionadvisor.com/online-advertising, accessed August 2022; Jennifer Mellon, "What You Need to Know about Using Facebook When Trying to Adopt," May 17, 2017, https://adoption.com/use-facebook-when-trying-to-adopt.

70 *Adoptimist is a great way:* "Parent Profiles, Adoption Advertising & Marketing for Adoptive Parents," Adoptimist, https://www.adoptimist.com/hopeful-parents, accessed August 16, 2022.

70 *Many states regulate the extent:* "Use of Advertising and Facilitators in Adoptive Placements," Child Welfare Information Gateway, Children's Bureau, Office of the Administration for Children & Families, Department of Health and Human Services, https://www.childwelfare.gov/pubpdfs/advertising.pdf.

70 *One industry exploration found:* J. Cucullu, K. Monroe, K. Vander Vliet Ranyard, and C. Liversidge, "The Impact of Nationwide Advertising," presentation, National Council for Adoption Annual Conference, 2021.

71 *The banner ads Copley offered:* Naquanna Comeaux, "Target Marking to Reach Clients . . . in a Planned Parenthood Waiting Room," Pregnancy Help News, July 22, 2015, https://www.pregnancyhelpnews.com/news/item/512-target-marketing-to-reach-clients-in-planned-parenthood-waiting-room.

71 *this practice was quickly shut down:* Bob Salsberg, "Agreement Bars Ad Firm from Targeting Women Entering Clinics," AP News, April 4, 2017, https://www.wwlp.com/news/agreement-bars-ad-firm-from-targeting-women-entering-clinics/; Catie L'Heureux, "Your Phone Knows When You're at an Abortion Clinic and Will Serve You Pro-Life Ads," *The Cut,* May 26, 2016, https://www.thecut.com/2016/05/pro-life-ads-target-women-at-abortion-clinics.html.

71 *Virtual geofencing allows adoption agencies:* "All About Geofencing," Choose Life Marketing, https://www.chooselifemarketing.com/all-about-geofencing/; "Is Virtual Geofencing Right for Your Center?," Choose Life Marketing, https://www.chooselifemarketing.com/is-virtual-geofencing-right-for-your-center/.

72 *While the profiles are designed to help prospective adoptive parents:* Gretchen Sisson and Jessica Harrison, "'That Picture Perfect Life': *Dear Birthmother* Letters as Sites of Power and Persuasion," *Adoption & Culture,* in press, 2023.

74 *One survey found:* Elissa Madden, Scott Ryan, S., Donna Aguiniga, and Marcus Crawford, "Understanding Options Counseling Experiences in Adoption: A Quantitative Analysis of First/Birth Parents and Professionals," Donaldson Adoption Institute, November 2016, http://www.adoptioninstitute.org/wp-content/uploads/2016/11/Understanding-Options-Counseling-Experiences-in-Adoption-Phase-One-Report.pdf.

77 *A survey of birth mothers found:* Madden, Ryan, Aguiniga, and Crawford, "Understanding Options Counseling Experiences in Adoption."

78 *the potential loss of social support from family:* Madden, Ryan, Aguiniga, and Crawford, "Understanding Options Counseling Experiences in Adoption."

80 *adoptive parents frequently use their prospective family profiles:* Sisson and Harrison, "'That picture perfect life': *Dear Birthmother* Letters as Sites of Power and Persuasion."

81 *pregnancy options counseling:* Valerie A. French, Jody E. Steinauer, and Katrina Kimport, "What Women Want from Their Health Care Providers about Pregnancy Options Counseling," *Women's Health Issues* 27, no. 6 (2017): 715–20; Nancy F. Berglas, Valerie Williams, Katrina Mark, and Sarah C. M. Roberts, "Should Prenatal Care Providers Offer Pregnancy Options Counseling?," *BMC Pregnancy and Childbirth* 18 (2018): article no. 384; Kristen Nobel, Katherine Ahrens, Amy Handler, and Kelsey Holt, "Patient-Reported Experience with Discussion of All Options

During Pregnancy Options Counseling in the US South," *Contraception* 106 (2022): 68–74.

81 **when expectant parents receive good options counseling:** Susan Smith et al., "Safeguarding the Rights and Well-Being of Birthparents in the Adoption Process," Evan B. Donaldson Adoption Institute, November 2006.

82 **Only seven states require counseling prior to relinquishment:** "Consent to Adoption," Child Welfare Information Gateway, Children's Bureau, Office of the Administration for Children & Families, Department of Health and Human Services, https://www.childwelfare.gov/pubpdfs/consent.pdf.

82 **One survey of birth parents found:** Madden, Ryan, Aguiniga, and Crawford, "Understanding Options Counseling Experiences in Adoption."

82 **requiring the U.S. Department of Health and Human Services:** "Infant Adoption Awareness Training Program," Children's Bureau, Office of the Administration for Children & Families, U.S. Department of Health and Human Services, May 17, 2012, https://www.acf.hhs.gov/cb/grant-funding/infant-adoption-awareness-training -program.

82 **The bill received bipartisan support:** "Consider the Possibilities," National Council for Adoption, https://adoption.mclms.net/en/package/2924/course/1697/view.

83 **In practice, over $6 million of the original $8.6 million:** Cynthia Dailard, "Out of Compliance? Implementing the Infant Adoption Awareness Act," *Guttmacher Policy Review* 7, no. 3 (2004), https://www.guttmacher.org/gpr/2004/08/out -compliance-implementing-infant-adoption-awareness-act.

83 **The NCFA's training materials describe:** "Consider the Possibilities," National Council for Adoption.

84 **The trainings were overtly religious:** Dailard, "Out of Compliance? Implementing the Infant Adoption Awareness Act."

84 **Of the approximately 4,000 centers:** Family Research Council, "A Passion to Serve: How Pregnancy Resource Centers Empower Women, Help Families, and Strengthen Communities," Pregnancy Resource Center Service Report, 2nd ed., 2010.

84 **most people who visit and use crisis pregnancy centers:** Katrina Kimport, J. Parker Dockray, and Shelly Dodson, "What Women Seek from a Pregnancy Resource Center," *Contraception* 94, no. 2 (2016): 168–72; Katrina Kimport, Rebecca Kriz, and Sarah C. M. Roberts, "The Prevalance and Impacts of Crisis Pregnancy Center Visits Among a Population of Pregnant Women," *Contraception* 98, no. 1 (2018): 69–73; Amy G. Bryant, Subarsi Narasimhan, Katelyn Bryant-Comstock, and Erika E. Levi, "Crisis Pregnancy Center Websites: Information, Misinformation and Disinformation," *Contraception* 90, no. 6 (2016): 601–605.

84 **closely affiliated with adoption providers:** Family Research Council, "A Passion to Serve."

84 **As sociologist Kimberly Kelly:** Kimberly Kelly, "In the Name of the Mother: Renegotiating Conservative Women's Authority in the Crisis Pregnancy Center Movement," *Signs: Journal of Women in Culture and Society* 38, no. 1 (2012): 218.

85 **anti-abortion centers receive public funding in fourteen states:** Teddy Wilson, "State-Level Republicans Pour Taxpayer Money into Fake Clinics at an Unprecedented Pace," *Rewire*, February 16, 2018, https://rewirenewsgroup.com/article/2018 /02/16/state-level-republicans-pour-taxpayer-money-fake-clinics-unprecedented -pace/.

86 **being spent on biased options counseling:** Frederica Mathewes-Green, "Pro-Life Dilemma: Pregnancy Centers and the Welfare Trap," *Policy Review* 78 (July/August 1996): 40–43.

86 *in 2021, Arizona, Maine, and New Hampshire:* Rachel Wormer, "Mapping Deception: A Closer Look at How States' Anti-Abortion Center Programs Operate," Equity Forward, 2021, https://equityfwd.org/research/mapping-deception-closer -look-how-states-anti-abortion-center-programs-operate.

3. The Family My Heartbreak Made Possible

106 *Nearly 70 percent of relinquishing mothers say they wish:* Elissa Madden, Scott Ryan, S., Donna Aguiniga, and Marcus Crawford, "Understanding Options Counseling Experiences in Adoption: A Quantitative Analysis of First/Birth Parents and Professionals," Donaldson Adoption Institute, November 2016, http:// www.adoptioninstitute.org/wp-content/uploads/2016/11/Understanding-Options -Counseling-Experiences-in-Adoption-Phase-One-Report.pdf.

108 *mothers who felt pressure from their agency or attorney:* Linda F. Cushman, Debra Kalmuss, and Pearila B. Namerow, "Placing an Infant for Adoption: The Experiences of Young Birthmothers," *Social Work* 38, no. 3 (1993): 264–72.

108 *Mothers who were isolated and had poor social support:* Michael De Simone, "Birth Mother Loss: Contributing Factors to Unresolved Grief," *Clinical Social Work Journal* 24, no. 1 (1996): 65–76; Madden, Ryan, Aguiniga, and Crawford, "Understanding Options Counseling Experiences in Adoption"; Elissa Madden, Scott Ryan, Donna Aguiniga, Olga Verbovaya, Marcus Crawford, and Chandler Gobin, "Understanding Options Counseling Experiences in Adoption: A Qualitative Analysis of First/Birth Parents and Professionals," Donaldson Adoption Institute, March 2017, http://www.adoptioninstitute.org/wp-content/uploads/2017/03 /Understanding-Options-Counseling-Experiences-in-Adoption-Qualitative -Study.pdf.

109 *were often clearly traumatized by these losses:* Merry Bloch Jones, *Birthmothers: Women Who Have Relinquished Babies for Adoption Tell Their Stories* (Chicago: Chicago Review Press, 1993; Open Road Media, 2016); Ann Fessler, *The Girls Who Went Away: The Hidden History of Women Who Surrendered Children for Adoption in the Decades Before* Roe v. Wade (New York: Penguin, 2006).

109 *report more traumatic dreams:* Mary O'Leary Riley and Amanda L. Baden, "Birth Parents in Adoption: Research, Practice, and Counseling Psychology," *The Counseling Psychologist* 33, no. 1 (2005): 13–50.

109 *The ability to choose the adoptive family:* Linda F. Cushman, Debra Kalmuss, and Pearila B. Namerow, "Placing an Infant for Adoption: The Experiences of Young Birthmothers," *Social Work* 38, no. 3 (1993): 264–72.

109 *Many studies have shown that openness:* Xiaojia Ge, Misaki N. Natsuaki, David Martin, et al., "Bridging the Divide: Openness in Adoption and Post-Adoption Psychosocial Adjustment Among Birth and Adoptive Parents," *Journal of Family Psychology* 22, no. 4 (2008): 529-40; Cinda L. Christian, Ruth G. McRoy, Harold D. Grotevant, and Chalandra M. Bryant, "Grief Resolution of Birthmothers in Confidential, Time-Limited Mediated, Ongoing Mediated, and Fully Disclosed Adoptions," *Adoption Quarterly* 1, no. 2 (1997): 35–58.

109 *These studies include my own research:* Gretchen Sisson, Lauren Ralph, Heather Gould, and Diana Greene Foster, "Adoption Decision Making Among Women Seeking Abortion," *Women's Health Issues* 27, no. 2 (2017): 136–44.

112 *Once parental rights are relinquished:* "Postadoption Contact Agreements Between Birth and Adoption Families," Child Welfare Information Gateway, Children's Bureau, U.S. Department of Health and Human Services, https://www.childwelfare.gov /pubpdfs/cooperative.pdf.

112 *A 2014 study found:* David Brodzinsky and Susan Livingston Smith, "Post-Placement Adjustment and the Needs of Birthmothers Who Place an Infant for Adoption," *Adoption Quarterly* 17, no. 3 (2014): 165–84.

112 *Another recent survey found that:* Madden, Ryan, Aguiniga, and Crawford, "Understanding Options Counseling Experiences in Adoption."

112 *Adopted children in open adoptions have:* Deborah Lewis Fravel, Ruth G. McRoy, and Harold D. Grotevant, "Birthmother Perceptions of the Psychologically Present Adopted Child: Adoption Openness and Boundary Ambiguity," *Family Relations* 49, no. 4 (2000): 425–33.

114 *Research has found adopted people experience increased rates:* For details on the challenges of adoption for adoptee mental health and well-being, please see Kristin Gärtner Askeland, Mari Hysing, Leif Edvard Aarø, et al., "Mental Health Problems and Resilience in International Adoptees: Results from a Population-Based Study of Norwegian Adolescents Aged 16–19 Years," *Journal of Adolescence* 44 (2015): 48–56; Mattias Strand, Ruyue Zhang, L. M. Thornton, et al., "Risk of Eating Disorders in International Adoptees: A Cohort Study Using Swedish National Population Registers," *Epidemiology and Psychiatric Sciences* 29 (2020): e131; Joseph Westermeyer, Gihyun Yoon, Carla Amundson, et al., "Personality Disorders in Adopted Versus Non-Adopted Adults," *Psychiatry Research* 226, no. 2–3 (2015): 446–50; Sandra Melero and Yolanda Sánchez-Sandoval, "Mental Health and Psychological Adjustment in Adults Who Were Adopted During Their Childhood: A Systematic Review," *Children and Youth Services Review* 77 (2017): 188–96; Brent C. Miller, Xitao Fan, Mathew Christensen, et al., "Comparisons of Adopted and Nonadopted Adolescents in a Large, Nationally Representative Sample," *Child Development* 71, no. 5 (2000): 1458–73; Amanda L. Baden, Sunanda M. Sharma, Samantha Balducci, et al., "A Trauma-Informed Substance Use Disorder Prevention Program for Transracially Adopted Children and Adolescents," *Child Abuse & Neglect* 130, pt. 2 (2022): 105598; Gihyun Yoon, Joseph Westermeyer, Marion Warwick, and Michael A. Kuskowski, "Substance Use Disorders and Adoption: Findings from a National Sample," *PLoS One* 7, no. 11 (2012): e49655; Adalberto Campo-Arias, Jorge Armando Egurrola-Pedraza, and Edwin Herazo, "Relationship Between Adoption and Suicide Attempts: A Meta-Analysis," *International Journal of High Risk Behaviors and Addiction* 9, no. 4 (2020); Margaret A. Keyes, Stephen M. Malone, Anu Sharma, et al., "Risk of Suicide Attempt in Adopted and Nonadopted Offspring," *Pediatrics* 132, no. 4 (2013): 639–46; Anna W. Wright, Kiri Carlson, and Harold D. Grotevant, "Internalizing Symptoms and Use of Mental Health Services Among Domestic Adoptees," *Children and Youth Services Review* 138 (2022): 106499.

114 *Adopted people are about twice as likely to seek out counseling:* Brent C. Miller, Xitao Fan, Harold D. Grotevant, et al., "Adopted Adolescents' Overrepresentation in Mental Health Counseling: Adoptees' Problems or Parents' Lower Threshold for Referral?," *Journal of the American Academy of Child & Adolescent Psychiatry* 39, no. 12 (2000): 1504–11; Amanda L. Baden, Andrew Kitchen, Jonathan R. Mazza, et al., "Addressing Adoption in Counseling: A Study of Adult Adoptees' Counseling Satisfaction," *Families in Society* 98, no. 3 (2017): 209–16.

114 *With regard to their physical health:* Shannon Gibney, "An Unfinished Story, an Unfinished Body: How Missing Health Histories Predispose Adoptees to Illness," *Narrative Inquiry in Bioethics* 8, no. 2 (2018): 109–11; Pat C. Lord, "Family Health History: Invaluable for Adoptees' Medical Care and Self Identity," *Narrative Inquiry in Bioethics* 8, no. 2 (2018): 143–49; Heewon Lee, Rachel I. Vogel, Bonnie LeRoy, and Heather A. Zierhut, "Adult Adoptees and Their Use of Direct-to-Consumer Genetic

Testing: Searching for Family, Searching for Health," *Journal of Genetic Counseling* 30, no. 1 (2021): 144–57.

114 **We should not overly pathologize adopted people:** David S. Cubito and Karen Obremski Brandon, "Psychological Adjustment in Adult Adoptees: Assessment of Distress, Depression, and Anger," *American Journal of Orthopsychiatry* 70, no. 3 (2021): 408–13; Karine Côté and Martin L. Lalumière, "Psychological Adjustment of Domestic Adult Adoptees," *Journal of Adult Development* 27, no. 2 (2020): 118–34; Margaret A. Keyes, Anu Sharma, Irene J. Elkins, et al., "The Mental Health of US Adolescents Adopted in Infancy," *Archives of Pediatrics & Adolescent Medicine* 162, no. 5 (2008): 419–25.

114 **Many adopted activists draw on key texts:** Nancy Newton Verrier, *The Primal Wound: Understanding the Adopted Child* (Baltimore: Gateway Press, 1993); Betty Jean Lifton, *Lost and Found: The Adoption Experience* (New York: Dial Press, 1979).

115 **openness mitigates some of these risks:** For impact of open adoptions on adoptees, please see Amanda L. Baden, Doug Shadel, Ron Morgan, et al., "Delaying Adoption Disclosure: A Survey of Late Discovery Adoptees," *Journal of Family Issues* 40, no. 9 (2019): 1154–80; Tai J. Mendenhall, Jerica M. Berge, Gretchen M. Wrobel, et al., "Adolescents' Satisfaction with Contact in Adoption," *Child and Adolescent Social Work Journal* 21, no. 2 (2004): 175–90; Rachel H. Farr, Holly A. Grant-Marsney, Danila S. Musante, et al., "Adoptees' Contact with Birth Relatives in Emerging Adulthood," *Journal of Adolescent Research* 29, no. 1 (2014): 45–66; Gretchen M. Wrobel, Harold D. Grotevant, Jerica Berge, et al., "Contact in Adoption: The Experience of Adoptive Families in the USA," *Adoption & Fostering* 27, no. 1 (2003): 57–67; Jerica M. Berge, Tai J. Mendenhall, Gretchen M. Wrobel, et al., "Adolescents' Feelings About Openness in Adoption: Implications for Adoption Agencies," *Child Welfare* 85, no. 6 (2006): 1011–39; Harriet E. Gross, "Open Adoption: A Research-Based Literature Review and New Data," *Child Welfare* 72, no. 3 (1993): 269–84; Harold D. Grotevant, Ruth G. McRoy, Gretchen M. Wrobel, and Susan Ayers-Lopez, "Contact Between Adoptive and Birth Families: Perspectives from the Minnesota/Texas Adoption Research Project," *Child Development Perspectives* 7, no. 3 (2013): 193–98; Jerica M. Berge, Tai J. Mendenhall, Gretchen M. Wrobel, et al., "Adolescents' Feelings About Openness in Adoption: Implications for Adoption Agencies," *Child Welfare* 85, no. 6 (2006): 1011–39; Julie K. Kohler, Harold D. Grotevant, and Ruth G. McRoy, "Adopted Adolescents' Preoccupation with Adoption: The Impact on Adoptive Family Relationships," *Journal of Marriage and Family* 64, no. 1 (2002): 93–104.

117 **with household incomes over $100,000 per year:** Xiaojia Ge, Misaki N. Natsuaki, David Martin, et al., "Bridging the Divide: Openness in Adoption and Postadoption Psychosocial Adjustment Among Birth and Adoptive Parents," *Journal of Family Psychology* 22, no. 4 (2008): 529–40.

119 **"childlike in their dependence":** Riley and Baden, "Birth Parents in Adoption: Research, Practice, and Counseling Psychology."

124 **Today, it's about 55 percent:** Gretchen Sisson, "Who Are the Women Who Relinquish Infants for Adoption? Domestic Adoption and Contemporary Birth Motherhood in the United States," *Perspectives on Sexual and Reproductive Health* 54, no. 2 (2022): 46–53.

124 **most adoptive parents in the private adoption system:** Ryan Hanlon and Matthew Quade, *Profiles in Adoption: A Survey of Adoptive Parents and Secondary Data Analysis of Federal Adoption Files,* National Council for Adoption, 2022, https:// adoptioncouncil.org/research/profiles-in-adoption.

124 **Critical adoption scholar Kimberly McKee has written:** Kimberly D. McKee,

"White Supremacy, Christian Americanism, and Adoption," *Adoption & Culture* 9, no. 1 (2021): 84–111.

125 **the unique work of transracially adopted people:** JaeRan Kim, "'Forever Family Is Like a Manufactured Hallmark Idea': Adoption Discontinuity Experiences of Intercountry Adoptees," *Child Abuse & Neglect* 130, pt. 2 (2022): 105184. JaeRan Kim's blog *Harlow's Monkey* includes important perspectives on transracial and transnational adoption: https://harlows-monkey.com/.

125 **the National Association of Black Social Workers released a strong statement:** National Association of Black Social Workers, "Position Statement on Trans-Racial Adoptions," September 1972, https://cdn.ymaws.com/nabsw.site-ym.com/resource /collection/E1582D77-E4CD-4104-996A-D42D08F9CA7D/NABSW_Trans-Racial _Adoption_1972_Position_(b).pdf.

125 **why the Hague Convention on Intercountry Adoption:** "Convention of 29 May 1993 on Protection of Children and Co-operation in Respect of Intercountry Adoption," Hague Conference on Private International Law, May 29, 1993, https://www .hcch.net/en/instruments/conventions/full-text/?cid=69.

125 **The accounts of transracially adopted people are:** For accounts of transracial adoptees, I recommend several memoirs: Nicole Chung's *All You Can Ever Know* (New York: Catapult, 2018), Susan Devan Harness's *Bitterroot: A Salish Memoir of Transracial Adoption* (Lincoln: University of Nebraska Press, 2018), Lauren Sharkey's *Inconvenient Daughter: A Novel* (Brooklyn: Kaylie Jones Books/Akashic Books, 2020), Rebecca Carroll's *Surviving the White Gaze* (New York: Simon & Schuster, 2022), Harrison Mooney's *Invisible Boy: A Memoir of Self-Discovery* (Lebanon, NH: Steerforth Press/Truth to Power Books, 2022), and Angela Tucker's *"You Should Be Grateful": Stories of Race, Identity, and Transracial Adoption* (Boston: Beacon Press, 2023). Additionally, Melissa Guida-Richards's *What White Parents Should Know about Transracial Adoption: An Adoptee's Perspective on Its History, Nuances, and Practices* (Berkeley, CA: North Atlantic Books, 2021) is another important adoptee perspective, and *Outsiders Within: Writing on Transracial Adoption,* edited by Jane Jeong Trenka, Julia Chinyere Oparah, and Sun Yung Shin (Minneapolis: University of Minnesota Press, 2006), is essential.

125 **Nicole Chung, a domestically adopted person:** Chung, *All You Can Ever Know*, 7.

126 **In her memoir, "You Should Be Grateful":** Tucker, *"You Should Be Grateful."*

128 **In her memoir, Surviving the White Gaze:** Carroll, *Surviving the White Gaze,* 65.

128 **Joe tells Carroll he wanted to raise her:** Rebecca Carroll is not the only adopted person to comment specifically on her Black birth father's feeling wholly shut out of the adoption process. Adoptees Angela Tucker and Lisa Marie Simmons co-authored an essay on how their Black fathers wanted to raise them, but were shut out by a system that failed to acknowledge and honor their rights. See Angela Tucker and Lisa Marie Simmons, "Institutional Racism and the Rights of Black Fathers," Bill of Health, Petrie-Flom Center Staff, Harvard Law School, May 10, 2022, https:// blog.petrieflom.law.harvard.edu/2022/05/10/institutional-racism-and-the-rights-of -black-fathers/.

129 **"After meeting Joe":** Carroll, *Surviving the White Gaze,* 266–67.

132 **In the Haaland case, white adoptive parents:** The most comprehensive reporting on the *Haaland v. Brackeen* case is from Rebecca Nagle's podcast *This Land,* Crooked Media, 2021, https://crooked.com/podcast-series/this-land. See also Kathryn E. Fort, "The Indian Child Welfare Act: Preserving Families Is in Children's Best Interests," Bill of Health, Petrie-Flom Center Staff, Harvard Law School, May 12,

2022, https://blog.petrieflom.law.harvard.edu/2022/05/12/the-indian-child-welfare-act-preserving-families-is-in-childrens-best-interests; Lauren van Schilfgaarde, "Native Reproductive Justice: Practices and Policies from Relinquishment to Family Preservation," Bill of Health, Petrie-Flom Center Staff, Harvard Law School, May 12, 2022, https://blog.petrieflom.law.harvard.edu/2022/05/12/native-reproductive-justice-adoption-relinquishment-family-preservation/.

136 *One study found that teen mothers are heavily influenced:* Newlyn B. Moore and J. Kenneth Davidson Sr., "A Profile of Adoption Placers: Perceptions of Pregnant Teens During the Decision-Making Process," *Adoption Quarterly* 6, no. 2 (2002): 29–41.

137 *One adoption marketing site:* "Adoption Advertising," https://www.adoptionadvertising.org/.

137 *Legal scholar Malinda Seymore has written about how openness:* Malinda L. Seymore, "Sixteen and Pregnant: Minors' Consent in Abortion and Adoption," *Yale Journal of Law and Feminism* 25 (2016), 99.

138 *Sociologist Elizabeth Raleigh has noted that in moments of economic recession:* Elizabeth Yoon Hwa Raleigh, *Selling Transracial Adoption: Families, Markets, and the Color Line* (Philadelphia: Temple University Press, 2018), 43–44.

139 *are already involved with the family regulation system:* For a full analysis impact of these systems on American families, and particularly for Black families, please see Dorothy Roberts's *Torn Apart: How the Child Welfare System Destroys Black Families—and How Abolition Can Build a Safer World* (New York: Basic Books, 2022).

139 *As reported by Rebecca Nagle on her podcast* This Land: Nagle, *This Land*, https://crooked.com/podcast-series/this-land. I highly recommend the second season of Nagle's podcast, which explores the *Haaland v. Brackeen* case in great detail—including discussion of the Brackeens' son's adoption, as well as their attempts to adopt his biological sister (ICWA applied in both cases).

141 *The agency's materials share:* Shari Levine, *Empowering Expectant Parents: Pregnancy Options Counseling and Open Adoption as an Alternative to State Adoption,* Open Adoption & Family Services, 2016, https://www.oregon.gov/oha/ph/healthypeoplefamilies/babies/homevisiting/Documents/EmpoweringExpectantParentswebinar.PDF.

4. Ten Years Later

163 *a majority of mothers reported:* Susan M. Henney, Susan Ayers-Lopez, Ruth G. McRoy, and Harold D. Grotevant, "Evolution and Resolution: Birthmothers' Experience of Grief and Loss at Different Levels of Adoption Openness," *Journal of Social and Personal Relationships* 24, no. 6 (2007): 875–89.

163 *another study found that over a quarter of relinquishing mothers:* Robin Winkler and Margaret Van Keppel, *Relinquishing Mothers in Adoption: Their Long-Term Adjustment,* Institute of Family Studies Monograph No. 3, Melbourne, Australia, May 1, 1984.

163 *Another onetime survey of mothers:* Elissa E. Madden, Scott Ryan, Deborah Aguiniga, et al., "The Relationship Between Time and Birth Mother Satisfaction with Relinquishment," *Families in Society: The Journal of Contemporary Social Services* 99, no. 2 (2018).

163 *This dissatisfaction was particularly true:* Madden, Ryan, Aguiniga, et al., "The Relationship Between Time and Birth Mother Satisfaction with Relinquishment."

163 *Mothers who are satisfied with their careers:* Michael De Simone, "Birth Mother

Loss: Contributing Factors to Unresolved Grief," *Clinical Social Work Journal* 24, no. 1 (1996): 65–76.

168 **Betty Jean Lifton's book:** Betty Jean Lifton, *Lost and Found: The Adoption Experience* (New York: Dial Press, 1979).

168 **"allows adoptees the opportunity to critically explore":** Susan F. Branco, JaeRan Kim, Grace Newton, Stephanie Kripa Cooper-Lewter, and Paula O'Loughlin, "Out of the Fog and into Consciousness: A Model of Adoptee Awareness," June 2022, https://intercountryadopteevoices.com/wp-content/uploads/2022/06/adoptee -consciousness-model.pdf.

168 **Openness is most protective:** Harold D. Grotevant, Ruth G. McRoy, Gretchen M. Wrobel, and Susan Ayers-Lopez, "Contact Between Adoptive and Birth Families: Perspectives from the Minnesota/Texas Adoption Research Project," *Child Development Perspectives* 7, no. 3 (2013): 193–98.

169 **In a survey of birth mothers who had some contact with their child:** Elissa Madden, Scott Ryan, S., Donna Aguiniga, and Marcus Crawford, "Understanding Options Counseling Experiences in Adoption: A Quantitative Analysis of First/Birth Parents and Professionals," Donaldson Adoption Institute, November 2016, http:// www.adoptioninstitute.org/wp-content/uploads/2016/11/Understanding-Options -Counseling-Experiences-in-Adoption-Phase-One-Report.pdf.

169 **The social supports and skills:** Grotevant, McRoy, Wrobel, and Ayers-Lopez, "Contact Between Adoptive and Birth Families: Perspectives from the Minnesota/ Texas Adoption Research Project"; David Brodzinsky and Susan Livingston Smith, "Post-Placement Adjustment and the Needs of Birthmothers Who Place an Infant for Adoption," *Adoption Quarterly* 17, no. 3 (2014): 165–84.

169 **and over 40 percent of birth mothers:** Madden, Ryan, Aguiniga, and Crawford, "Understanding Options Counseling Experiences in Adoption."

174 **This pattern is consistent with a survey of birth mothers:** Madden, Ryan, Aguiniga, and Crawford, "Understanding Options Counseling Experiences in Adoption."

176 **my colleagues found that women who relinquish infants:** Diana Greene Foster, *The Turnaway Study: Ten Years, a Thousand Women, and the Consequences of Having—or Being Denied—an Abortion* (New York: Scribner, 2020).

177 **research shows that 95 percent of women who receive an abortion:** Corinne H. Rocca, Katrina Kimport, Sarah C. M. Roberts, et al., "Decision Rightness and Emotional Responses to Abortion in the United States: A Longitudinal Study," *PLoS One* 10, no. 7 (2015): e0128832.

177 **anti-abortion messaging that has centered on abortion regret:** J. Shoshanna Ehrlich and Alesha E. Doan, *Abortion Regret: The New Attack on Reproductive Freedom* (Santa Barbara, CA: Praeger, 2019).

5. Mothers, Martyrs, Myths

193 **In 2009, seventeen-year-old Catelynn and her boyfriend:** The quotes from this section are drawn from *16 and Pregnant* episodes "Catelynn" (July 16, 2009) and "Life After Labor" (July 23, 2009).

197 **One frequently recalled story line was the final episode of Friends:** "The Last One," *Friends*, May 6, 2004.

197 **The trope of the birth mother who easily, happily walks away:** Jason Reitman, *Juno*, Mandate Pictures, 2007.

199 **The character in question is Dr. Jing-Mei Chen:** "The Greatest of Gifts," *ER*, December 14, 2000.

199 *mentioned a 2006 episode of* **Grey's Anatomy:** "Time After Time," *Grey's Anatomy,* April 19, 2007.

200 *On* **Desperate Housewives** *(2006), Gabrielle:* "It Wasn't Meant to Happen," *Desperate Housewives,* April 30, 2006.

200 *On* **Glee** *(2011), mean girl cheerleader:* "I Am a Unicorn," *Glee,* September 27, 2011.

200 *The outlandish plot device prompted activists:* "Produce a PSA About Adoption Reality," https://www.change.org/p/ask-glee-and-fox-to-separate-adoption-fact-from -fiction-produce-a-psa-about-adoption-reality.

200 *On* **Downton Abbey** *(2014), when Edith:* "A Moorland Holiday," *Downton Abbey,* December 25, 2014.

201 *After the episodes aired, one adoptive parent wrote:* Daniel Summers, "*Downton Abbey's* Alarming Adoption Plot," *The Daily Beast,* January 18, 2015, https://www .thedailybeast.com/downton-abbeys-alarming-adoption-plot.

201 *Another plotline on* **Grey's Anatomy** *(2010) included young mother Sloan Riley:* "Hook, Line, and Sinner," *Grey's Anatomy,* April 29, 2010.

201 *In contrast, on a 2012 episode of* **Parenthood,** *Zoe decides:* "Remember Me, I'm the One Who Loves You," *Parenthood,* February 21, 2012; "My Brother's Wedding," *Parenthood,* February 28, 2012.

202 *Similarly, on* **A Million Little Things** *(2020) Eve devastates:* "'Til Death Do Us Part," *A Million Little Things,* March 26, 2020.

202 *One exception—which was remembered by multiple participants:* "Rock and a Hard Place," *NCIS,* March 18, 2014.

203 *On yet another* **Grey's Anatomy** *episode (2019), surgeon Jo Wilson:* *Grey's Anatomy,* "Silent All These Years," *Grey's Anatomy,* March 28, 2019.

204 **This Is Us** *also explored much of this complexity:* *This Is Us,* "Birth Mother," *This Is Us,* January 12, 2021.

205 *in which fertile woman called handmaids are forced to bear children for infertile couples:* For sources of the legacies of slave narratives and important commentary on the connections to Native parents' experiences with *The Handmaid's Tale,* see Emily O'Malley and Paul Reich, "'A Prison of Our Own Sins': The Unacknowledged Legacy of 19th Century Slave Narratives in HBO's *Westworld* and Hulu's *The Handmaid's Tale,*" *Popular Culture Review* 32, no. 1 (2021): 1–36, https://www .popularculturereview.org/a-prison-of-our-own-sins.html; Tiffany Midge, *Bury My Heart at Chuck E. Cheese's* (Lincoln: University of Nebraska Press, 2019).

206 *Critical adoption scholar Kimberly McKee makes this connection clear:* Kimberly McKee, "Adoption as a Reproductive Justice Issue," *Adoption & Culture* 6, no 1. (2018): 74–93.

206 *the conservative Family Research Council (FRC) released a report:* Curtis J. Young, "The Missing Piece: Adoption Advocacy and Pregnancy Resource Centers," Family Research Council, 2000.

207 *The Dave Thomas Foundation has found in:* Dave Thomas Foundation for Adoption, "2022 US Adoption Attitudes Survey," February 2022.

207 *A 2007 follow-up report from the Family Research Council:* Charles T. Kenny, "Birthmother, Good Mother: Her Story of Heroic Redemption," Family Research Council and National Council for Adoption, 2007, https://www.adoptionbirthmothers .com/wp-content/uploads/2012/12/Birthmother-Good-Mother-PDF.pdf.

208 *Sociologist Elizabeth Raleigh found that one agency:* Elizabeth Yoon Hwa Raleigh, *Selling Transracial Adoption: Families, Markets, and the Color Line* (Philadelphia: Temple University Press, 2018), 3.

208 *in her study of an adoption agency, anthropologist Kathryn Mariner:* Kathryn A. Mariner, *Contingent Kinship: The Flows and Futures of Adoption in the United States* (Oakland: University of California Press, 2019), 166.

209 *In Utah (where the state requires that each student:* "School Presentations," United for Adoption, https://unitedforadoption.org/school-presentations/.

209 *while in Tennessee and Alabama:* "Public Education," Decisions, Choices, and Options, https://dcoinc.org/programs/public-education/.

209 *Both federal and state governments invest in advertising:* "New PSAs Showcase Heartwarming 'Moments' for Adopted Teens and Their Families," press release, October 23, 2019, Children's Bureau, Administration for Children & Families, U.S. Department of Health and Human Services, Washington, DC, https://www.acf.hhs.gov/media/press/2019/new-psas-showcase-heartwarming-moments-adopted-teens-and-their-families.

209 *Save the Storks, an anti-abortion organization that dispatches vans:* "Save the Storks Kicks Off 'Life's About Choice' Campaign Celebrating National Adoption Awareness Month," November 2, 2021, https://www.prnewswire.com/news-releases/save-the-storks-kicks-off-lifes-about-choice-campaign-celebrating-national-adoption-awareness-month-301413846.html.

209 *LDS Family Services, an organization established:* Sarah Jane Weaver, "Ad Campaign Send Message: 'Adoption—It's About Love,'" *Deseret News,* March 10, 2001, https://www.thechurchnews.com/2001/3/10/23244758/ad-campaign-sends-message-adoption-151-its-about-love; "Adoption Commercial Receives National Award," Church of Jesus Christ of Latter-Day Saints, March 2003, https://www.churchofjesuschrist.org/study/ensign/2003/03/news-of-the-church/adoption-commercial-receives-national-award.

210 *Founded in 2012, BraveLove works:* All quotes from BraveLove are pulled from their website, including their "About," "FAQ," and "Manifesto" pages, bravelove.org.

210 *BraveLove asserts that they are "not an adoption agency":* Elizabeth Quinn, "BraveLove Founder Ellen Porter Started a Pro-Adoption Movement in Dallas (and Around the Nation)," DFW Child, November 21, 2019, https://dfwchild.com/bravelove-ellen-porter-adoption/.

210 *A recent tax filing from BraveLove:* As a tax-exempt organization, BraveLove's 990 forms are publicly available. Their 2019 filing, from which this quotation is pulled, was accessed via GuideStar.

211 *One Instagram post included a quote from Katie:* Each of these quotes is drawn from posts on BraveLove's Instagram page, available: instagram.com/bravelove.

213 *during President Donald Trump's 2018 State of the Union address:* The White House, "President Donald J. Trump's State of the Union Address," Trump White House Archives, January 30, 2018, trumpwhitehouse.archives.gov/briefings-statements/president-donald-j-trumps-state-union-address.

214 *This small family unit assembled through adoption:* I am borrowing here from my own words, as published in Gretchen Sisson, "The Good Plaintiff," *Adoption and Culture* 10, no. 2 (2022).

214 *In his 2021 proclamation:* The White House, "A Proclamation on National Adoption Month," Washington, DC, October 29, 2021, https://www.whitehouse.gov/briefing-room/presidential-actions/2021/10/29/a-proclamation-on-national-adoption-month-2021/.

215 *A year later, his 2022 proclamation:* The White House, "A Proclamation on National Adoption Month," Washington, DC, October 31, 2022, https://www.whitehouse

.gov/briefing-room/presidential-actions/2022/10/31/a-proclamation-on-national
-adoption-month-2022.

217 **Offscreen, Dawn partners with the anti-abortion:** "Why Open Adoption Is a
Good Thing with Dawn Baker," Students for Life, https://www.youtube.com/watch
?v=ZVVBspGRfPM&ab_channel=StudentsforLife.

6. To Parent the Children We Have

235 **that prioritized the professionalized voices:** Renee Bracey Sherman and Tracy
Weitz, "The Fall of *Roe* Was Driven by Our Country's Original Sin: Anti-Blackness,"
Rewire News Group, September 20, 2021, https://rewirenewsgroup.com/2021/09/20
/the-fall-of-roe-was-driven-by-this-countrys-original-sin-anti-blackness/.

236 **CUB was established in 1976:** E. Wayne Carp, *Jean Paton and the Struggle to
Reform American Adoption* (Ann Arbor: University of Michigan Press, 2014), 183;
"Concerned United Birthparents," Adoption History Project, University of Oregon,
https://pages.uoregon.edu/adoption/people/CUB.htm.

236 **Mary Anne Cohen reflected decades later:** Mary Anne Cohen, "A Personal
History of Birthmother Activism," Adoption and Culture, annual meeting, May 1,
2010, Cambridge, Massachusetts, http://www.mit.edu/~shaslang/ASAC2010/papers
/CohenPHBA.pdf.

236 **As researcher and writer Liz Latty argues:** Liz Latty, "Adoption Is a Feminist
Issue, But Not for the Reasons You Think." The Establishment, April 19, 2017, https:
//theestablishment.co/adoption-is-a-feminist-issue-but-not-for-the-reasons-you-think
-93ba3824bcbb/.

237 **In the early summer of 1994:** This articulation of the history of the emergence
of reproductive justice as a theory and movement is drawn from "The Herstory of
Reproductive Justice," https://www.sistersong.net/reproductive-justice; Victoria Guer-
rero, "The Black History of Reproductive Justice," Progress Texas, February 25, 2021,
https://progresstexas.org/blog/black-history-reproductive-justice.

237 **a group of Black women gathered in Chicago:** This group included Toni M.
Bond Leonard, Reverend Alma Crawford, Evelyn S. Field, Terri James, Bisola Marig-
nay, Cassandra McConnell, Cynthia Newbille, Loretta Ross, Elizabeth Terry, "Able"
Mable Thomas, Winnette P. Willis, and Kim Youngblood.

237 **describes how reproductive justice goes beyond the debates about pregnancy:**
Loretta Ross, "Understanding Reproductive Justice: Transforming the Pro-Choice
Movement," *Off Our Back* 36, no. 4 (2006): 14–19.

238 **In Outsiders Within: Writing on Transracial Adoption:** Jane Jeong Trenka,
Julia Chinyere Oparah, and Sun Yung Shin, eds., *Outsiders Within: Writing on Transracial Adoption* (Minneapolis: University of Minnesota Press, 2020), 13.

240 **T. Sheri Amore Dickerson, an adopted person:** T. Sheri Amore Dickerson,
"Adoption Justice Must Center Adoptees," in Tina Vásquez, ed., *Prism,* December 12,
2022, https://prismreports.org/2022/12/12/adoption-justice-must-center-adoptees.

240 **"Right-wing movements have taken hold of adoption narratives":** Tiffany
HyeonBrooks, "Reproductive Justice Must Recognize Adoption as Violence," in
Tina Vásquez, ed., *Prism,* November 29, 2022, https://prismreports.org/2022/11/29
/reproductive-justice-must-recognize-adoption-as-violence/.

241 **dissertation on the role of anti-abortion politics:** Katherine Grace Livingston,
*Adoptee Access to Original Birth Certificates and the Politics of Birthmotherhood in
Ohio, 1963–2014,* Ph.D. dissertation, Ohio State University, 2016, https://etd.ohiolink
.edu/apexprod/rws_etd/send_file/send?accession=osu1461068976&disposition
=inline.

242 *Around the time of our first conversation:* "About OBG," www.ohiobirthparents .org.

242 *critical adoption scholar Kimberly McKee cites:* Kimberly McKee, "Adoption as a Reproductive Justice Issue," *Adoption & Culture* 6, no. 1 (2018): 74–93.

243 *In December 2021, Kate and I participated:* Irin Carmon, "Amy Coney Barrett's Adoption Myths," *The Intelligencer: New York Magazine,* December 3, 2021, https://nymag.com/intelligencer/2021/12/amy-coney-barrett-adoption-myths .html.

246 *Historically, birth mother activism has always been rooted in adoptee activism:* A full review of the broad and robust history of adoptee activism is beyond the scope of this project, but for those interested in learning more, I suggest: E. Wayne Carp, *Jean Paton and the Struggle to Reform American Adoption* (Ann Arbor: University of Michigan Press, 2014), 139; E. Wayne Carp, *Adoption Politics: Bastard Nation and Ballot Initiative 58* (Lawrence: University of Kansas Press, 2004); Merritt, M., "Adoptees Online: Community-Building, Collective Affect, and a New Generation of Activists," *Adoption & Culture* 9, no. 1 (2022): 219–46; Hollee McGinnis, "All Grown Up: Rise of Korean Adult Adoptee Movement and Implications for Practice," in *Intercountry Adoption: Policies, Practices, and Outcomes,* Judith L. Gibbons and Karen Smith Rotabi, eds. (Burlington, VT: Ashgate, 2012); Lina Vanegas, "Organizing and Activism of Adopted and Displaced People," *Bill of Health,* Petrie-Flom Center Staff, Harvard Law School, May 13, 2022, https://blog.petrieflom.law.harvard .edu/2022/05/13/organizing-and-activism-of-adopted-and-displaced-people. I also suggest Bastard Nation, Adoptees Rising, Adoptees United, and—perhaps most important—the diverse and candid voices that participate on social media (particularly Twitter, Instagram, and TikTok) with #AdopteeVoices.

249 *"was awarded the Angels in Adoption award":* The Angels in Adoption award is given annually by the Congressional Coalition on Adoption Institute to "celebrat[e] the extraordinary efforts of individuals, couples, families, and organizations who work tirelessly to advocate for children and youth in need of a safe and nurturing family," https://www.ccainstitute.org/programs/view/angels-in-adoption -honorees.

250 *In a 2020 lawsuit:* "Faith Based Adoption Service Sues Former Client for Defamation," *MyNewsLA,* July 28, 2020, https://mynewsla.com/crime/2020/07/28/faith -based-adoption-service-sues-former-client-for-defamation/.

250 *Susan Dusza Guerra Leksander, an adopted person, birth mother, and adoption provider:* Susan Dusza Guerra Leksander, "Striving Toward Ethical Adoption Practice," Bill of Health, Petrie-Flom Center Staff, Harvard Law School, May 11, 2022, https://blog.petrieflom.law.harvard.edu/2022/05/11/striving-towards-ethical -adoption-practice/.

251 *In her ethnographic study of a nonprofit adoption agency, anthropologist Kathryn Mariner described:* Kathryn A. Mariner, *Contingent Kinship: The Flows and Futures of Adoption in the United States* (Oakland: University of California Press, 2019), 33.

254 *For both groups, the most common reasons are financial:* M. Antonia Biggs, Heather Gould, and Diana Greene Foster, "Understanding Why Women Seek Abortions in the US," *BMC Women's Health* 13, no. 9 (2013): 29.

255 *Of countries in the Organisation for Economic Co-operation and Development:* All OECD ranking information is available from the OECD Family Database, oe.cd/fdb.

256 *Many Americans are having fewer children:* Brigid Schulte and Rebecca Gale,

"These Parents Dreamed of Having More Children. Financial Worries Are Holding Them Back," The Lily at *The Washington Post,* November 23, 2021, https://www.thelily.com/these-parents-dreamed-of-having-more-children-financial-worries-are-holding-them-back/.

256 **Sociologist Sarah Cowan examined the impact:** Sarah K. Cowan and Kiara Wyndham Douds, "Examining the Effects of a Universal Cash Transfer on Fertility," *Social Forces* 101, no. 2 (2022): 1003–30.

256 **Research has found that a 5 percent increase:** Michelle Johnson-Motoyama, Donna K. Ginther, Patricia Oslund, et al., "Association Between state Supplemental Nutrition Assistance Program Policies, Child Protective Services Involvement, and Foster Care in the US, 2004–2016," *JAMA Network Open* 5, no. 7 (2022): e2221509.

256 **raising the minimum wage by just one dollar:** Kerri M. Raissian and Lindsey Rose Bullinger, "Money Matters: Does the Minimum Wage Affect Child Maltreatment Rates?" *Children and Youth Services Review* 72 (2017): 60–70.

257 **were all part of President Joe Biden's 2021 American Rescue Plan:** Gloria Oladipo, "US Child Poverty Rate Fell by Half in 2021, US Census Data Show," *The Guardian,* September 14, 2022, https://www.theguardian.com/us-news/2022/sep/14/us-child-poverty-rate-tax-credit-census.

257 **the Adoption Tax Credit for adoptive families:** "Budget of the U.S. Government: Fiscal Year 2023," The White House, Office of Management and Budget, https://www.whitehouse.gov/wp-content/uploads/2022/03/budget_fy2023.pdf; "Adoption Tax Credit FAQs," North American Council on Adoptable Children, https://nacac.org/help/adoption-tax-credit/adoption-tax-credit-faqs/; "What Is the Adoption Tax Credit?," *Key Elements of the U.S. Tax System,* Tax Policy Center Briefing Book, Urban Institute and Brookings Institution, https://www.taxpolicycenter.org/briefing-book/what-adoption-tax-credit.

258 **None of these beliefs are supported by our best evidence:** For information on the physical, psychological, and emotional sequelae of having an abortion, please see Diana Greene Foster, *The Turnaway Study: Ten Years, a Thousand Women, and the Consequences of Having—or Being Denied—an Abortion* (New York: Scribner, 2020), and also: M. Antonia Biggs, John M. Neuhaus, and Diana G. Foster, "Mental Health Diagnoses 3 Years After Receiving or Being Denied an Abortion in the United States," *American Journal of Public Health* 105, no. 12 (2015): 2557–63; M. Antonia Biggs, Brenly Rowland, Charles E. McCulloch, and Diana G. Foster, "Does Abortion Increase Women's Risk for Post-Traumatic Stress? Findings from a Prospective Longitudinal Cohort Study," *BMJ Open* 6, no. 2 (2016): e009698; M. Antonia Biggs, Ushma D. Upadhyay, Charles E. McCulloch, C. E., and Diana G. Foster, "Women's Mental Health and Well-Being 5 Years After Receiving or Being Denied an Abortion: A Prospective, Longitudinal Cohort Study," *JAMA Psychiatry* 74, no. 2 (2017): 169–78; M. Antonia Biggs, Ushma D. Upadhyay, Julia R. Steinberg, and Diana G. Foster, "Does Abortion Reduce Self-Esteem and Life Satisfaction?," *Quality of Life Research* 23, no. 9 (2014): 2505–13; Diana G. Foster, Julia R. Steinberg, Sarah C. M. Roberts, et al., "A Comparison of Depression and Anxiety Symptom Trajectories Between Women Who Had an Abortion and Women Denied One," *Psychological Medicine* 45, no. 10 (2015): 2073–82; Caitlin Gerdts, Loren Dobkin, Diana Greene Foster, and Eleanor Bimla Schwarz, "Side Effects, Physical Health Consequences, and Mortality Associated with Abortion and Birth After an Unwanted Pregnancy," *Women's Health Issues* 26, no. 1 (2016): 55–59; Laura F. Harris, Sarah C. M. Roberts, M. Antonia Biggs, et al., "Perceived Stress and Emotional Social Support Among Women Who Are Denied or Receive Abortions in the United States: A Prospective Cohort Study," *BMC*

Women's Health 14, no. 1 (2014): 1–11; Corinne H. Rocca, Katrina Kimport, Sarah C. M. Roberts, et al., "Decision Rightness and Emotional Responses to Abortion in the United States: A Longitudinal Study," *PLoS One* 10, no. 7 (2015): e0128832; Corinne H. Rocca, Heidi Moseson, Heather Gould, et al., "Emotions over Five Years After Denial of Abortion in the United States: Contextualizing the Effects of Abortion Denial on Women's Health and Lives," *Social Science & Medicine* 269 (2021): 113567; Corinne H. Rocca, Goleen Samari, Diana G. Foster, et al., "Emotions and Decision Rightness over Five Years Following an Abortion: An Examination of Decision Difficulty and Abortion Stigma," *Social Science & Medicine* 248 (2020): 112704.

258 *Stephanie Drenka, an internationally adopted person, offers this response:* Stephanie Drenka, "I'm Adopted and Pro-Choice," *Korean Quarterly,* Fall 2020, https://www.koreanquarterly.org/front_page_below_fold/im-adopted-and-pro-choice/.

258 *Adoption abolition:* Throughout this section on abolition, I am relying on the theorizing and scholarship of Angela Davis, *Are Prisons Obsolete?* (New York: Seven Stories Press, 2003); Ruth Wilson Gilmore, *Golden Gulag: Prisons, Surplus, Crisis, and Opposition in Globalizing California* (Berkeley: University of California Press, 2007) and *Abolition Geography: Essays Towards Liberation* (London: Verso, 2022); Mariame Kaba, *We Do This 'Til We Free Us* (Chicago: Haymarket Books, 2021); and Dorothy Roberts, *Torn Apart: How the Child Welfare System Destroys Black Families—and How Abolition Can Build a Safer World* (New York: Basic Books, 2022).

259 *Amanda Transue-Woolston, a social worker and activist:* I originally quoted Amanda Transue-Woolston's words in a piece coauthored with Jessica Harrison entitled "What We Get Wrong About Adoption" and published in *The Nation* on December 7, 2021, https://www.thenation.com/article/society/adoption-politics. Transue-Woolston's valuable perspectives are also available on Twitter @AmandaTDA and on Instagram at @amandawoolstonadoption.

259 *As prison abolitionist Ruth Wilson Gilmore describes:* Ruth Wilson Gilmore, December 5, 2019, "Keynote Conversation" with Mariame Kaba and James Kilgore, Making and Unmaking Mass Incarceration Conference, University of Mississippi.

260 *Transnational adoptee Nicole Eigbrett reflects on her growing connection:* Nicole Eigbrett, "Adoption Abolition Envisions a World Without 'Organized Abandonment,'" in Tina Vásquez, ed., *Prism,* December 1, 2022, https://prismreports.org/2022/12/01/adoption-abolition-organized-abandonment/.

260 *Daniel Drennan ElAwar reflects on global activist efforts:* Daniel Drennan ElAwar, "The New Abolition: Ending Adoption in Our Time," *Dissident Voice,* August 18, 2012, https://dissidentvoice.org/2012/08/the-new-abolition-ending-adoption-in-our-time/.

261 *Adoption abolitionist Joon Ae Haworth-Kaufka describes a series of abolition tactics:* These tactics are drawn from Joon Ae Haworth-Kaufka's Instagram page @joonae.jk, https://www.instagram.com/p/CecT2X2pbmc. Her interview on Jo Luehmann's podcast *The Living Room* (episode title: "The Unseen Side of Adoption") is also an essential listen. More information about her important work and writing is available: https://joonaehk.com/.

261 *For Benjamin Lundberg Torres Sánchez, an adoption abolitionist:* Lundberg Torres Sánchez's work with the abolitionist zine *We Are Holding This,* created by "people directly impacted by systems of family regulation, surveillance, and policing to gather our creative expressions and to know one another through the liberatory practice of independent publishing." More information is available: https://www.weareholdingthis.org. In August 2022, Lundberg Torres Sánchez spoke on the

panel "Abolishing the Child Welfare System (and Its Algorithms!)" with Dorothy Roberts and Victoria Copeland at the International Summer Festival Kampnagel in Hamburg, Germany, which is available at https://www.youtube.com/watch?v =joSP9n5kdoc&ab. Their thoughts are also shared on Twitter @b_lts_.

262 *They argue that many approaches:* For those interested in learning more about adoption abolition, I suggest (in addition to the sources cited in the text): the abolition zine *We Are Holding This*; matthew anthony's podcast *little did u know*; the episodes of Jo Luehmann's podcast *The Living Room with Jo Luehmann* that include interviews with Joon Ae Haworth-Kaufka and matthew anthony; and the work of Liz Latty, Benjamin Lundberg Torres Sánchez, and Daniel Drennan ElAwar, on which I have only begun to touch here. Additionally, on social media: matthew anthony (IG @matthewanthonywriter; Twitter @CantBurntheSun), Joon Ae Haworth-Kaufka (IG @joonae.hk), Tiffany HyeonBrooks (IG @tea.hyeon), Mila Konomos (IG/Twitter @the_empress_han), Karen Leonard (IG @karenwangareleonard), Benjamin Lundberg Torres Sánchez (IG/Twitter @b_lts___), Ferera Swan (IG @fereraswan), Lina Vanegas (IG/Twitter @LinaLeadsWithLove), Kirsta Bowman (IG @karpoozy), and so many others frequently share their thinking on abolition and adoptee-led advocacy. The conversation around adoption abolition is collectively built by and rooted in the leadership of adopted people; connecting to these essential thinkers online— where these conversations are happening—is part of forging a connection to it.

262 *"demands that the state . . . not unduly interfere":* Loretta J. Ross and Rickie Solinger, *Reproductive Justice: An Introduction* (Oakland: University of California Press, 2017), 169.

Appendix B: A Note on Adoption Language

268 *"positive adoption language" (PAL), as formalized:* Marietta E. Spencer, "The Terminology of Adoption," *Child Welfare* 58, no. 7 (1979): 451–59.

268 *"honest adoption language" (HAL), a counterpoint:* Origins Canada, "Honest Adoption Language," Origins Canada Supporting People Separated by Adoption, 2003, https://www.originscanada.org/adoption-practices/adoption-language/honest -adoption-language/.

269 *wrote in her book* **The Baby Scoop Era** *that PAL:* Karen Wilson-Buterbaugh, *The Baby Scoop Era: Unwed Mothers, Infant Adoption, and Forced Surrender* (Karen Wilson-Buterbaugh, 2017), 335.

269 *the website of the National Council for Adoption:* National Council for Adoption, "Correct Adoption Terminology," 2010, https://www.adoptioncouncil.org /resources/adoption_terms.html (accessed 2010).

269 *By 2018, the NCFA website acknowledged:* National Council for Adoption, "Using Accurate Adoption Language," January 22, 2018, https://adoptioncouncil.org /article/using-accurate-adoption-language/.

269 *The advocacy group Concerned United Birthparents (CUB):* Concerned United Birthparents, "Separated by Adoption? What Is CUB?" Des Moines, 1976; E. Wayne Carp, *Jean Paton and the Struggle to Reform American Adoption* (Ann Arbor: University of Michigan Press, 2014), 183.

270 *In contrast, BraveLove, the "pro-adoption movement":* BraveLove, "About BraveLove." https://www.bravelove.org/about.

Index